Hymns and sacred poems.
– Primary Source Edition

John Wesley, Charles Wesley

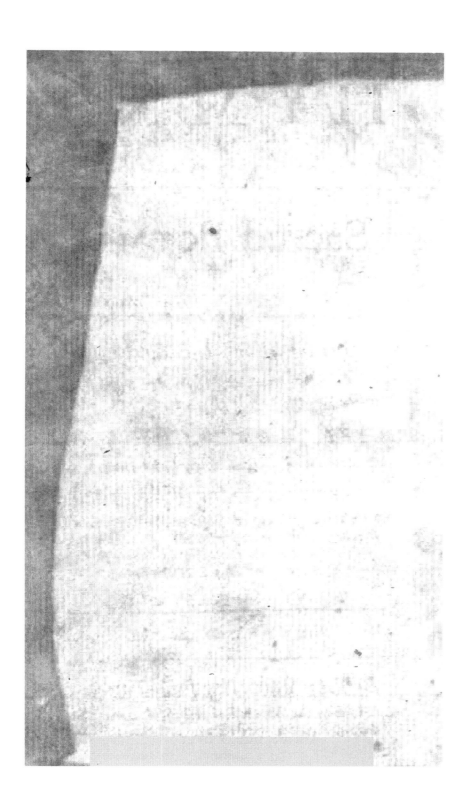

HYMNS

AND

Sacred Poems.

BY

JOHN WESLEY, M.A.
Fellow of *Lincoln* College, OXFORD.

AND

CHARLES WESLEY, M.A.
Student of *Christ-Church*, OXFORD.

Let the Word of CHRIST *dwell in You richly in all
Wisdom, teaching and admonishing one another,
in Psalms and Hymns and Spiritual Songs, singing
with Grace in your Hearts to the* LORD.
Col. iii. 16.

The FOURTH Edition.

Bristol: Printed by *Felix Farley.*
And sold by the Booksellers of *Bristol, Bath, London, Newcastle* upon *Tyne,* and *Exeter;*—as also by *A. Bradford,* in *Philadelphia.*

M. DCC. XLIII.

The PREFACE.

1. *SOME Verses, it may be observ'd, in the following Collection, were wrote upon the Scheme of the Mystick Divines. And these 'tis own'd, we had once in great Veneration, as the best Explainers of the Gospel of* CHRIST. *But we are now convinced that we therein* greatly err'd; not knowing the Scriptures, neither the Power of GOD. *And because this is an Error which many serious Minds are sooner or later exposed to, and which indeed most easily besets those, who seek the* LORD JESUS *in Sincerity; we believe ourselves indispensibly obliged, in the Presence of GOD and Angels, and Men, to declare wherein we apprehend those Writers,* Not to teach *the Truth as it is in* JESUS.

2. *And first, we apprehend them to lay* Another Foundation. *They are careful indeed to pull down our own Works, and to prove, that by the* DEEDS of the Law shall no Flesh be justified. *But why is this? Only,* to establish our own Righteousness *in the Place of our own Works. They speak largely and well, against expecting to be accepted of* GOD *for our Virtuous Actions: And then teach,* That we *are to be accepted, For our Virtuous Habits or Tempers. Still the Ground of our Acceptance is placed in ourselves. The Difference is only this: Common Writers suppose we are to be justified, for the Sake of our Outward Righteousness: These suppose we are to be justified, for the Sake of our Inward Righteousness: Whereas in Truth, we are no more justified, for the Sake of one than of the other. For neither our own Inward nor Outward Righteousness, is the Ground of our Justification. Holiness of Heart, as well as Holiness of Life, is not the Cause, but the Effect of it. The Sole Cause of our Acceptance with* GOD *(or, That for the Sake of which, on the Account of which we are accepted) is the*

Righ-

Righteousness and the Death of CHRIST, *who fulfilled* GOD'*s Law, and died in our Stead. And even the Condition of it, is not (as they suppose) our Holiness either of Heart or Life: But our* FAITH ALONE; *Faith contradistinguish'd from Holiness as well as from Good Works. Other Foundation therefore can no Man lay, without being an Adversary to* CHRIST *and his Gospel, than* FAITH ALONE, *Faith, though necessarily producing both, yet not including either Good Works, or Holiness.*

3. *But supposing them to have laid the Foundation right, the Manner of building thereon which they advise, is quite opposite to that prescribed by* CHRIST. *He commands to* build up one another. *They advise,* " *To the Desert, to the Desert, and* GOD " *will build you up.*" *Numberless are the Commendations that occur in all their Writings, not of Retirement intermix'd with Conversation, but of an intire Seclusion from Men, (perhaps for Months or Years) in order to purify the Soul. Whereas, according to the Judgment of our Lord, and the Writings of his Apostles, it is only when we are* knit together, *that we* have Nourishment from Him, and increase with the Increase of GOD. *Neither is there any time, when the weakest Member can say to the strongest, or the strongest to the weakest,* " I " have no Need of Thee." *Accordingly our Blessed Lord, when his Disciples were in their weakest State, sent them forth, not alone, but* Two by Two. *When they were strengthen'd a little, not by Solitude, but by abiding with him and one another, he commanded them to* wait, *not separate but* being assembled together, for the Promise of the Father. *And* they were all with one Accord in one Place, *when they received the Gift of the Holy Ghost. Express mention is made in the same Chapter, that when* there were added unto them Three Thousand Souls, all that believed were together, and continued stedfastly *not only* in the A-

postles

postles Doctrine *but also* in Fellowship and in breaking of Bread *and in praying* with one Accord. *Agreeable to which is the Account the Great Apostle gives of the Manner which he had been taught of* GOD, for the perfecting of the Saints, for the edifying of the Body of CHRIST, *even to the End of the World. And according to St.* Paul, all *who will ever* come, in the Unity of the Faith, unto a perfect Man, unto the Measure of the Stature of the Fulness of CHRIST, *must* together grow up into Him: From whom the whole Body fitly join'd together and compacted *(or strengthen'd)* by that which every Joint supplieth, according to the effectual Working in the Measure of every Part, maketh Increase of the Body, unto the Edifying of itself in Love. *Ephesians* iv. 15, 16.

4. *So widely distant is the Manner of Building up Souls in* CHRIST *taught by St.* Paul, *from that taught by the Mysticks! Nor do they differ as to the Foundation, or the Manner of Building thereon, more than they do with Regard to the Superstructure. For the Religion these Authors would edify us in, is Solitary Religion. If Thou wilt be Perfect, say they,* " *trouble not thyself about Outward Works. It is* " *better to work Virtues in the Will. He hath at-* " *tained the True Resignation, who hath estranged* " *himself from all Outward Works, that* GOD " *may work inwardly in him, without any turning* " *to Outward Things. These are the true Wor-* " *shippers, who worship* GOD, *in Spirit and in* " *Truth." For Contemplation is with them, the fulfilling of the Law, even a Contemplation that* " *consists in a Cessation from all Works.*"

5. *Directly opposite to this is the Gospel of* CHRIST. *Solitary Religion is not to be found there.* " *Holy Solitaries" is a Phrase no more consistent with the Gospel than Holy Adulterers. The Gospel of* CHRIST *knows of no Religion, but Social; no Holiness but Social Holiness.* Faith working by Love, *is the Length and Breadth and Depth and Heighth of Christian Perfection.* This Command-

ment have we from CHRIST, that he who love GOD, love his Brother also: *And that we mani-fest our Love* by doing good unto all Men; especially to them that are of the Houshold of Faith. *And in truth, whosoever loveth his Brethren not in Word only, but as* CHRIST *loved him, cannot but be zealous of Good Works.* He feels in his Soul a burning, restless Desire, of spending and being spent for them. My Father, *will he say,* worketh hitherto and I work. *And at all possible Opportunities, he is, like his Master,* going about doing good.

6. *This then is the Way: Walk Ye in it, whosoever Ye are that have believed in his Name.* Ye know, Other Foundation can no Man lay, than that which is laid, even JESUS CHRIST. *Ye feel that by Grace Ye are saved thro' Faith; saved from Sin, by* CHRIST *form'd in your Hearts, and from Fear, by* his Spirit bearing Witness with your Spirit, that Ye are the Sons of GOD. *Ye are taught of GOD,* not to forsake the assembling of yourselves together, as the Manner of some is; *but to instruct, admonish, exhort, reprove, comfort, confirm and every Way* build up one another. Ye have an Unction from the Holy One, *that teach-eth you to renounce any other or higher Perfection, than* Faith working by Love, *Faith* zealous of Good Works, *Faith* as it hath Opportunity doing good unto all Men. As Ye have therefore received JESUS CHRIST the LORD, so Walk ye in Him, rooted and built up in Him, and stablish'd in the Faith and abounding therein *more and more. Only,* beware lest any Man spoil you thro' Philosophy and vain Deceit, after the Tradition of Men, after the Rudiments of the World, and not after CHRIST. *For* Ye are complete in Him. He is Alpha and Omega, the Beginning and the Ending, the First and the Last. *Only* continue in *Him,* grounded and settled and be not moved away from the Hope of the Gospel: And when CHRIST, who is our Life shall appear, then shall Ye also appear with Him in Glory!   H Y M N S

HYMNS
AND
SACRED POEMS.

PART I.

EUPOLIS' *Hymn to the Creator.*

From the Greek.

AUTHOR of Being, Source of Light,
With unfading Beauties bright,
Fulnefs, Goodnefs, rolling round
Thy own fair Orb without a Bound:
Whether Thee Thy Suppliants call
Truth, or Good, or One, or All,
Ei, or *Iao;* Thee we hail
Effence that can never fail,
Grecian or *Barbaric* Name,
Thy ftedfaft Being ftill the fame.

Thee, when Morning greets the Skies
With rofy Cheeks and humid Eyes;
Thee, when fweet-declining Day
Sinks in purple Waves away;
Thee will I fing, O Parent *Jove,*
And teach the World to praife and love.

Yonder azure Vault on high,
Yonder blue, low, liquid Sky,
Earth on its firm Bafis plac'd,
And with circling Waves embrac'd,
All Creating Pow'r confefs,
All their mighty Maker blefs.

Thou

Thou shak'st all Nature with thy Nod,
Sea, Earth, and Air confess the GOD:
Yet does Thy pow'rful Hand sustain
Both Earth and Heaven, both Firm and Main.

Scarce can our daring Thought arise
To thy Pavilion in the Skies;
Nor can *Plato*'s self declare
The Bliss, the Joy, the Rapture there.
Barren above Thou dost not reign,
But circled with a glorious Train,
The Sons of GOD, the Sons of Light,
Ever joying in Thy Sight:
(For Thee their silver Harps are strung,)
Ever beauteous, ever young,
Angelic Forms their Voices raise,
And thro' Heav'ns Arch resound Thy Praise.

The Feather'd Souls that swim the Air,
And bathe in liquid Ether there,
The Lark, Precentor of their Choir
Leading them higher still and higher,
Listen and learn; th' angelic Notes
Repeating in their warbling Throats:
And e're to soft Repose they go,
Teach them to their Lords below:
On the green Turf, their mossy Nest,
The Ev'ning Anthem swells their Breast.
Thus like thy Golden Chain from high,
Thy Praise unites the Earth and Sky.

Source of Light, Thou bidst the Sun
On his burning Axles run;
The Stars like Dust around him fly,
And strew the Area of the Sky.
He drives so swift his Race above,
Mortals can't perceive him move:
So smooth his Course, oblique or strait,
Olympus shakes not with his Weight.

As

As the Queen of folemn Night
Fills at his Vafe her Orb of Light,
Imparted Luftre; Thus we fee,
The Solar Virtue fhines by Thee.

Eirefione we'll no more,
Imaginary Pow'r, adore;
Since Oil, and Wool, and chearful Wine,
And Life-fuftaining Bread are thine.

Thy Herbage, O Great *Pan,* fuftains
The Flocks that graze our *Attic* Plains;
The Olive, with frefh Verdure crown'd,
Rifes pregnant from the Ground;
At Thy Command it fhoots and fprings,
And a thoufand Bleffings brings.
Minerva, only is thy Mind,
Wifdom, and Bounty to Mankind.
The fragrant Theme, the bloomy Rofe,
Herb, and Flow'r, and Shrub that grows.
On *Theffalian Tempe's* Plain,
Or where the rich *Sabeans* reign,
That treat the Tafte, or Smell, or Sight,
For Food, for Med'cine or Delight;
Planted by Thy Parent Care,
Spring, and fmile, and flourifh there.

O ye Nurfes of foft Dreams,
Reedy Brooks, and winding Streams,
Or murm'ring o'er the Pebbles fheen,
Or fliding thro' the Meadows green,
Or where thro' matted Sedge you creep,
Travelling to your Parent Deep:
Sound his Praife, by whom you rofe,
That Sea, which neither ebbs nor flows.

O ye immortal Woods and Groves,
Which the enamour'd Student loves;
Beneath whofe venerable Shade,
For Thought and friendly Converfe made,

Fam'd *Hecadem*, old Hero, lies,
Whose Shrine is shaded from the Skies,
And thro' the Gloom of silent Night
Projects from far its trembling Light;
You, whose Roots descend as low,
As high in Air your Branches grow;
Your leafy Arms to Heav'n extend,
Bend your Heads, in Homage bend:
Cedars, and Pines that wave above,
And the Oak belov'd of *Jove*.

Omen, Monster, Prodigy,
Or nothing are, or *Jove* from Thee!
Whether various Nature play,
Or re-invers'd thy Will obey,
And to Rebel Man declare
Famine, Plague or Wasteful War.
Laugh, ye Profane, who dare despise
The Threatning Vengeance of the Skies,
Whilst the Pious, on his Guard,
Undismay'd is still prepar'd:
Life or Death, his Mind's at rest,
Since what Thou send'st must needs be best.

No Evil can from Thee proceed:
'Tis only suffer'd, not Decreed.
Darkness is not from the Sun,
Nor mount the Shades 'till he is gone;
Then does Night obscene arise
From *Erebus*, and fill the Skies,
Fantastic Forms the Air invade,
Daughters of Nothing and of Shade.

Can we forget Thy Guardian Care,
Slow to punish, prone to spare!
Thou brak'st the haughty *Persian*'s Pride,
That dar'd old Ocean's Pow'r deride;
Their Shipwrecks strew'd the *Eubean* Wave,
At *Marathon* they found a Grave.

O ye

O ye bleſt *Greeks* who there expir'd,
For *Greece* with pious Ardour fir'd,
What Shrines or Altars ſhall we raiſe
To ſecure your endleſs Praiſe?
Or need we Monuments ſupply,
To reſcue what can never die!

    And yet a Greater Hero far
(Unleſs Great *Socrates* could err)
Shall riſe to bleſs ſome future Day,
And teach to live, and teach to pray.
Come, Unknown Inſtructor, come!
Our leaping Hearts ſhall make Thee Room:
Thou with *Jove* our Vows ſhalt ſhare,
Of *Jove* and Thee We are the Care.

    O Father King, whoſe heav'nly Face
Shines ſerene on All Thy Race,
We Thy Magnificence adore,
And Thy well-known Aid implore:
Nor vainly for Thy Help we call;
Nor can we want: For Thou art All!

SOLITUDE.

From the Latin.

SOLITUDE! where ſhall I find
  Thee, pleaſing to the thoughtful Mind!
Sweet Delights to Thee belong,
 Untaſted by the vulgar Throng.
Weary of Vice and Noiſe I flee,
Sweeteſt Comforter, to Thee.
Here the Mild and Holy Dove
Peace inſpires, and Joy, and Love.
Thy unmoleſted, ſilent Shade
No tumultuous Sounds invade:
No Stain of Guilt is ſeen in Thee,
To ſoil thy ſpotleſs Purity.

Here

Here the smiling Fields around
Softest Harmony resound.
Here with Angel Quires combin'd,
The Lord of his own peaceful Mind
Glides thro' Life, from Business far,
And noisy Strife; and eating Care.
Here retir'd from Pomp and State
(The envy'd Torment of the Great)
Innocent he leads his Days,
Far from giddy Thirst of Praise.
Here his Accounts with studious Care
Preparing for the last great Bar,
He weeps the Stains of Guilt away,
And ripens for Eternal Day.

Hoarded Wealth desire who please,
'Tow'rs and gilded Palaces.
Fraudless Silence may I find,
Solitude and Peace of Mind;
To all the busy World unknown,
Seen and lov'd by GOD alone.

Ye Rich, ye Learn'd, ye Great, confess
This in Life is Happiness,
To live (unknown to all abroad)
To myself only and my GOD.

_____

The Mystery of Life.

1 SO many Years I've seen the Sun,
    And call'd these Eyes and Hands my own,
A thousand little Acts I've done,
    And Childhood have and Manhood known:
O what is Life! and this dull Round
To tread, why was a Spirit bound?

2 So many airy Draughts and Lines,
    And warm Excursions of the Mind,
Have fill'd my Soul with great Designs,
    While Practice grovel'd far behind:

O

O what is Thought! and where withdraw
The Glories which my Fancy faw?

3 So many tender Joys and Woes
    Have on my quiv'ring Soul had Pow'r;
Plain Life with height'ning Paffions rofe,
    The Boaft or Burden of their Hour:
O what is All we feel! why fled
Thofe Pains and Pleafures o'er my Head?

4 So many human Souls Divine,
    Some at one Interview difplay'd,
Some oft and freely mixt with mine,
    In lafting Bonds my Heart have laid:
O what is Friendfhip! why impreft
On my weak, wretched, dying Breaft?

5 So many wond'rous Gleams of Light,
    And gentle Ardors from above,
Have made me fit, like Seraph bright,
    Some Moments on a Throne of Love:
O what is Virtue! why had I,
Who am fo low, a Tafte fo high?

6 Ere long, when Sov'reign Wifdom wills,
    My Soul an unknown Path fhall tread,
And ftrangely leave, who ftrangely fills
    This Frame, and waft me to the Dead:
O what is Death?----'tis Life's laft Shore,
Where Vanities are vain no more;
Where all Purfuits their Goal obtain,
And Life is all retouch'd again;
Where in their bright Refult fhall rife
Thoughts, Virtues, Friendfhips, Griefs and
    Joys.

EPITAPH.

ASK not, who ended here his Span?
   His Name, Reproach and Praife, was Man.
Did no great Deeds adorn his Courfe?
No Deed of His, but fhew'd him worfe:
One Thing was great, which GOD fupply'd,
He fuffer'd Human Life----and Dy'd.
What Points of Knowledge did he gain?
That Life was facred all----and Vain:
Sacred how high, and vain how low?
He knew not here, but dy'd to know.

VIRTUE.

Alter'd from HERBERT.

1 SWEET Day, fo cool, fo calm, fo bright,
    The Bridal of the Earth and Sky:
The Dew fhall weep thy Fall to Night,
    For Thou with all thy Sweets muft die!

2 Sweet Rofe, fo fragrant and fo brave,
    Dazling the rafh Beholder's Eye:
Thy Root is ever in its Grave,
    And Thou with all thy Sweets muft die!

3 Sweet Spring, fo beauteous and fo gay,
    Storehoufe, where Sweets unnumber'd lie:
Not long thy fading Glories ftay,
    But Thou with all thy Sweets muft die!

4 Only a Sweet and Virtuous Mind,
    When Nature all in Ruins lies,
When Earth and Heav'n a Period find,
    Begins a Life that never dies!

Upon

Upon lift'ning to the Vibrations of a Clock.

INSTRUCTIVE Sound! I'm now convinc'd by
    Thee
Time in its Womb may bear Infinity.
How the paft Moment dies, and throbs no more!
What Worlds of Parts compofe the rolling Hour!
The leaft of thefe a ferious Care demands;
For tho' they're little, yet they're Golden Sands:
By fome great Deeds diftinguifh'd all in Heav'n,
For the fame End to me by Number given!
Ceafe, Man, to lavifh Sums thou ne'er haft told!
Angels, tho' Deathlefs, dare not be fo bold!

DOOMSDAY.

From HERBERT.

1 "COme to Judgment, come away!"
    (Hark, I hear the Angel fay,
Summoning the Duft to rife)
  " Hafte, refume, and lift your Eyes;
  " Hear, ye Sons of *Adam*, hear,
  " Man, before thy GOD appear!

2   Come to Judgment, come away!
This, the Laft, the Dreadful Day.
Sov'reign Author, Judge of all,
Duft obeys Thy quick'ning Call,
Duft no other Voice will heed:
Thine the Trump that wakes the Dead.

3   Come to Judgment, come away!
Ling'ring Man no longer ftay;

Thee let Earth at length reſtore,
Priſ'ner in her Womb no more;
Burſt the Barriers of the Tomb,
Riſe to meet thy inſtant Doom!

4   Come to Judgment, come away!
Wide diſperſt howe'er ye ſtray,
Loſt in Fire, or Air, or Main,
Kindred Atoms meet again;
Sepulchred where'er ye reſt,
Mix'd with Fiſh, or Bird, or Beaſt.

5   Come to Judgment, come away!
Help, O CHRIST, thy Works Decay:
Man is out of Order hurl'd,
Parcel'd out to all the World;
LORD, thy broken Concert raiſe,
And the Muſick ſhall be Praiſe.

SPIRITUAL SLUMBER.

From the German.

1 O Thou, who all Things canſt controul,
     Chaſe this dead Slumber from my Soul;
With Joy and Fear, with Love and Awe
Give me to keep thy perfect Law.

2   O may one Beam of Thy bleſt Light
Pierce thro', diſpel the Shades of Night:
Touch my cold Breaſt with heav'nly Fire,
With holy, conq'ring Zeal inſpire.

3   For Zeal I ſigh, for Zeal I pant;
Yet heavy is my Soul and faint:
With Steps unwav'ring, undiſmay'd
Give me in all thy Paths to tread.

With

4   With out-ftretch'd Hands, and ftreaming
       Eyes
Oft I begin to grafp the Prize ;
I groan, I ftrive, I watch, I pray:
But ah! how foon it dies away !

5   The deadly Slumber foon I feel
Afrefh upon my Spirit fteal:
Rife, LORD; ftir up Thy quick'ning Pow'r,
And wake me that I fleep no more.

6   Single of Heart O may I be,
Nothing may I defire but Thee :
Far, far from me the World remove,
And all that holds me from Thy Love !

ZEAL.

1 DEAD as I am, and cold my Breaft,
      Untouch'd by Thee, Celeftial Zeal,
How fhall I fing th' unwonted Gueft ?
   How paint the Joys I cannot feel ?

2 Affift me Thou, at whofe Command
   The Heart exults, from Earth fet free?
'Tis Thine to raife the drooping Hand,
   Thine to confirm the feeble Knee.

3 'Tis Zeal muft end this inward Strife,
   Give to know That Warmth Divine!
Thro' all my Verfe, thro' all my Life
   The Active Principle fhall fhine.

4 Where fhall we find its high Abode ?
   To Heav'n the Sacred Ray afpires,
With ardent Love embraces GOD,
   Parent, and Object of its Fires.

B 3   There

5 There its peculiar Influence known
    In Breasts Seraphic learns to glow;
  Yet darted from th' Eternal Throne,
    It sheds a chearing Light below.

6 'Thro' Earth diffus'd, the Active Flame
    Intensely for GOD's Glory burns,
  And always mindful whence it came,
    To Heav'n in ev'ry Wish returns.

7 Yet vain the fierce Enthusiast's Aim
    With This to sanctify his Cause;
  To skreen beneath this Awful Name
    The persecuting Sword he draws.

8 In vain the mad Fanatick's Dreams
    To this mysteriously pretend;
  On Fancy built, his airy Schemes
    Or slight the Means, or drop the End.

9 Where Zeal holds on its even Course,
    Blind Rage, and Bigotry retires;
  Knowledge assists, not checks its Force,
    And Prudence guides, not damps its Fires.

10 Resistless then it wins its Way;
    Yet deigns in humble Hearts to dwell:
  The Humble Hearts confess its Sway,
    And pleas'd the strange Expansion feel.

11 Superiour far to mortal Things,
    In grateful Extasy they own,
  (Such antedated Heav'n it brings)
    That Zeal and Happiness are one.

12 Now vary'd Deaths their Terrors spread,
    Now threat'ning Thousands rage--- In vain!
  Nor Tortures can arrest its Speed,
    Nor Worlds its Energy restrain.

13 That Energy, which quells the Strong,
    Which cloaths with Strength the abject
        Weak,
  Looses the stamm'ring Infant's Tongue,
    And bids the Sons of Thunder speak.

14 While Zeal its heav'nly Influence sheds,
    What Light o'er *Moses*' Visage plays!
  It wings th' immortal Prophet's Steeds,
    And brightens fervent *Stephen*'s Face.

15 Come then, bright Flame, my Breast inspire;
    To me, to me be Thou but giv'n,
  Like them I'll mount my Car of Fire,
    Or view from Earth an op'ning Heav'n.

16 Come then, if mighty to redeem,
    CHRIST purchas'd thee with Blood Divine:
  Come, Holy Zeal! for Thou thro' Him,
    JESUS Himself thro' Thee is Mine!

On Reading Monsr. de Renty's *Life*.

WE deem the Saints, from mortal Flesh
        releas'd,
With brighter Day, and bolder Raptures blest:
Sense now no more precludes the distant Thought,
And naked Souls now feel the GOD they sought,
But thy great Soul, which walk'd with GOD on
        Earth
Can scarce be nearer by that second Birth:
By Change of Place dull Bodies may improve,
But Spirits to their Bliss advance by Love.
Thy Change insensible brought no Surprize,
Inur'd to Innocence and Paradise:
For Earth, not Heav'n, thou thro' a Glass
    didst view,
The Glass was Love; and Love no Evil knew,
But in all Places only Heav'n did shew.

Can'st

Can'ft Thou love more, when from a Body
        freed,
Which fo much Life, fo little had of Need?
So pure, it feem'd for This alone defign'd,
To ufher forth the Virtues of the Mind!
From Nature's Chain, from Earthly Drofs fet
        free,
One only Appetite remain'd in Thee:
That Appetite it mourn'd but once deny'd,
For when it ceas'd from ferving GOD, it dy'd.

FAREWEL *to the* WORLD.

From the French.

1. WORLD adieu, Thou real Cheat!
        Oft have thy deceitful Charms
Fill'd my Heart with fond Conceit,
    Foolifh Hopes and falfe Alarms:
Now I fee as clear as Day,
How thy Follies pafs away.

2. Vain thy entertaining Sights,
    Falfe thy Promifes renew'd,
All the Pomp of thy Delights
    Does but flatter and delude:
Thee I quit for Heav'n above,
Object of the noblest Love.

3. Farewel Honour's empty Pride!
    Thy own nice, uncertain Guft,
If the leaft Mifchance betide,
    Lays thee lower than the Duft:
Worldly Honours end in Gall,
Rife to Day, to Morrow fall.

4 Foolifh Vanity farewel,
 More inconftant than the Wave!
Where thy foothing Fancies dwell,
 Pureft Tempers they deprave:
He, to whom I fly, from Thee
JESUS CHRIST fhall fet me free.

5 Never fhall my wand'ring Mind
 Follow after fleeting Toys,
Since in GOD alone I find
 Solid and fubftantial Joys:
Joys that never overpaft,
Thro' Eternity fhall laft.

6 LORD, how happy is a Heart
 After Thee while it afpires!
True and faithful as Thou art,
 Thou fhalt anfwer its Defires:
It fhall fee the glorious Scene
Of Thine Everlafting Reign.

GIDDINESS.

From HERBERT.

1 O WHAT a Thing is Man! from Reft
 How widely diftant, and from Pow'r!
Some twenty fev'ral Men at leaft
 He feems, he is, each fev'ral Hour.

2 Heav'n his fole Treafure now he loves;
 But let a tempting Thought creep in,
His Coward Soul he foon reproves,
 That ftarts t'admit a pleafing Sin.

3 Eager he rufhes now to War;
 Inglorious now diffolves in Eafe;
Wealth now engroffes all his Care;
 And lavifh now he fcorns Increafe.

4. A stately Dome he raises now:
    But soon the Dome his Change shall feel;
See, level lies its lofty Brow,
    Crush'd by the Whirlwind of his Will!

5 O what were Man, if his Attire
    Still vary'd with his varying Mind!
If we his ev'ry new Desire
    Stamp'd on his alt'ring Form could find.

6 Could each one see his Neighbour's Heart,
    Brethren and Social made in vain,
All would disband and range apart,
    And Man detest the Monster Man.

7 If GOD refuse our Heart to turn,
    Vain will his first Creation be:
O make us daily! Or we spurn
    Our own Salvation, LORD, and Thee!

To a FRIEND *in* LOVE.

ACCEPT, dear Youth, a sympathizing Lay,
    The only Tribute pitying Love can pay:
Tho' vain the Hope thine Anguish to asswage,
Charm down Desire; or calm fierce Passion's Rage;
Yet still permit me in thy Griefs to grieve,
Relief to offer, if I can't relieve;
Near thy sick Couch with fond Concern t'attend,
And reach out Cordials to my Dying Friend.

    Poor hapless Youth! what Words can ease thy
        Pain,
When Reason pleads, and Wisdom cries in vain!
Can feeble Verse impetuous Nature guide,
Or stem the Force of blind Affection's Tide?
If Reason checks, or Duty disallows,
" Reason, you cry, and Duty are my Foes:
              " Religion's

" Religion's Dictates ineffectual prove,
" And GOD Himself's Impertinence in Love.

What art Thou, Love? Thou strange myfte-
　　rious Ill,
Whom none aright can know, tho' all can feel.
From careless Sloth thy dull Exiftence flows,
And feeds the Fountain whence itself arofe:
Silent its Waves with baleful Influence roll,
Damp the young Mind, and fink th' afpiring Soul,
Poifon its Virtues, all its Pow'rs reftrain,
And blaft the Promife of the future Man.
'To Thee, curft Fiend, the captive Wretch con-
　　fign'd,
" His Paffions rampant, and his Reafon blind,
Reafon, Heav'ns great Vicegerent, dares difown,
And place a foolifh Idol in its Throne:
Or wildly raife his frantick Raptures higher,
And pour out Blafphemies at thy Defire.
At thy Defire he bids a Creature fhine,
He decks a Worm with Attributes Divine;
Hers to Angelic Beauties dares prefer,
" Angels are painted fair to look like Her!
Before her Shrine the lowly Suppliant laid,
Adores the Idol that himfelf has made:
From her Almighty Breath his Doom receives,
Dies by her Frown, as by her Smile he lives.
Supreme fhe reigns in all-fufficient State, ⎫
To her he bows, from her expects his Fate, ⎬
" Heav'n in her Love, Damnation in her Hate. ⎭
He rears unhallow'd Altars to her Name,
Where Luft lights up a black, polluted Flame;
Where Sighs impure, as impious Incenfe rife, ⎫
Himfelf the Prieft, his Heart the Sacrifice: ⎬
And thus GOD's Sacred Word his Horrid Pray'r ⎭
　　fupplies.

" Center of all Perfection, Source of Blifs,
" In whom thy Creature lives, and moves, and is,
　　　　　　　　　" Save,

" Save, or I perifh! hear my humble Pray'r,
" Spare Thy poor Servant---O in Mercy fpare.
" Thou art my Joy, on Thee alone I Truft,
" Hide not Thy Face, nor frown me into Duft.
" Send forth Thy Breath, and rais'd again I fee
" My Joy, my Life, my Final Blifs in Thee.
" For Thee I Am: for Thee I all refign,
" Be Thou my One thing Needful, Ever Mine!

But O forbear, prefumptuous Mufe forbear,
Nor wound with Rant prophane the Chriftian Ear:
A juft Abhorrence in my Friend I fee,
He ftarts from Love, when Love's Idolatry.
" Give me thy Heart," if the Creator cries,
" 'Tis given the Creature," What bold Wretch
    replies?
Not fo my Friend---he wakes, he breaths again,
And " Reafon takes once more the flacken'd
    Rein."
In vain rebellious Nature claims a Part,
When Heav'n requires, he gives up All his Heart:
(" For Love-Divine no Partnerfhip allows,
" And Heav'n averfe rejects divided Vows)
Fixt tho' fhe be, he rends the Idol thence,
Nor lets her Pow'r exceed Omnipotence.
Commands his GOD, " Cut off th' offending
    Hand?"
He hears, Obedient to his GOD's Command:
" Pluck out thine Eye," let the Redeemer fay;
He tears, and cafts the bleeding Orb away.
Victorious now to Nobler Joys afpires,
His Bofom, touch'd with more than Earthly Fires:
He leaves rough Paffion for calm Virtue's Road,
Gives Earth for Heav'n, and quits a Worm for
    GOD.

1 TIM. v. 6.

She that liveth in Pleasure, is Dead while She liveth.

HOw haplefs is th' applauded Virgin's Lot,
    Her GOD forgetting, by her GOD forgot!
Stranger to Truth, unknowing to obey,
In Error nurft, and difciplin'd to ftray;
Swoln with Self-will, and principled with Pride,
Senfe all her Good, and Paffion all her Guide:
Pleafure its Tide, and Flatt'ry lends its Breath,
And fmoothly waft her to Eternal Death!

A Goddefs Here, fhe fees her Vo'tries meet,
Crowd to her Shrine, and tremble at her Feet;
She hears their Vows, Believes their Life and Death
Hangs on the Wrath and Mercy of her Breath;
Supreme in fancy'd State fhe reigns her Hour,
And glories in her Plenitude of Pow'r:
Herfelf the Only Object worth her Care,
Since all the kneeling World was made for Her.

For Her, Creation all its Stores difplays,
The Silkworms labour, and the Diamonds blaze:
Air, Earth, and Sea confpire to tempt her Tafte,
And ranfack'd Nature furnifhes the Feaft.
Life's gaudieft Pride attracts her willing Eyes,
And Balls, and Theaters, and Courts arife:
Italian Songfters pant her Ear to pleafe,
Bid the firft Cries of infant Reafon ceafe,
Save her from Thought, and lull her Soul to Peace.

Deep funk in Senfe th'imprifon'd Soul remains,
Nor knows its Fall from GOD, nor feel its Chains:
Unconfcious ftill, fleeps on in Errors Night,
Nor ftrives to rife, nor ftruggles into Light:
Heav'n-born in vain, degen'rate cleaves to Earth,
(No Pangs experienc'd of the Second Birth)
She only Feln, yet Unawaken'd found,
While all th'enthrall'd Creation groans around.

C

Know

Know ye not that the Friendfhip of the World is Enmity with GOD.

JAMES iv. 4.

1 WHERE has my flumb'ring Spirit been,
    So late emerging into Light?
So imperceptible, within,
    The Weight of this *Egyptian* Night!

2 Where have they hid the WORLD fo long,
    So late prefented to my View?
Wretch! tho' myfelf encreas'd the Throng,
    Myfelf a Part I never knew.

3 Secure beneath its Shade I fat,
    To me were all its Favours fhown:
I could not tafte its Scorn or Hate;
    Alas, it ever lov'd its Own!

4 JESUS, if half difcerning now,
    From Thee I gain this glimm'ring Light,
Retouch my Eyes, anoint them Thou,
    And grant me to receive my Sight.

5 O may I of Thy Grace obtain
    The World with other Eyes to fee:
Its Judgments falfe, its Pleafures vain,
    Its Friendfhip Enmity with Thee.

6 Delufive World, thy Hour is paft,
    The Folly of thy Wifdom fhew!
It cannot now retard my Hafte,
    I leave thee for the Holy Few.

7 No! Thou blind Leader of the Blind,
    I bow my Neck to Thee no more;
I caft thy Glories all behind,
    And flight thy Smiles, and dare thy Pow'r

8 Ex·

8 Excluded from my SAVIOUR's Pray'r,
   Stain'd, yet not hallow'd, with His Blood,
Shalt Thou my fond Affection share,
   Shalt Thou divide my Heart with GOD?

9 No! Tho' it rouze thy utmost Rage,
   Eternal Enmity I vow:
Tho' Hell with thine its Pow'rs engage,
   Prepar'd I meet your Onset now.

10 Load me with Scorn, Reproach and Shame;
   My patient Master's Portion give:
As Evil still cast out my Name,
   Nor suffer such a Wretch to live.

11 Set to thy Seal that I am His;
   Vile as my LORD I long to be:
My Hope, my Crown, my Glory this,
   Dying to conquer Sin, and Thee!

HYMN *to* CONTEMPT.

1 WELCOME, Contempt! Stern, faithful Guide,
   Unpleasing, healthful Food!
Hail pride-sprung Antidote of Pride,
   Hail Evil turn'd to Good!

2 Thee when with awful Pomp array'd
   Ill-judging Mortals see,
Perverse they fly with coward Speed,
   To Guilt they fly from Thee.

3 Yet if one haply longing stands
   To choose a Nobler Part,
Ardent from Sin's ensnaring Bands
   To vindicate his Heart:

C   4. Present

4 Present to end the doubtful Strife,
    Thy Aid he soon shall feel;
  Confirm'd by Thee, tho' warm in Life,
    Bid the vain World farewel.

5 Thro' Thee he treads the shining Way
    That Saints and Martyrs trod,
  Shakes off the Frailty of his Clay,
    And wings his Soul for GOD.

6 His Portion Thou, he burns no more,
    With fond Desire to please;
  The fierce, distracting Conflict's o'er,
    And all his Thoughts are Peace.

7 Sent by Almighty Pity down,
    To Thee alone 'tis giv'n
  With glorious Infamy to crown
    The Favourites of Heav'n.

8 With Thee Heav'n's Fav'rite Son, when made
    Incarnate, deign'd t'abide;
  To Thee He meekly bow'd his Head,
    He bow'd His Head, and dy'd.

9 And shall I still the Cup decline,
    His Suff'rings disesteem,
  Disdain to make this Portion mine
    When sanctify'd by Him?

0 Or firm thro' Him and undismay'd,
    Thy sharpest Darts abide?
  Sharp as the Thorns that tore His Head,
    The Spear that pierc'd His Side.

1 Yes---since with Thee my Lot is cast,
    I bless my GOD's Decree,
  Embrace with Joy what He embrac'd,
    And live and die with Thee!

12 So when before th' Angelic Host
   To each his Lot is giv'n,
Thy Name shall be in Glory lost,
   And Mine be found in Heav'n!

GRACE *before* MEAT.

1. FOUNTAIN of Being, Source of Good!
   At whose Almighty Breath
The Creature proves our Bane or Food,
   Dispensing Life or Death:

2 Thee we address with humble Fear,
   Vouchsafe Thy Gifts to crown;
Father of All, Thy Children hear,
   And send a Blessing down.

3 O may our Souls for ever pine
   Thy Grace to taste and see;
Athirst for Righteousness Divine,
   And hungry after Thee!

4 For this we lift our longing Eyes,
   We wait the Gracious Word;
Speak---and our Hearts from Earth shall rise,
   And feed upon the LORD.

Another.

1. ENSLAV'D to Sense, to Pleasure prone,
   Fond of Created Good;
Father, our Helplessness we own,
   And trembling taste our Food.

2 Trembling we taste: for ah! no more
   To Thee the Creatures lead;
Chang'd they exert a Fatal Pow'r,
   And poison while they feed.

C 3   3 Curst

3 Curſt for the Sake of wretched Man,
　　They now engroſs Him whole,
With pleaſing Force on Earth detain,
　　And ſenſualize His Soul.

4 Grov'ling on Earth we ſtill muſt lie,
　　'Till CHRIST the Curſe repeal ;
'Till CHRIST deſcending from on high
　　Infected Nature heal.

5 Come then, our Heav'nly *Adam*, come !
　　Thy healing Influence give ;
Hallow our Food, reverſe our Doom,
　　And bid us eat and live.

6 The Bondage of Corruption break !
　　For this our Spirits groan ;
Thy only Will we fain would ſeek ;
　　O ſave us from our own.

7 Turn the full Stream of Nature's Tide :
　　Let all our Actions tend
To Thee their Source ; Thy Love the Guide,
　　Thy Glory be the End.

8 Earth then a Scale to Heav'n ſhall be,
　　Senſe ſhall point out the Road ;
The Creatures all ſhall lead to Thee,
　　And all we taſte be GOD !

GRACE *after* MEAT.

1 BEING of Beings, GOD of Love,
　　To Thee our Hearts we raiſe ;
Thy all-ſuſtaining Pow'r we prove,
　　And gladly ſing Thy Praiſe.

2 Thine,

2 Thine, wholly Thine we pant to be,
 Our Sacrifice receive ;
Made, and preferv'd, and fav'd by Thee,
 To Thee Ourfelves we give.

3 Heav'nward our ev'ry Wifh afpires:
 For all Thy Mercy's Store
The fole Return Thy Love requires,
 Is that we afk for more.

4 For more we afk, we open then
 Our Hearts t'embrace Thy Will :
Turn and beget us, LORD, again,
 With all Thy Fulnefs fill !

5 Come, Holy Ghoft, the SAVIOUR's Love
 Shed in our Hearts abroad ;
So fhall we ever live and move,
 And Be, with CHRIST, in GOD.

On Clemens Alexandrinus's *Defcription of a Perfect Chriftian.*

1 HERE from afar the finifh'd Height
 Of Holinefs is feen :
But O, what heavy Tracts of Toil,
 What Deferts lie between ?

2 Man for the Simple Life Divine
 What will it coft to break ;
Ere Pleafure foft and willy Pride
 No more within him fpeak ?

3 What ling'ring Anguifh muft corrode
 The Root of Nature's Joy ?
What fecret Shame and dire Defeats
 The Pride of Heart deftroy ?

4 Learn

4 Learn Thou the whole of Mortal State
　　In Stilnefs to fuftain;
Nor footh with falfe Delights of Earth
　　Whom GOD hath doom'd to Pain.

5 Thy Mind now Multitude of Thoughts,
　　Now Stupor fhall diftrefs;
The Venom of each latent Vice
　　Wild Images imprefs.

6 Yet darkly fafe with GOD thy Soul
　　His Arm ftill onward bears,
'Till thro' each Tempeft on her Face
　　A Peace beneath appears.

7 'Tis in that Peace we fee and act
　　By Inftincts from above;
With finer Tafte of Wifdom fraught,
　　And myftick Pow'rs of Love.

8 Yet afk not in mere Eafe and Pomp
　　Of Ghoftly Gifts to fhine:
'Till Death the Lownefles of Man,
　　And Pitying Griefs are Thine.

The C O L L A R.

From HERBERT.

1 NO more, I cry'd, fhall Grief be mine,
　　I will throw off the Load;
No longer weep, and figh, and pine
　　To find an abfent GOD.

2 Free as the Mufe, my Wifhes move,
　　Thro' Nature's Wilds they roam:
Loofe as the Wind, ye Wand'rers rove,
　　And bring me Pleafures home!

3 Still shall I urge with endless Toil,
    Yet not obtain my Suit?
  Still shall I plant th' ungrateful Soil,
    Yet never taste the Fruit?

4 Not so, my Heart!---for Fruit there is,
    Seize it with eager Haste;
  Riot in Joys, dissolve in Bliss,
    And pamper ev'ry Taste.

5 On Right and Wrong thy Thoughts no more
    In cold Dispute employ;
  Forsake thy Cell, the Bounds pass o'er,
    And give a Loose to Joy.

6 Conscience and Reason's Pow'r deride,
    Let stronger Nature draw,
  Self be thy End, and Sense thy Guide,
    And Appetite thy Law.

7 Away, ye Shades, while light I rise,
    I tread you all beneath!
  Grasp the dear Hours my Youth supplies,
    Nor idly dream of Death.

8 Whoe'er enslav'd to Grief and Pain,
    Yet starts from Pleasure's Road,
  Still let him weep, and still complain,
    And sink beneath his Load----

9 But as I rav'd, and grew more wild
    And fierce at ev'ry Word,
  Methought I heard One calling "Child!"
    And I reply'd----"My Lord!"

G R A C E.

From the same.

1. MY Stock lies dead, and no Increase
   Does Thy Paſt Gifts improve:
O let Thy Graces without ceaſe
   Drop gently from above.

2. If ſtill the Sun ſhould hide His Face,
   Earth would a Dungeon prove,
Thy Works Night's Captives: O let Grace
   Drop gently from above.

3. The Dew unſought each Morning falls,
   Leſs bounteous is Thy Dove?
The Dew for which my Spirit calls
   Drop gently from above.

4. Death is ſtill digging like a Mole
   My Grave, where'er I move;
Let Grace work too, and on my Soul
   Drop gently from above.

5. Sin is ſtill ſpreading o'er my Heart
   A Hardneſs void of Love;
Let ſuppling Grace, to croſs her Art,
   Drop gently from above.

6 O come; for Thou doſt know the Way?
   Or if Thou wilt not move,
Tranſlate me, where I need not ſay
   Drop gently from above.

GRATEFULNESS.

From the same.

1 THou, who hast giv'n so much to me,
　　O give a grateful Heart:
See how Thy Beggar works on Thee
　　By acceptable Art!

2 He makes thy Gifts occasion more;
　　And says, if here he's crost,
All Thou hast giv'n him heretofore,
　　Thyself, and All is lost.

3 But Thou didst reckon, when at first
　　Our Wants Thy Aid did crave,
What it would come to at the worst
　　Such needy Worms to save.

4 Perpetual Knockings at Thy Door,
　　Tears sullying all Thy Rooms;
Gift upon Gift; much would have more,
　　And still Thy Suppliant comes.

5 Yet Thy unweary'd Love went on;
　　Allow'd us all our Noise;
Nay Thou hast dignify'd a Groan,
　　And made a Sigh Thy Joys.

6 Wherefore I cry, and cry again,
　　Nor canst Thou quiet be,
'Till my repeated Suit obtain
　　A Thankful Heart from Thee.

7 Hear then, and Thankfulness impart
　　Continual as Thy Grace;
O add to all Thy Gifts a Heart
　　Whose Pulse may beat Thy Praise.

The

The F L O W E R.

From the same.

1 WHILE sad my Heart, and blasted mourns,
  How chearing, LORD, are Thy Returns,
How sweet the Life, the Joys they bring!
Grief in Thy Presence melts away:
Refresh'd I hail the gladsome Day,
  As Flow'rs salute the rising Spring.

2 Who would have thought my wither'd Heart
Again should feel Thy sov'reign Art,
  A kindly Warmth again should know?
Late like the Flow'r, whose drooping Head
Sinks down, and seeks its native Bed
  To see the Mother-Root below.

3 These are Thy Wonders, LORD of Pow'r,
Killing and Quick'ning! One short Hour
  Lifts up to Heav'n, and sinks to Hell:
Thy Will supreme disposes All;
We prove Thy Justice in our Fall,
  Thy Mercy in our Rise we feel.

4 O that my Latest Change were o'er!
  O were I plac'd where Sin no more
  With its Attendant Grief, could come!
Stranger to Change, I then should rise
Amidst the Plants of Paradise,
  And flourish in Eternal Bloom.

5 Many a Spring since here I grew,
I seem'd my Verdure to renew,
  And higher still to rise and higher:
Water'd by Tears, and fan'd by Sighs,
I pour'd my Fragrance thro' the Skies,
  And heav'nward ever seem'd t'aspire.

6 But while I grow, as Heav'n were mine,
Thine Anger comes, and I decline;
  Faded my Bloom, my Glory loft:
Who can the deadly Cold fuftain,
Or ftand beneath the chilling Pain
  When blafted by Thine Anger's Froft?

7 And now in Age I bud again,
Once more I feel the Vernal Rain,
  Tho' dead fo oft, I live, and write:
Sure I but dream! It cannot be
That I, my GOD, that I am He
  On whom Thy Tempefts fell all Night!

8 Thefe are Thy Wonders, LORD of Love,
Thy Mercy thus delights to prove
  We are but Flow'rs that bloom and die!
Soon as This faving Truth we fee,
Within Thy Garden plac'd by Thee,
  Time we furvive, and Death defy.

BITTER-SWEET.

From the fame.

1 AH my dear, angry LORD,
    Since Thou doft love, yet ftrike,
Caft down, and yet Thy Help afford,
    Sure I will do the like.

2   I will complain, yet praife,
    Bewail, and yet approve,
And all my mournful, joyful Days
    I will lament, and love.

D   *A* MID-

A MIDNIGHT-HYMN *for one under the Law.*

1 WHile Midnight Shades the Earth o'erspread,
    And veil the Bosom of the Deep,
Nature reclines her weary Head,
    And Care respires, and Sorrows sleep:
My Soul still aims at Nobler Rest,
Aspiring to her Saviour's Breast.

2 Aid me, ye hov'ring Spirits near,
    Angels and Ministers of Grace:
Who ever, while you guard us here,
    Behold your Heav'nly Father's Face!
Gently my raptur'd Soul convey
To Regions of Eternal Day.

3 Fain would I leave this Earth below,
    Of Pain and Sin the dark Abode;
Where shadowy Joy, or solid Woe
    Allures, or tears me from my GOD:
Doubtful, and insecure of Bliss,
Since Death alone confirms me His.

4 'Till then, to Sorrow born I sigh,
    And gasp, and languish after Home;
Upward I send my streaming Eye,
    Expecting 'till the Bridegroom come:
Come quickly, LORD! Thy own receive,
Now let me see Thy Face, and live.

5 Absent from Thee, my exil'd Soul
    Deep in a Fleshly Dungeon groans;
Around me Clouds of Darkness roll,
    And lab'ring Silence speaks my Moans:
Come quickly, LORD! Thy Face display,
And look my Midnight into Day.

6 Error

6 Error and Sin, and Death are o'er,
    If Thou reverfe the Creature's Doom,
Sad *Rachel* weeps her Lofs no more,
    If Thou the GOD, the Saviour come:
Of Thee poffeft, in Thee we prove
The Light, the Life, the Heav'n of Love.

After confidering fome of his Friends.

1 WHY do the Deeds of happier Men
        Into a Mind return,
Which can, oppreft by Bands of Sloth,
    With no fuch Ardors burn?

2 GOD of my Life and all my Pow'rs,
    The Everlafting Friend!
Shall Life, fo favour'd in its Dawn,
    Be fruitlefs in its End?

3 To Thee, O LORD, my tender Years
    A trembling Duty paid,
With Glimpfes of the mighty GOD
    Delighted and afraid.

4 From Parent's Eye, and Paths of Men,
    Thy Touch I ran to meet;
It fwell'd the Hymn, and feal'd the Pray'r,
    'Twas calm, and ftrange, and fweet!

5 Oft when beneath the Work of Sin
    Trembling and dark I ftood,
And felt the Edge of eager Thought,
    And felt the kindling Blood:

6 Thy Dew came down—my Heart was Thine,
    It knew nor Doubt nor Strife;
Cool now, and peaceful as the Grave,
    And ftrong to Second Life.

D 2   7 Full

7 Full of myfelf I oft forfook
    The Now, the Truth, and Thee,
  For fanguine Hope, or fenfual Guft,
    Or earth-born Sophiftry :

8 The Folly thriv'd, and came in Sight
    Too grofs for Life to bear;
  I fmote the Breaft for Man too bafe,
    I fmote— and GOD was there!

9 Still will I hope for Voice and Strength
    To glorify thy Name;
  Tho' I muft die to all that's Mine,
    And fuffer All my Shame.

RELIGIOUS DISCOURSE.

TO fpeak for GOD, to found Religion's Praife,
  Of facred Paffions the wife Warmth to raife ;
T''infufe the Contrite Wifh to Conqueft nigh,
And point the Steps myfterious as they lie ;
To feize the Wretch in full Career of Luft,
And footh the filent Sorrows of the Juft :
Who would not blefs for this the Gift of Speech,
And in the Tongue's Beneficence be rich ?

  But who muft talk ? Not the mere modern Sage,
Who fuits the foften'd Gofpel to the Age ;
Who ne'er to raife degen'rate Practice ftrives,
But brings the Precept down to Chriftian Lives.
Not He, who Maxims from cold Reading took,
And never faw Himfelf but thro' a Book :
Not He, who Hafty in the Morn of Grace,
Soon finks extinguifh'd as a Comet's Blaze.
Not He, who ftrains in Scripture phrafe t'abound,
Deaf to the Senfe, who ftuns us with the Sound :
But He, who Silence loves; and never dealt
In the falfe Commerce of a Truth Unfelt.

Guilty

Guilty you speak, if subtle from within
Blows on your Words the Self-admiring Sin:
If unresolv'd to choose the Better Part,
Your forward Tongue belies your languid Heart:
But then speak safely, when your peaceful Mind
Above Self-seeking blest, on GOD reclin'd,
Feels Him at once suggest unlabour'd Sense,
And ope a Sluce of sweet Benevolence.
Some high Behests of Heav'n you then fulfil,
Sprung from His Light your Words, and issuing by
      His Will.

Nor yet expect so *Mystically* long,
'Till Certain Inspiration loose your Tongue:
Express the Precept runs, " Do good to all; "
Nor adds, " Whene'er you find an inward Call."
'Tis GOD commands: no farther Motive seek,
Speak or without, or with Reluctance speak:
To Love's Habitual Sense by Acts aspire,
And kindle, 'till you catch the Gospel-Fire.

Discoveries immature of Truth decline,
Nor prostitute the Gospel Pearl to Swine.
Beware, too rashly how you speak the whole,
The Vileness, or the Treasures of your Soul.
If spurn'd by some, where weak on Earth you lie,
If judg'd a Cheat or Dreamer, where you fly;
Here the Sublimer Strain, th'exerted Air
Forego; you're at the Bar, not in the Chair.

To the pert Reas'ner if you speak at all,
Speak what within his Cognizance may fall:
Expose not Truths Divine to Reason's Rack,
Give him his own belov'd Ideas back,
Your Notions 'till they look like His, dilute;
Blind he must be----but save him from Dispute!
But when we're turn'd of Reason's noontide Glare,
And Things begin to shew us what they are,

D 3   More

More free to such your true Conceptions tell;
Yet graft them on the Arts where they excel.
If sprightly Sentiments detain their Taste;
If Paths of various Learning they have trac'd;
If their cool Judgment longs, yet fears to fix:
Fire, Erudition, Hesitation mix.

All Rules are dead: 'tis from the Heart you
 draw
The living Lustre, and unerring Law.
A State of Thinking in your Manner shew,
Nor fiercely soaring, nor supinely low:
Others their Lightness and each inward Fault
Quench in the Stilness of your deeper Thought.
Let all your Gestures fixt Attention draw,
And wide around diffuse infectious Awe;
Present with GOD by Recollection seem,
Yet present, by your Chearfulness, with Them.

Without Elation Christian Glories paint,
Nor by fond am'rous Phrase assume the Saint.
Greet not frail Men with Compliments untrue;
With Smiles to Peace confirm'd and Conquest due,
There are who watch t'adore the Dawn of Grace,
And pamper the young Proselyte with Praise:
Kind, humble Souls! They with a right good
 Will
Admire His Progress---'till he stands stock still.

Speak but to Thirsty Minds of Things Divine,
Who strong for Thought, are free in yours to
 join.
The Busy from his Channel parts with Pain,
The Languid loaths an Elevated Strain:
With these you aim but at good-natur'd Chat,
Where all, except the Love, is low and flat.

Not one Address will diff'rent Tempers fit,
The Grave and Gay, the Heavy and the Wit.
         Wits

Wits will fift you; and moft Conviction find
Where leaft 'tis urg'd, and feems the leaft defign'd.
Slow Minds are merely paffive; and forget
Truths not inculcated: to thefe repeat,
Avow your Counfel, nor abftain from Heat.

Some gentle Souls to gay Indiff'rence true,
Nor hope, nor fear, nor think the more for you:
Let Love turn Babler here, and Caution fleep,
Blufh not for fhallow Speech, nor mufe for deep;
Thefe to your Humour, not your Senfe attend,
'Tis not th'Advice that fways them, but the
      Friend.

Others have large Receffes in their Breaft:
With penfive Procefs all they hear digeft:
Here well-weigh'd Words with wary Forefight fow,
For all you fay will fink, and ev'ry Seed will grow.

At firft Acquaintance prefs each Truth fevere,
Stir the whole Odium of your Character:
Let harfheft Doctrines all your Words engrofs,
And Nature bleeding on the Daily Crofs.
Then to yourfelf th'Afcetic Rule enjoin,
To others ftoop furprizingly benign;
Pitying, if from Themfelves with Pain they part,
If ftubborn Nature long holds out the Heart.
Their Outworks now are gain'd; forbear to prefs;
The more you urge them, you prevail the lefs;
Let Speech lay by its Roughnefs to oblige,
Your fpeaking Life will carry on the Siege:
By your Example ftruck, to GOD they ftrive
To live, no longer to Themfelves alive.

To pofitive Adepts infidious yield,
T'enfure the Conqueft, feem to quit the Field:
Large in your Grants; be their Opinion fhown:
Approve, amend----and wind it to your own.
                          Couch

Couch in your Hints, if more resign'd they hear,
Both what they will be soon, and what they are:
Pleasing These Words now to their conscious Breast,
Th'anticipating Voice hereafter blest.

In Souls just wak'd the Paths of Light to choose,
Convictions keen, and Zeal of Pray'r infuse.
Let them love Rules; 'till freed from Passion's
    Reign,
'Till blameless Moral Rectitude they gain.

But lest reform'd from each Extremer Ill,
They should but Civilize old Nature still,
The loftier Charms and Energy display
Of Virtue model'd by the Godhead's Ray;
The Lineaments Divine, Perfection's Plan,
And all the Grandeur of the Heavenly Man.
Commences thus the Agonizing Strife
Previous to Nature's Death, and second Life:
Struck by their own inclement piercing Eye,
Their feeble Virtues blush, subside, and die:
They view the Scheme that mimick Nature made,
A fancy'd Goddess, and Religion's Shade;
With angry Scorn they now reject the whole,
Unchang'd their Heart, undeify'd their Soul;
'Till Indignation sleeps away to Faith,
And GOD's own Pow'r and Peace take Root in sa-
    cred Wrath.

Aim less to Teach than Love. The Work begun
In Words, is crown'd by artless Warmth alone.
Love to your Friend a Second Office owes,
Yourself and Him before Heav'ns Footstool throws:
You place his Form as Suppliant by your Side,
(A helpless Worm, for whom the Saviour dy'd)
Into his Soul call down th'Etherial Beam,
And longing ask to spend, and to be spent for Him.

MISERY.

M I S E R Y.

From the same.

1 LORD, let the Angels praise thy Name,
    Man is a Feeble, Foolish Thing!
Folly and Sin play all his Game,
    Still burns his House, He still doth sing:
To-day he's here, To-morrow gone,
The Madman knows it—and sings on.

2 How canst Thou brook his Foolishness?
    When heedless of the Voice Divine,
Himself alone he seeks to please,
    And carnal Joys prefers to Thine;
Eager thro' Nature's Wilds to rove,
Nor aw'd by Fear, nor charm'd by Love.

3 What strange Pollutions does he wed,
    Slave to his Senses and to Sin!
Naked of GOD, his Guilty Head
    He strives in Midnight Shades to skreen:
Fondly he hopes from Thee to fly,
Unmark'd by Thine all-seeing Eye.

4 The best of Men to Evil yield,
    If but the slightest Trial come:
They fall, by Thee no more upheld:
    And when Affliction calls them home,
Thy gentle Rod they scarce endure,
And murmur to accept their Cure.

5 Wayward they haste, while Nature leads,
    T'escape Thee; but thy gracious Dove
Still mildly o'er their Folly spreads
    The Wings of his expanded Love:
Thou bring'st them back, nor suff'rest those
Who Would be, to Remain Thy Foes.

6 My

6 My GOD, Thy Name Man cannot praise,
    All Brightness Thou, all Purity!
The Sun in his Meridian Blaze
    Is Darkness, if compar'd to Thee.
O how shall sinful Worms proclaim,
Shall Man presume to speak Thy Name?

7 Man cannot serve Thee: All his Care
    Engross'd by grov'ling Appetite,
Is fixt on Earth; his Treasure there,
    His Portion, and his base Delight:
He starts from Virtue's thorny Road,
Alive to Sin, but dead to GOD!

8 Ah, foolish Man, where are thine Eyes?
    Lost in a Crowd of Earthly Cares:
Thy Indolence neglects to rise,
    While Husks to Heav'n thy Soul prefers;
Careless the starry Crown to seize,
By Pleasure bound, or lull'd by Ease.

9 To GOD, thro' all Creation's Bounds
    Th' Unconscious Kinds their Homage bring;
His Praise thro' Ev'ry Grove resounds,
    Nor know the Warblers whom they sing:
But Man, Lord of the Creatures, knows
The Source from whence their Being flows.

10 He owns a GOD —but eyes him not,
    But lets his mad Disorders reign:
They make his Life a constant Blot,
    And Blood Divine an Off'ring vain.
Ah Wretch! thy Heart unsearchable,
Thy Ways mysterious who can tell!

11 Perfect at first, and blest his State,
    Man in his Maker's Image shone;
In Innocence divinely great
    He liv'd; he liv'd to GOD alone:

His

His Heart was Love, his Pulse was Praise,
And Light and Glory deck'd his Face.

12 But alter'd now and *faln* he is,
　　Immerst in Flesh, and *dead within*;
Dead to the Taste of native Bliss,
　　And ever sinking into Sin:
Nay by his wretched Self undone.
Such is Man's State—and such *my own!*

The SINNER.

From the same.

1 WHEN all the Secrets of my Heart
　　With Horror, LORD, I see,
Thine is, I find, the smallest Part,
　　Tho' All be due to Thee.
Thy Footsteps scarce appear within,
　　But Lusts a countless Crowd;
Th'immense Circumference is Sin,
　　A Point is all my Good.

2 O break my Bonds, let Sin enthrall
　　My struggling Soul no more;
Hear thy fall'n Creature's feeble Call,
　　Thine Image now restore!
And tho' my Heart senseless and hard
　　To Thee can scarcely groan,
Yet O remember, gracious LORD,
　　Thou once didst write in Stone!

HOME.

H O M E.

From the same.

1 FAINT is my Head, and sick my Heart,
    While Thou dost ever, ever stay!
Fixt in my Soul I feel Thy Dart,
    Groaning I feel it Night and Day:
Come, LORD, and shew Thyself to me,
Or take, O take me up to Thee!

2 Canst Thou with-hold Thy healing Grace,
    So kindly lavish of Thy Blood;
When swiftly trickling down Thy Face,
    For Me the purple Current flow'd!
Come, LORD, and shew, &c.

3 When Man was lost, *LOVE* look'd about,
    To see what Help in Earth or Sky:
In vain; for none appear'd without;
    The Help did in Thy Bosom lie!
Come, LORD, &c.

4 There lay Thy Son: But left His Rest
    Thraldom and Mis'ry to remove
From those who Glory once possest,
    But wantonly abus'd Thy Love.
Come, LORD, &c.

5 He came —— O my dear Redeemer dear!
    And canst Thou after this be strange?
Not yet within my Heart appear!
    Can Love like Thine or fail or change?
Come, LORD, &c,

6 But if Thou tarriest, why must I?
    My GOD, what is this World to me!
This World of Woe—— hence let them fly,
    The Clouds that part my Soul and Thee.
Come, LORD, &c.   Why

7 Why should this weary World delight,
  Or Sense th'immortal Spirit bind!
Why should frail Beauty's Charms invite,
  The trifling Charms of Womankind?
Come, Lord, &c.

8 A Sigh Thou breath'st into my Heart,
  And earthly Joys I view with Scorn:
Far from my Soul, ye Dreams depart,
  Nor mock me with your vain Return!
Come, Lord, &c.

9 Sorrow and Sin, and Loss and Pain
  Are all that here on Earth we see;
Restless we pant for Ease in vain,
  In vain------'till Ease we find in Thee.
Come, Lord, &c.

10 Idly we talk of Harvests here,
  Eternity our Harvest is:
Grace brings the great Sabbatick Year,
  When ripen'd into Glorious Bliss.
Come, Lord, &c.

11 O loose this Frame, Life's Knot untie,
  That my free Soul may use her Wing;
Now pinion'd with Mortality,
  A weak, entangled, wretched Thing!
Come, Lord, &c.

12 Why should I longer stay and groan?
  The most of me to Heav'n is fled:
My Thoughts and Joys are thither gone;
  To all below I now am dead.
Come, Lord, &c.

E   Come,

13 Come, dearest LORD! my Soul's Desire
　　With eager Pantings gasps for Home:
Thee, Thee my restless Hopes require;
　　My Flesh and Spirit bid Thee come!
Come, LORD, and shew Thyself to me,
Or take, O take me up to Thee!

L O N G I N G.

From the same.

1 WIHT bending Knees, and aking Eyes,
　　　Weary and faint, to Thee my Cries,
To Thee my Tears, my Groans I send:
O when shall my Complainings end?

2　Wither'd my Heart, like barren Ground
Accurst of GOD; my Head turns round,
My Throat is hoarse: I faint, I fall,
Yet falling still for Pity call.

3　Eternal Streams of Pity flow
From Thee their Source to Earth below:
Mothers are kind, because Thou art,
Thy Tenderness o'erflows their Heart.

4　LORD of my Soul, bow down thine Ear,
Hear, Bowels of Compassion, hear!
O give not to the Winds my Pray'r:
Thy Name, thy Hallow'd Name is there!

5　Look on my Sorrows, mark them well,
The Shame, the Pangs, the Fires I feel:
Consider, LORD, thine Ear incline!
Thy Son hath made my Suff'rings Thine.

6　Thou, JESU, on th'accursed Tree
Didst bow thy Dying Head for me;

Incline

Incline it now! Who made the Ear,
Shall He, shall He forget to hear!

7   See Thy poor Duft, in Pity fee,
It ftirs, it creeps, it aims at Thee!
Hafte, fave it from the greedy Tomb!
Come! —Ev'ry Atom bids Thee come!

8   'Tis Thine to help! Forget me not!
O be thy Mercy ne'er forgot!
Lock'd is thy Ear? Yet ftill my Plea
May fpeed: For Mercy keeps the Key.

9   Thou tarrieft, while I fink, I die,
And fall to Nothing! Thou on high
Seeft me Undone: Yet am I ftil'd
By Thee (loft as I am) thy Child!

10   Didft Thou for This forfake thy Throne?
Where are thy antient Mercies gone?
Why fhould my Pain, my Guilt furvive,
And Sin be dead, yet Sorrow live?

11   Yet Sin is dead; and yet abide
Thy Promifes; they fpeak, they chide:
They in thy Bofom pour my Tears,
And my Complaints prefent as Theirs.

12   Hear, JESU! hear my broken Heart!
Broken fo long, that ev'ry Part
Hath got a Tongue that ne'er fhall ceafe,
'Till Thou pronounce " Depart in Peace."

13   My Love, my SAVIOUR, hear my Cry;
By thefe dear Feet, at which I lie!
Pluck out thy Dart, regard my Sighs;
Now heal my Soul, or now it dies.

The

The SEARCH.

From the same.

1 WHITHER, O whither art Thou fled,
   My Saviour and my Love?
My Searches are my daily Bread,
   Yet unsuccessful prove.
My Knees on Earth, on Heav'n mine Eye
   Is fixt; and yet the Sphere,
And yet the Center both deny
   That Thou, my GOD, art there.

2 Yet can I mark that Herbs below
   Their fragrant Greens display,
As if to meet Thee They did know,
   While wither'd I decay.
Yet can I mark how Stars above
   With conscious Lustre shine,
Their Glories borrowing from thy Love,
   While I in Darkness pine.

3 I sent a Sigh to seek Thee out,
   Drawn from my Heart in Pain,
Wing'd like an Arrow; but my Scout
   Return'd, alas! In vain.
Another from my endless Store
   I turn'd into a Groan,
Because the Search was dumb before:
   But all, alas! was one.

4 Where is my GOD? What secret Place
   Still holds, and hides Thee still?
What Covert dares eclipse thy Face?—
   Is it thy Awful Will?
O let not That thy Presence bound:
   Rather let Walls of Brass,
Let Seas and Mountains gird Thee round,
   And I thro' all will pass.

                                   5 Thy

5 Thy Will so vast a Distance is,
    Remotest Points combine,
East touches West, compar'd to this,
    And Heav'n and Hell conjoin.
Take then these Bars, these Lengths away,
    Turn and restore my Soul:
Thy Love Omnipotent display,
    Approach, and make me whole.

6 When Thou, my LORD, my GOD art nigh,
    Nor Life, nor Death can move,
Nor deepest Hell, nor Pow'rs on high
    Can part me from thy Love.
For as thy Absence passes far
    The widest Distance known,
Thy Presence brings my Soul so near,
    That Thou and I are One!

DISCIPLINE.

From the same.

1   O THROW away thy Rod,
      O throw away thy Wrath!
My Gracious SAVIOUR and my GOD,
    O take the gentle Path.

2   Thou seest, my Heart's Desire
    Still unto Thee is bent:
Still does my longing Soul aspire
    To an entire Consent.

3   Not ev'n a Word or Look
    Do I approve or own,
But by the Model of thy Book,
    Thy sacred Book alone.

E 3   4 Altho'

4   Altho' I fail, I weep;
       Altho' I halt in pace,
   Yet ftill with trembling Steps I creep
       Unto the Throne of Grace.

5   O then let Wrath remove:
       For Love will do the Deed!
   Love will the Conqueft gain; with Love
       E'en ftony Hearts will bleed.

6   For Love is fwift of Foot,
       Love is a Man of War;
   Love can refiftlefs Arrows fhoot,
       And hit the Mark from far.

7   Who can efcape his Bow?
       That which hath wrought on Thee,
   Which brought the King of Glory low,
       Muft furely work on me.

8   O throw away thy Rod;
       What tho' Man frailties hath?
   Thou art my SAVIOUR and my GOD!
       O throw away thy Wrath!

DIVINE LOVE

From the German.

1 THou hidden Love of GOD, whofe Height,
     Whofe Depth unfathom'd no Man knows,
  I fee from far thy beauteous Light,
     Inly I figh for thy Repofe:
  My Heart is pain'd, nor can it be
  At reft, 'till it finds Reft in Thee.

2 Thy secret Voice invites me still
    The Sweetness of thy Yoke to prove;
And fain I would: But tho' my Will
    seem fixt, yet wide my Passions rove:
Yet Hindrances strew all the Way;
I aim at Thee, yet from Thee stray.

3 'Tis Mercy all, that Thou hast brought
    My Mind to seek her Peace in Thee!
Yet while I seek, but find Thee not,
    No Peace my wandring Soul shall see.
O when shall all my Wandrings end,
And all my Steps to Thee-ward tend?

4 Is there a Thing beneath the Sun,
    That strives with Thee my Heart to share?
Ah tear it thence, and reign alone,
    The LORD of ev'ry Motion there:
Then shall my Heart from Earth be free,
When it has found Repose in Thee.

5 O hide this SELF from me, that I
    No more, but CHRIST in me may live!
My vile Affections crucify,
    Nor let one darling Lust survive.
In all Things nothing may I see,
Nothing desire, or seek but Thee!

6 O LOVE, thy Sov'reign Aid impart,
    To save me from low-thoughted Care:
Chase this Self-will thro' all my Heart,
    Thro' all its latent Mazes there:
Make me Thy duteous Child, that I
Ceaseless may Abba Father cry.

7 Ah no! ne'er will I backward turn:
    Thine wholly, Thine alone I am!
Thrice happy He, who views with Scorn
    Earth's Toys for Thee his constant Flame.

O help

O help, that I may never move
From the bleſt Footſteps of thy Love!

8 Each Moment draw from Earth away
   My Heart, that lowly waits thy Call:
Speak to my inmoſt Soul, and ſay
   I am thy Love, thy GOD, thy All!
To feel thy Pow'r, to hear thy Voice,
To taſte thy Love is all my Choice!

_____

Written in the Beginning of a Reco-
very from Sickneſs.

1 PEACE, flutt'ring Soul! the Storm is o'er,
   Ended at laſt the doubtful Strife:
Reſpiring now, the Cauſe explore
   That bound thee to a wretched Life.

2 When on the Margin of the Grave,
   Why did I doubt my SAVIOUR's Art?
Ah! why miſtruſt his Will to ſave?
   What meant that Fault'ring of my Heart?

3 'Twas not the ſearching Pain within
   That fill'd my coward Fleſh with Fear;
Nor Conſciouſneſs of Outward Sin;
   Nor Senſe of Diſſolution near.

4 Of Hope I felt no Joyful Ground,
   The Fruit of Righteouſneſs alone;
Naked of CHRIST my Soul I found,
   And ſtarted from a GOD unknown.

5 Corrupt my Will, nor half ſubdu'd,
   Could I his purer Preſence bear?
Unchang'd, unhallow'd, unrenew'd
   Could I before his Face appear?

6 Father

6 Father of Mercies, hear my Call!
    Ere yet returns the Fatal Hour,
Repair my Loſs, retrieve my Fall,
    And raiſe me by thy quick'ning Pow'r.

7 My Nature re-exchange for Thine;
    Be Thou my Life, my Hope, my Gain;
Arm me in Panoply Divine,
    And Death ſhall ſhake his Dart in vain.

8 When I thy promis'd CHRIST have ſeen,
    And claſp'd Him in my Soul's Embrace,
Poſſeſt of my Salvation, Then ——
    Then, let me, LORD, depart in Peace!

After a Recovery from Sickneſs.

1 AND live I yet by Pow'r Divine!
    And have I ſtill my Courſe to run?
Again brought back in its Decline
    The Shadow of my parting Sun?

2 Wondring I aſk, Is This the Breaſt
    Struggling ſo late and torn with Pain!
The Eyes that upward look'd for Reſt,
    And dropt their weary Lids again!

3 The recent Horrors ſtill appear:
    O may they never ceaſe to awe!
Still be the King of Terrors near,
    Whom late in all his Pomp I ſaw.

4 Torture and Sin prepar'd his Way,
    And pointed to a yawning Tomb!
Darkneſs behind eclips'd the Day,
    And check'd my forward Hopes of Home.

5 My feeble Flesh refus'd to bear
    Its strong redoubled Agonies:
When Mercy heard my speechless Pray'r,
    And saw me faintly gasp for Ease.

6 JESUS to my Deliv'rance flew,
    Where sunk in mortal Pangs I lay:
Pale Death his Ancient Conq'ror knew,
    And trembled, and ungrasp'd his Prey!

7 The Fever turn'd its backward Course,
    Arrested by Almighty Pow'r;
Sudden expir'd its Fiery Force,
    And Anguish gnaw'd my Side no more.

8 GOD of my Life, what just Return
    Can sinful Dust and Ashes give?
I only live my Sin to mourn,
    To love my GOD I only live!

9 To Thee, benign and saving Power,
    I consecrate my lengthen'd Days;
While mark'd with Blessings, ev'ry Hour
    Shall speak thy co-extended Praise.

10 How shall I teach the World to love,
    Unchang'd myself, unloos'd my Tongue?
Give me the Pow'r of Faith to prove,
    And Mercy shall be all my Song.

11 Be all my Added Life employ'd
    Thy Image in my Soul to see:
Fill with Thyself the Mighty Void;
    Enlarge my Heart to compass Thee!

12 O give me, SAVIOUR, give me more!
    Thy Mercies to my Soul reveal:
Alas! I *see* their endless Store,
    Yet O! I cannot, cannot *feel!*

13 The

13 The Blessing of thy Love bestow,
    For this my Cries shall never fail;
Wrestling I will not let Thee go,
    I will not, 'till my Suit prevail.

14 I'll weary Thee with my Complaint;
    Here at thy Feet for ever lie,
With longing sick, with groaning faint
    O give me Love, or else I die!

15 Without this best, divinest Grace
    'Tis Death, 'tis worse than Death to live;
'Tis Hell to want thy Blissful Face,
    And Saints in Thee their Heav'n receive.

16 Come then, my Hope, my Life, my LORD,
    And fix in me thy lasting Home!
Be mindful of thy gracious Word,
    Thou with thy promis'd Father, come!

17 Prepare, and then possess my Heart,
    O take me, seize me from above:
Thee do I love, for GOD Thou art;
    Thee do I feel, for GOD is Love!

A Prayer *under Convictions.*

1 FATHER of Light, from whom proceeds
    Whate'er thy Ev'ry Creature needs,
Whose Goodness providently nigh
Feeds the young Ravens when they cry;
To thee I look; my Heart prepare,
Suggest, and hearken to my Pray'r.

2   Since by thy Light Myself I see
Naked, and poor, and void of Thee,
Thine Eyes must all my Thoughts survey,
Preventing what my Lips would say:

                          Thou

Thou feeſt my Wants; for Help they call,
And e'er I ſpeak, Thou know'ſt them all.

3   Thou know'ſt the Baſeneſs of my Mind
Wayward, and impotent, and blind,
Thou know'ſt how unſubdu'd my Will,
Averſe to Good, and prone to Ill:
Thou know'ſt how wide my Paſſions rove,
Nor check'd by Fear, nor charm'd by Love.

4   Fain would I know, as known by Thee,
And feel the Indigence I ſee;
Fain would I all my Vileneſs own,
And deep beneath the Burthen groan:
Abhor the Pride that lurks within,
Deteſt and loath myſelf and Sin.

5   Ah give me, Lord, myſelf to feel,
My total Miſery reveal:
Ah give me, Lord, (I ſtill would ſay)
A Heart to mourn, a Heart to pray;
My Buſineſs this, my only Care,
My Life, my ev'ry Breath be Pray'r.

6   Scarce I begin my ſad Complaint,
When all my warmeſt Wiſhes faint;
Hardly I lift my weeping Eye,
When all my kindling Ardors die;
Nor Hopes nor Fears my Boſom move,
For ſtill I cannot, cannot love.

7   Father, I want a thankful Heart;
I want to taſte how good Thou art,
To plunge me in thy Mercy's Sea,
And comprehend thy Love to me;
The Breadth, and Length, and Depth, and Height,
Of Love divinely infinite.

8 Father

8   Father, I long my Soul to raise,
And dwell for ever on thy Praise;
Thy Praise with Glorious Joy to tell,
In Extasy unspeakable;
While the Full Pow'r of FAITH I know,
And reign triumphant here below.

The 53ᵈ Chapter of Isaiah.

1 WHO hath believ'd the Tidings? Who?
      Or felt the Joys our Words impart?
Gladly confess'd our Record true,
    And found the Saviour in his Heart?
Planted in Nature's barren Ground,
    And cherish'd by JEHOVAH's Care,
There shall th'Immortal Seed be found,
    The Root Divine shall flourish there!

2 See, the Desire of Nations comes;
    Nor outward Pomp bespeaks him near:
A Veil of Flesh the GOD assumes,
    A Servant's Form he stoops to wear;
He lays his every Glory by;
    Ignobly low, obscurely mean,
Of Beauty void, in Reason's Eye,
    The Source of Loveliness is seen.

3 Rejected and despis'd of Men,
    A Man of Griefs, enur'd to Woe;
His only Intimate is Pain,
    And Grief is all his Life below.
We saw, and from the irksome Sight
    Disdainfully our Faces turn'd;
Hell follow'd Him with fierce Despight,
    And Earth the humble Abject scorn'd.

F

4 Surely for Us He humbled was,
    And griev'd with Sorrows, not his own:
Of all his Woes were We the Cause,
    We fill'd his Soul with Pangs unknown.
Yet Him th'Offender we esteem'd,
    Striken by Heav'ns vindictive Rod,
Afflicted for Himself we deem'd,
    And punish'd by an Angry GOD.

5 But O! with our Transgressions stain'd,
    For our Offence He wounded was;
Ours were the Sins that bruis'd, and pain'd,
    And scourg'd, and nail'd Him to the Cross.
The Chastisement that bought our Peace,
    To Sinners due, on Him was laid:
Conscience be still! thy Terrors cease!
    The Debt's discharg'd, the Ransom's paid.

6 What tho' we All, as wand'ring Sheep,
    Have left our GOD, and lov'd to stray,
Refus'd his mild Commands to keep,
    And madly urg'd the downward Way;
Father, on Him thy Bolt did fall,
    The mortal Law thy Son fulfill'd,
Thou laid'st on Him the Guilt of All,
    And by his Stripes we All are heal'd.

7 Accus'd, his Mouth He open'd not,
    He answer'd not by Wrongs oppress'd;
Pure tho' He was from sinful Spot,
    Our Guilt He *Silently* confest!
Meek as a Lamb to Slaughter led,
    A Sheep before his Shearers dumb,
To suffer in the Sinner's Stead,
    Behold the Spotless Victim come!

8 Who could his Heavenly Birth declare,
　　When bound by Man He silent stood,
　When Worms arraign'd Him at their Bar,
　　And doom'd to Death th'Eternal GOD!
　Patient the Sufferings to sustain
　　The Vengeance to Transgressors due,
　Guiltless He groan'd, and died for Man:
　　Sinners rejoice, He died for you!

9 For your *imputed* Guilt He bled,
　　Made Sin a sinful World to save;
　Meekly He sunk among the Dead:
　　The Rich supplied an Honour'd Grave:
　For O! devoid of Sin, and free
　　From Actual or Intail'd Offence,
　No Sinner in Himself was He,
　　But pure and perfect Innocence.

10 Yet Him th'Almighty Father's Will
　　With bruising Chastisements pursu'd,
　Doom'd Him the Weight of Sin to feel,
　　And sternly just requir'd his Blood.
　But lo! the Mortal Debt is paid,
　　The costly Sacrifice is o'er,
　His Soul for Sin an Offering made
　　Revives, and He shall die no more.

11 His numerous Seed He now shall see,
　　Scatter'd thro' all the Earth abroad,
　Blest with His Immortality,
　　Begot by him, and born of GOD.
　Head to his Church o'er all below,
　　Long shall He here his Sons sustain;
　Their bounding Hearts his Power shall know,
　　And bless the lov'd Messiah's Reign.

12 'Twixt GOD and Them He still shall stand,
　　The Children whom his Sire hath given,
　Their Cause shall prosper in his Hand,　　[ven:
　While RIGHTEOUSNESS looks down from Hea-
　　　　　F 2　　　　　　　　While

While pleas'd He counts the ransom'd Race,
  And calls, and draws them from above;
The Travail of his Soul surveys,
  And rests in his Redeeming Love.

13 'Tis done! my Justice asks no more,
  The Satisfaction's fully made:
Their Sins He in his Body bore;
  Their Surety all the Debt has paid.
My Righteous Servant and my Son
  Shall each believing Sinner clear,
And All, who stoop t'abjure their own,
  Shall in his Righteousness appear.

14 Them shall He claim his just Desert,
  Them his Inheritance receive,
And many a contrite humble Heart
  Will I for his Possession give.
Satan He thence shall chase away,
  Assert his Right, his Foes o'ercome;
Stronger than Hell retrieve the Prey,
  And bear the Spoil triumphant Home.

15 For charg'd with all their Guilt he stood,
  Sinners from Suffering to redeem,
For Them He pour'd out all his Blood,
  Their Substitute, He died for Them.
He died; and rose his Death to plead,
  To testify Their Sins forgiven —
And still I hear Him interceed,
  And still He makes Their Claim to Heaven!

Waiting for Redemption.

1 WEARY of struggling with my Pain,
  Hopeless to burst my Nature's Chain,
                Hardly

Hardly I give the Conteſt o'er,
I ſeek to free myſelf no more.

2   From my own Works at laſt I ceaſe,
GOD muſt create and ſeal my Peace;
Fruitleſs my Toil, and Vain my Care,
For all my Fitneſs is Deſpair.

3   LORD, I deſpair myſelf to heal,
I ſee my Sin, but cannot feel:
I cannot, 'till thy Spirit blow,
And bid th'Obedient Waters flow.

4   'Tis Thine an Heart of Fleſh to give,
Thy Gifts I only can receive:
Here then to Thee I all reſign,
To draw, redeem, and ſeal is Thine.

5   With ſimple Faith, to Thee I call,
My Light, my Life, my LORD, my All:
I wait the Moving of the Pool;
I wait the Word that ſpeaks me Whole.

6   Speak, gracious LORD, my Sickneſs cure,
Make my infected Nature pure:
Peace, Righteouſneſs, and Joy impart,
And pour Thyſelf into my Heart.

GAl. iii. 22.

The Scripture hath concluded all un-
der Sin, that the Promiſe by Faith
of JESUS CHRIST *might be given*
to them that believe.

1 JESU, the Sinner's Friend, to Thee
Loſt and undone for Aid I flee.

F 3

Weary of Earth, Myfelf, and Sin:
Open thine Arms, and take me in.

2   Pity, and heal my Sin-fick Soul,
'Tis Thou alone canft make me whole,
Fal'n, 'till in Me thine Image fhine,
And curft I am, 'till Thou art mine.

3   Hear, JESU, hear my helplefs Cry,
O fave a Wretch condemn'd to die!
The Sentence in Myfelf I feel,
And all my Nature teems with Hell.

4   When fhall Concupifcence and Pride
No more my tortur'd Heart divide!
When fhall this Agony be o'er,
And the Old *Adam* rage no more!

5   Awake, the Woman's Conqu'ring Seed,
Awake, and bruife the Serpent's Head,
Tread down thy Foes, with Power controul
The Beaft and Devil in my Soul.

6   The Manfion for Thyfelf prepare,
Difpofe my Heart by Ent'ring there!
'Tis This alone can make me clean,
'Tis This alone can caft out Sin.

7   Long have I vainly hop'd and ftrove
To force my Hardnefs into Love,
To give Thee all thy Laws require;
And labour'd in the Purging Fire:

8   A thoufand fpecious Arts effay'd,
Call'd the deep *Myftic* to my Aid:
His boafted Skill the Brute refin'd,
But left the fubtler Fiend behind.

9 Frail, dark, impure, I ftill remain,
Nor hope to break my Nature's Chain:
The fond felf-emptying Scheme is paft,
And lo! conftrain'd I yield at laft.

10 At laft I own it cannot be
That I fhould fit Myfelf for Thee:
Here then to Thee, I all refign,
Thine is the Work, and only Thine.

11 No more to lift my Eyes I dare
Abandon'd to a juft Defpair;
I Have my Punifhment in View,
I Feel a thoufand Hells my Due.

12 What fhall I fay thy Grace to move?
LORD I am Sin----but Thou art Love:
I give up every Plea befide,
LORD I am damn'd----but Thou haft died!

13 While groaning at thy Feet I fall
Spurn me away, refufe my Call,
If *Love* permit, contract thy Brow,
And, if Thou canft, deftroy me now!

Hoping for GRACE.

From the German.

1 MY Soul before Thee proftrate lies,
  To Thee her Source my Spirit flies,
My Wants I mourn, my Chains I fee:
O let thy Prefence fet me free!

2 Loft and undone, for Aid I cry;
In thy Death, SAVIOUR, let me die!
Griev'd with thy Grief, pain'd with thy Pain,
Ne'er may I feel Self-love again.

3 JESU, vouchsafe my Heart and Will
With thy meek Lowliness to fill;
No more her Pow'r let Nature boast,
But in thy Will may mine be lost.

4 In Life's short Day let me yet more
Of thy enliv'ning Pow'r implore:
My Mind must deeper sink in Thee,
My Foot stand firm from Wandring free.

5 Ye Sons of Men, here nought avails
Your Strength, here all your Wisdom fails;
Who bids a sinful Heart be clean?
Thou only, LORD, supreme of Men.

6 And well I know thy tender Love;
Thou never didst unfaithful prove:
And well I know Thou stand'st by me,
Pleas'd from Myself to set me free.

7 Still will I watch, and labour still
To banish ev'ry Thought of Ill;
'Till Thou in thy good Time appear,
And sav'st me from the Fowler's Snare.

8 Already springing Hope I feel;
GOD will destroy the Pow'r of Hell;
GOD from the Land of Wars and Pain
Leads me where Peace and Safety reign.

9 One only Care my Soul shall know,
Father, all thy Commands to do:
Ah deep engrave it on my Breast,
That I in Thee ev'n now am blest.

10 When my warm Thought I fix on Thee,
And plunge me in thy Mercy's Sea,
Then ev'n on me thy Face shall shine,
And quicken this dead Heart of mine.

11 So ev'n in Storms my Zeal shall grow;
    So shall I thy Hid Sweetness know;
And feel (what endless Age shall prove)
    That Thou, my LORD, my GOD, art Love.

The DAWNING.

From HERBERT.

1 AWAKE, sad Heart, whom Sorrows drown,
    Lift up thine Eyes, and cease to mourn,
Unfold thy Forehead's settled Frown;
    Thy SAVIOUR, and thy Joys return.

2 Awake, sad drooping Heart awake!
    No more lament, and pine, and cry:
His Death Thou ever dost partake,
    Partake at last his Victory.

3 Arise; if thou dost not withstand,
    CHRIST's Resurrection Thine may be:
O break not from the Gracious Hand
    Which, as it rises, raises Thee.

4 Chear'd by thy SAVIOUR's Sorrows rise;
    He griev'd, that Thou mayst cease to grieve;
Dry with his Burial Cloths thine Eyes,
    He dy'd Himself that Thou mayst live!

PSAL. CXXXIX. 23.

Try me, O GOD, and seek the Ground of my Heart.

1 JESU! my great High-priest above,
    My Friend before the Throne of Love!
If now for Me prevails thy Prayer,
If now I find Thee pleading there;

If Thou the Secret Wish convey,
And sweetly prompt my Heart to pray,
Hear; and my weak Petitions join,
Almighty Advocate, to Thine!

2   Fain would I know my utmost Ill,
And groan my Nature's Weight to feel,
To feel the Clouds that round me roll,
The Night that hangs upon my Soul;
The Darkness of my Carnal Mind,
My Will perverse, my Passions blind,
Scatter'd o'er all the Earth abroad,
Immeasurably far from GOD.

3   JESU! my Heart's Desire obtain,
My earnest Suit present, and gain,
My Fulness of Corruption shew,
The Knowledge of Myself bestow;
A deeper Displicence at Sin,
A sharper Sense of Hell within,
A stronger Struggling to get free,
A keener Appetite for Thee.

4   For Thee my Spirit often pants,
Yet often in pursuing faints,
Drooping it soon neglects t'aspire,
Nor fans the ever-dying Fire:
No more thy Glory's Skirts are seen,
The World, the Creature steals between;
Heavenward no more my Wishes move,
And I forget that Thou art Love.

5   O Sovereign Love, to Thee I cry,
Give me thyself, or else I die.
Save me from Death, from Hell set free,
Death, Hell, are but the Want of Thee:
Quicken'd by thy imparted Flame,
Sav'd, when possest of Thee, I am;
My Life, my only Heav'n Thou art:
O might I feel Thee in my Heart!   *The*

The C H A N G E.

From the German.

1 JEsu, whofe Glory's ftreaming Rays,
  Tho' duteous to thy high Command
Not Seraphs view with open Face,
  But veil'd before thy Prefence ftand:
How fhall weak Eyes of Flefh, weigh'd down
  With Sin, and dim with Error's Night,
Dare to behold thy awful Throne,
  Or view thy unapproached Light?

2 Reftore my Sight! let thy free Grace
  An Entrance to the Holieft give!
Open my Eyes of Faith! thy Face
  So fhall I fee; yet feeing live.
Thy Golden Scepter from above
  Reach forth; fee my whole Heart I bow:
Say to my Soul, Thou art my Love,
  My Chofen midft ten thoufand Thou.

3 O JESU, full of Grace! the Sighs
  Of a fick Heart with Pity view!
Hark how my Silence fpeaks; and cries,
  Mercy, Thou GOD of Mercy, fhew!
I know Thou canft not but be Good!
  How fhouldft Thou, LORD, thy Grace reftrain?
Thou, LORD, whofe Blood fo largely flow'd
  To fave me from all Guilt and Pain.

4 Into thy gracious Hands I fall,
  And with the Arms of Faith embrace!
O King of Glory, hear my Call!
  O raife me, heal me by thy Grace!
---Now Righteous thro' thy Wounds I am:
  No Condemnation now I dread:
I tafte Salvation in thy Name,
  Alive in Thee my Living Head!

5 Still let thy Wisdom be my Guide,
  Nor take thy Light from me away:
Still with me let thy Grace abide,
  That I from Thee may never stray:
Let thy Word richly in me dwell;
  Thy Peace and Love my Portion be,
My Joy t'endure, and do thy Will,
  'Till perfect I am found in Thee!

6 Arm me with thy whole Armour, LORD,
  Support my Weakness with thy Might:
Gird on my Thigh thy conq'ring Sword,
  And shield me in the threat'ning Fight:
From Faith to Faith, from Grace to Grace,
  So in thy Strength shall I go on,
'Till Heav'n and Earth flee from thy Face,
  And Glory end what Grace begun.

HYMNS

HYMNS
AND
SACRED POEMS.

PART II.

CHRIST *the Friend of Sinners.*

1 WHERE shall my wondring Soul begin?
   How shall I All to Heav'n aspire?
A Slave redeem'd from Death and Sin,
   A Brand pluck'd from Eternal Fire;
How shall I equal Triumphs raise,
And sing my Great Deliverer's Praise!

2 O how shall I the Goodness tell,
   Father, which Thou to me hast show'd,
That I, a Child of Wrath, and Hell,
   I should be call'd a Child of GOD!
Should know, should feel my Sins forgiven,
Blest with this Antepast of Heaven!

3 And shall I slight my Father's Love,
   Or basely fear his Gifts to own?
Unmindful of his Favours prove?
   Shall I, the hallow'd Cross to shun,
Refuse his Righteousness t'impart,
By hiding it within my Heart?
                    G
                              4 No:

4 No: Tho' the Antient Dragon rage,
 And call forth all his Hoſt to War,
Tho' Earth's Self-righteous Sons engage?
 Them, and their God alike I dare:
JESUS, the Sinner's Friend proclaim,
JESUS, to Sinners ſtill the ſame.

5 Outcaſts of Men, to You I call,
 Harlots, and Publicans, and Thieves!
He ſpreads his Arms t'embrace you all;
 Sinners alone his Grace receives:
No Need of Him the Righteous have,
He came the Loſt to ſeek and ſave!

6 Come all ye *Magdalens* in Luſt,
 Ye Ruffians fell in Murders old;
Repent, and live; deſpair, and truſt!
 JESUS for you to Death was ſold;
Tho' Hell proteſt, and Earth repine,
He died for Crimes like Yours----and Mine.

7 Come, O my guilty Brethren, come,
 Groaning beneath your Load of Sin!
His bleeding Heart ſhall make you room,
 His open Side ſhall take you in:
He calls you Now, invites you home—
Come, O my guilty Brethren, come!

8 For you the purple Current flow'd
 In Pardons from his wounded Side:
Languiſh'd for you th'Eternal GOD,
 For you the Prince of Glory dy'd.
Believe; and All your Sin's forgiven,
Only Believe----and yours is Heaven.

On

On the Conversion of a Common Harlot.

LUKE xv. 10.

There is Joy in the Presence of the Angels of GOD over one Sinner that repenteth.

1 SING ye Heavens, and Earth rejoice,
   Make to GOD a chearful Noise;
He the Work alone hath done,
He hath glorified his Son.

2   Sons of GOD exulting rise,
Join the Triumph of the Skies,
See the Prodigal is come,
Shout to bear the Wanderer home!

3   Strive in Joy with Angels strive,
Dead She was, but now's alive,
Loud repeat the glorious Sound,
Lost She was, but now is found!

4   This through Ages all along,
This be still the Joyous Song,
Wide diffus'd o'er Earth abroad,
Musick in the Ears of GOD.

5   Rescued from the Fowler's Snare,
JESUS spreads his Arms for Her,
JESU's Arms her sacred Fence:
Come, ye Fiends, and pluck her thence!

6   Thence she never shall remove,
Safe in his Redeeming Love:
This the Purchase of his Groans!
This the Soul he died for once!

7   Now the gracious Father fmiles,
Now the SAVIOUR boafts his Spoils:
Now the Spirit grieves no more:
Sing ye Heav'ns, and Earth adore!

Looking unto JESUS *the Author and Finifher of our Faith.*

1   L ORD, if to Me thy Grace hath given,
     A Spark of Life, a Tafte of Heaven,
The Gofpel Pearl, the Woman's Seed,
The Bruifer of the Serpent's Head:

2   Why fleeps my Principle Divine?
Why haftens not my Spark to fhine?
The Saviour in my Heart to move,
And all my Soul to flame with Love?

3   Buried, o'erwhelm'd, and loft in Sin,
And feemingly extinct within,
Th'Immortal Seed unactive lies,
The Heav'nly *Adam* finks, and dies:

4   Dies, and revives the Dying Flame.
Caft down, but not deftroy'd I am,
'Midft thoufand Lufts I ftill refpire,
And tremble, unconfum'd, in Fire.

5   Suffer'd awhile to want my GOD,
To groan beneath my Nature's Load,
That All may own, that All may fee,
Th'Ungodly juftified in Me.

ANO.

ANOTHER.

1   SAVIOUR of Men, how long shall I
 Forgotten at thy Footstool lie!
Close by the Fountain of thy Blood,
Yet groaning still to be renew'd;

2   A Miracle of Grace and Sin,
Pardon'd, yet still, alas, unclean!
Thy Righteousness is *counted* Mine:
When will it in my Nature shine?

3   Darksome I still remain and void,
And painfully unlike my GOD,
'Till Thou diffuse a brighter Ray,
And turn the Glimm'ring into Day.

4   Why didst Thou the First Gift impart,
And sprinkle with thy Blood my Heart,
But that my sprinkled Heart might prove,
The Life and Liberty of Love?

5   Why didst Thou bid my Terrors cease,
And sweetly fill my Soul with Peace,
But that my peaceful Soul might know
The Joys that from Believing flow?

6   See then thy Ransom'd Servant, see,
I hunger, LORD, I thirst for Thee!
Feed me with Love, thy Spirit give,
I gasp, in Him, in Thee to live.

7   The Promis'd Comforter impart,
Open the Fountain in my Heart;
There let Him flow with springing Joys,
And into Life Eternal rise.

8 The

8   There let Him ever, ever dwell,
The Pledge, the Witnefs, and the Seal;
I'll glory then in Sin forgiven,
In CHRIST my Life, my Love, my Heaven!

HYMN *of* THANKSGIVING *to the* FATHER.

1   THEE, O my GOD and King,
      My Father, Thee I fing!
Hear well-pleas'd the joyous Sound,
   Praife from Earth and Heav'n receive;
Loft, I now in CHRIST am found,
   Dead, by Faith in CHRIST I live.

2   Father, behold thy Son,
      In CHRIST I am thy own.
Stranger long to Thee and Reft,
   See the Prodigal is come:
Open wide thine Arms and Breaft,
   Take the weary Wand'rer home.

3   Thine Eye obferv'd from far,
      Thy Pity look'd me near:
Me thy Bowels yearn'd to fee,
   Me thy Mercy ran to find,
Empty, poor, and void of Thee,
   Hungry, fick, and faint, and blind.

4   Thou on my Neck didft fall,
      Thy Kifs forgave me all:
Still the gracious Words I hear,
   Words that made the SAVIOUR mine,
Hafte, for him the Robe prepare,
   His be Righteoufnefs Divine!

5 Thee then, my GOD and King,
 My Father, Thee I fing!
Hear well-pleas'd the joyous Sound,
 Praife from Earth and Heav'n receive;
Loft, I now in CHRIST am found,
 Dead, by FAITH in CHRIST I live.

HYMN *to the* SON.

1 O Filial Deity,
 Accept my New-born Cry!
See the Travail of thy Soul,
 SAVIOUR, and be fatisfy'd;
Take me now, poffefs me whole,
 Who for Me, for Me haft dy'd!

2 Of Life Thou art the Tree,
 My Immortality!
Feed this tender Branch of Thine,
 Ceafelefs Influence derive,
Thou the true, the Heav'nly Vine,
 Grafted into Thee I live.

3 Of Life the Fountain Thou,
 I know----l feel it Now!
Faint and dead no more I droop:
 Thou art in me: Thy Supplies
Ev'ry Moment fpringing up
 Into Life Eternal rife.

4 Thou the Good Shepherd art,
 From Thee I ne'er fhall part:
Thou my Keeper and my Guide,
 Make me ftill thy tender Care,
Gently lead me by thy Side,
 Sweetly in thy Bofom bear.

5 Thou art my Daily Bread;
 O CHRIST, Thou art my Head:

Motion, Virtue, Strength to Me,
   Me thy Living Member flow;
Nourifh'd I, and fed by Thee,
   Up to Thee in all Things grow.

6   Prophet, to me reveal
      Thy Father's perfect Will.
Never Mortal fpake like Thee,
   Human Prophet like Divine :
Loud and ftrong their Voices be,
   Small and ftill and inward Thine!

7   On Thee my Prieft I call,
      Thy Blood aton'd for All.
Still the Lamb as flain appears,
   Still Thou ftand'ft before the Throne,
Ever off'ring up thy Pray'rs,
   Thefe prefenting with thy own.

8   JESU! Thou art my King,
      From Thee my Strength I bring!
Shadow'd by thy mighty Hand,
   SAVIOUR, who fhall pluck me thence?
FAITH fupports, by FAITH I ftand
   Strong as thy Omnipotence,

9   O Filial Deity,
      Accept my New-born Cry!
See the Travail of thy Soul,
   SAVIOUR, and be fatisfy'd ;
Take me now, poffefs me whole,
   Who for Me, for Me haft dy'd!

HYMN *to the* HOLY GHOST.

1   HEAR, Holy Spirit, hear,
     My Inward Comforter!

Loos'd

Loos'd by Thee my ftamm'ring Tongue
· Firft effays to praife Thee now,
This the New, the Joyful Song,
    Hear it in thy Temple Thou!

2   Long o'er my Formlefs Soul
    The dreary Waves did roll;
Void I lay, and funk in Night:
    Thou, the overfhadowing Dove,
Call'dft the Chaos into Light,
    Bad'ft me Be, and live, and love.

3   Thee I exult to Feel,
    Thou in my Heart doft dwell:
There Thou bear'ft thy Witnefs true,
    Shed'ft the Love of GOD abroad;
I in CHRIST a Creature New,
    I, ev'n I, am born of GOD!

4   Ere yet the Time was come
    To fix in Me thy Home,
With me oft Thou didft refide:
    Now, my GOD, Thou In me art!
Here Thou ever fhalt abide;
    One we are, no more to part.

5   Fruit of the SAVIOUR's Pray'r,
    My Promis'd Comforter!
Thee the World cannot receive,
    Thee they neither know nor fee,
Dead is all the Life they live,
    Dark their Light, while void of Thee.

6   Yet I partake thy Grace
    Thro' CHRIST my Righteoufnefs;
Mine the Gifts Thou doft impart,
    Mine the Unction from above,
Pardon written on my Heart,
    Light, and Life, and Joy, and Love.

7 Thy

7 Thy Gifts, beft Paraclete,
  I glory to repeat:
Sweetly Sure of Grace I am,
  Pardon to my Soul apply'd,
Int'reft in the fpotlefs Lamb;
  Dead for All, for me He dy'd.

8 Thou art Thyfelf the Seal;
  I more than Pardon feel:
Peace, Unutterable Peace,
  Joy that Ages ne'er can move,
Faith's Affurance, Hope's Increafe,
  All the Confidence of Love!

9 Pledge of the Promife giv'n,
  My Antepaft of Heav'n; –
Earneft Thou of Joys Divine,
  Joys Divine on Me beftow'd,
Heav'n, and CHRIST, and All is mine,
  All the Plenitude of G O D.

10 Thou art My Inward Guide,
  I afk no Help befide:
Arm of G O D, on Thee I call,
  Weak as Helplefs Infancy!
Weak I am ---- yet cannot fall
  Stay'd by FAITH, and led by Thee!

11 Hear, Holy Spirit, hear,
  My Inward Comforter!
Loos'd by Thee my ftamm'ring Tongue
  Firft effays to praife Thee now;
This the New, the Joyful Song,
  Hear it in thy Temple Thou!

The

The G L A N C E.

From HERBERT.

1 WHEN firſt thy gracious Eye's Survey,
  Ev'n in the midſt of Youth and Night,
Mark'd me, where ſunk in Sin I lay,
  I felt a ſtrange, unknown Delight.

2 My Soul, as all at once renew'd
  Own'd the Divine Phyſician's Art,
So ſwift the healing Look bedew'd,
  Embalm'd, o'er-ran, and fill'd my Heart.

3 Since then I many a bitter Storm
  Have felt, and feeling ſure had dy'd,
Had the malicious Fatal Harm
  Roll'd on its unmoleſted Tide:

4 But working ſtill, within my Soul,
  Thy ſweet Original Joy remain'd;
Thy Love did all my Griefs controul,
  Thy Love the Victory more than gain'd.

5 If the firſt Glance, but open'd now
  And now ſeal'd up, ſo pow'rful prove,
What wondrous Tranſports ſhall we know
  When glorying in thy full-ey'd Love!

6 When Thou ſhalt look us out of Pain,
  And raiſe us to thy Bliſsful Sight,
With open Face ſtrong to ſuſtain
  The Blaze of thy unclouded Light!

FREE

FREE GRACE.

1 AND can it be, that I should gain
    An Int'reſt in the Saviour's Blood!
Dy'd He for Me? ---- who caus'd his Pain!
    For Me? ---- who him to Death purſu'd!
Amazing Love! how can it be
That Thou, my GOD ſhouldſt die for Me?

2 'Tis Myſt'ry all! th'Immortal dies!
    Who can explore his ſtrange Deſign?
In vain the firſt-born Seraph tries
    To found the Depths of Love Divine.
'Tis Mercy all! let Earth adore;
Let Angel Minds enquire no more.

3 He left his Father's Throne above,
    (So free, ſo infinite his Grace!)
Empty'd himſelf of All but Love,
    And bled for *Adam*'s helpleſs Race:
'Tis Mercy all, immenſe and free!
For O my GOD! it found out Me!

4 Long my impriſon'd Spirit lay,
    Faſt bound in Sin and Nature's Night:
Thine Eye diffus'd a quick'ning Ray;
    I woke; the Dungeon flam'd with Light;
My Chains fell off, my Heart was free,
I roſe, went forth, and follow'd Thee.

5 Still the ſmall inward Voice I hear,
    That whiſpers all my Sins forgiv'n;
Still the Atoning Blood is near,
    That quench'd the Wrath of hoſtile Heav'n:
I feel the Life his Wounds impart;
I feel my SAVIOUR in my Heart.

6 No Condemnation now I dread,
    JESUS, and all in Him, is Mine :
Alive in Him, my Living Head,
    And cloath'd in Righteousnefs Divine,
Bold I approach th'Eternal Throne,
And claim the Crown, thro' CHRIST, my own.

The C A L L.

From HERBERT.

1 COME, O my Way, my Truth, my Life!
        A Way that gives us Breath,
    A Truth that ends its Followers Strife,
        A Life that conquers Death!

2 Come, O my Light, my Feaft, my Strength!
        A Light that fhews a Feaft ;
    A Feaft that ftill improves by Length,
        A Strength that makes the Gueft!

3 Come, O my Joy, my Love, my Heart!
        A Joy that none can move ;
    A Love that none can ever part,
        A Heart that joys in Love !

The D I A L O G U E.

From the fame.

1 SAVIOUR, if Thy precious Love
        Could be merited by mine,
    FAITH thefe Mountains would remove ;
        FAITH would make me ever Thine :
    But when all my Care and Pains,
        Worth can ne'er create in Me,
    Nought by me thy Fulnefs gains ;
        Vain the Hope to purchafe Thee.

H   2 C. Ceafe,

2 *C.* Ceafe, my Child, thy Worth to weigh,
    Give the needlefs Conteft o'er:
Mine Thou art! while thus I fay,
    Yield Thee up, and afk no more.
What thy Eftimate may be,
    Only can by Him be told,
Who to ranfom wretched Thee,
    Thee to gain, Himfelf was fold.

3 *S.* But when All in Me is Sin,
    How can I thy Grace obtain?
How prefume Thyfelf to win?
    GOD of Love, the Doubt explain —
Or if Thou the Means fupply,
    Lo! to Thee I All refign!
Make me, LORD, (I afk not why,
    How, I afk not) ever Thine!

4 *C.* This I would—That humbly ftill
    Thou fubmit to my Decree,
Meekly fubjecting thy Will,
    Clofely copying after Me:
That as I did leave my Throne;
    Freely from my Glory part;
Die, to make thy Heart my own —
    S. Ah! no more—Thou break'ft my Heart!

Subjection to CHRIST.

From the German.

1 JESU, to Thee my Heart I bow,
    Strange Flames far from my Soul remove;
Faireft among ten thoufand Thou,
    Be Thou my LORD, my Life, my Love.

2 All Heav'n Thou fill'ft with pure Defire;
    O fhine upon my frozen Breaft;
With facred Warmth my Heart infpire,
    May I too thy hid Sweetnefs tafte.

3 I fee thy Garments roll'd in Blood,
    Thy ftreaming Head, thy Hands, thy Side:
All hail, Thou Suff'ring Conqu'ring GOD!
    Now Man fhall live; for GOD hath dy'd.

4 O kill in Me this Rebel Sin,
    And triumph o'er my willing Breaft:
Reftore thy Image, LORD, therein,
    And lead me to my Father's Reft.

5 Ye earthly Loves, be far away!
    SAVIOUR, be Thou my Love alone;
No more may Mine ufurp the Sway,
    But in me thy great Will be done!

6 Yea, Thou true Witnefs, fpotlefs Lamb,
    All Things for Thee I count but Lofs;
My fole Defire, my conftant Aim,
    My only Glory be thy Crofs!

Renouncing all for CHRIST.

From the French.

1 COME, SAVIOUR JESU, from above,
    Affift me with thy heav'nly Grace,
Withdraw my Heart from worldly Love,
    And for Thyfelf prepare the Place.

2 O let thy facred Prefence fill
    And fet my longing Spirit free,
Which pants to have no other Will,
    But Night and Day to feaft on Thee.

H 2   3 While

3 While in thefe Regions here below,
   No other Good will I purfue;
I'll bid this World of Noife and Show
   With all its flatt'ring Snares, adieu.

4 That Path, with humble Speed I'll feek,
   Wherein my SAVIOUR's Footfteps fhine,
Nor will I hear, nor will I fpeak
   Of any other Love than Thine.

5 To Thee my earneft Soul afpires,
   To Thee I offer all my Vows,
Keep me from falfe and vain Defires,
   My GOD, my SAVIOUR, ard my Spoufe.

6 Henceforth may no prophane Delight
   Divide this confecrated Soul;
Poffefs it Thou, who haft the Right,
   As LORD and Mafter of the whole.

7 Wealth, Honour, Pleafure, or what elfe
   This fhort-enduring World can give,
Tempt as you will, my Heart repels,
   To CHRIST alone refolv'd to live.

8 Thee I can love, and Thee alone
   With holy Peace, and Inward Blifs;
To find Thou tak'ft me for thy own,
   O what a Happinefs is This!

9 Nor Heav'n nor Earth do I defire,
   But thy pure Love within my Breaft,
This, this I always will require,
   And freely give up all the reft.

10 Thy Gifts, if call'd for, I refign,
   Pleas'd to receive, pleas'd to reftore;
Gifts are thy Work; it fhall be mine
   The Giver only to adore.

The INVITATION.

From HERBERT.

1 COME hither All, whose grov'ling Taste
        Inslaves your Souls, and lays them waste;
    Save your Expence, and mend your Cheer:
    Here GOD Himself's prepar'd and drest,
    Himself vouchsafes to be your Feast,
        In whom Alone all Dainties are.

2 Come hither All, whom tempting Wine
    Bows to your Father *Belial*'s Shrine,
        Sin all your Boast, and Sense your GOD:
    Weep now for what you've drank amiss,
    And loose your Taste for sensual Bliss
        By drinking here your SAVIOUR's Blood.

3 Come hither All, whom searching Pain,
    Whom Conscience's loud Cries arraign
        Producing all your Sins to view:
    Taste; and dismiss your Guilty Fear,
    O taste and see that GOD is here
        To heal your Souls, and Sin subdue.

4 Come hither All, whom Careless Joy
    Does with alluring Force destroy,
        While loose ye range beyond your Bounds:
    True Joy is here, that passes quite,
    And all your transient mean Delight
        Drowns, as a Flood the lower Grounds.

5 Come hither All, whose Idol-love,
    While fond the pleasing Pain ye prove,
        Raises your foolish Raptures high:
    True Love is here; whose dying Breath
    Gave Life to Us; who tasted Death,
        And tasting once no more can die.

H 3   6 LORD

6 LORD, I have now invited All,
And inftant ftill the Guefts fhall call,
   Still fhall I All invite to Thee :
For O my GOD, it feems but right
In mine, thy meaneft Servants Sight,
   That where All Is, there All fhould be !

The BANQUET.

From the fame.

1 WELCOME, delicious Sacred Cheer,
   Welcome, my GOD, my SAVIOUR dear,
O with me, In me live and dwell !
Thine, Earthly Joy furpaffes quite,
The Depths of thy fupreme Delight
   Not Angel Tongues can tafte or tell.

2 What Streams of Sweetnefs from the Bowl
Surprize and deluge all my Soul,
   Sweetnefs that is, and makes Divine !
Surely from GOD's Right Hand they flow,
From thence deriv'd to Earth below,
   To chear us with Immortal Wine.

3 Soon as I tafte the Heav'nly Bread,
What Manna o'er my Soul is fhed,
   Manna that Angels never knew !
Victorious Sweetnefs fills my Heart,
Such as my GOD delights t'impart,
   Mighty to fave, and Sin fubdue.

4 I had forgot my Heav'nly Birth,
My Soul degen'rate clave to Earth,
   In Senfe and Sins bafe Pleafures drown'd :
When GOD affum'd Humanity,
And fpilt his Sacred Blood for me,
   To find me grov'ling on the Ground.

5 Soon as his Love has rais'd me up,
He mingles Bleſſings in a Cup,
    And ſweetly meets my raviſh'd Taſte,
Joyous I now throw off my Load,
I caſt my Sins and Care on GOD,
    And Wine becomes a Wing at laſt.

6 Upborn on This, I mount, I fly ;
Regaining ſwift my Native Sky,
    I wipe my ſtreaming Eyes, and ſee
Him, whom I ſeek, for whom I ſue,
My GOD, my SAVIOUR there I view,
    Him, who has done ſo much for me!

7 O let thy wondrous Mercy's Praiſe,
Inſpire, and conſecrate my Lays,
    And take up all my Lines and Life ;
Thy Praiſe my ev'ry Breath employ :
Be all my Buſineſs, all my Joy
    To ſtrive in This, and love the Strife !

Therefore with Angels, &c.

1 LORD and GOD of Heav'nly Pow'rs,
    Theirs ; yet O! benignly Ours;
Glorious King, let Earth proclaim,
Worms attempt to chaunt thy Name.

2   Thee to laud in Songs Divine,
Angels and Archangels join ;
We with them our Voices raiſe,
Echoing thy Eternal Praiſe:

3   Holy, Holy, Holy LORD,
Live by Heav'n and Earth ador'd !
Full of Thee, they ever cry,
Glory be to GOD moſt High '

Glory

Glory be to GOD on high, &c.

1 GLORY be to GOD on high,
    GOD whose Glory fills the Sky:
Peace on Earth to Man forgiv'n,
Man the Well-belov'd of Heav'n!

2   Sov'reign Father, Heav'nly King!
Thee we now prefume to fing;
Glad Thine Attributes confefs,
Glorious all, and numberlefs.

3   Hail! by all thy Works ador'd,
Hail! the everlafting LORD!
Thee, with thankful Hearts, we prove
LORD of Pow'r, and GOD of Love.

4   CHRIST our LORD and GOD we own,
CHRIST the Father's only Son!
Lamb of GOD, for Sinners flain,
SAVIOUR of offending Man!

5   Bow Thine Ear, in Mercy bow,
Hear, the World's Atonement Thou!
JESU, in thy Name we pray,
Take, O take our Sins away.

6   Pow'rful Advocate with GOD,
Juftify us by thy Blood!
Bow Thine Ear, in Mercy bow,
Hear, the World's Atonement Thou!

7   Hear; for Thou, O CHRIST alone
Art with thy great Father One;
One the Holy Ghoft with Thee,
One fupreme Eternal Three.

H Y M N

HYMN to CHRIST.

Alter'd from Dr. Hicks's Reform'd Devotions.

1　JESU, behold the Wife from far,
　　Led to thy Cradle by a Star,
　　　Bring Gifts to Thee, their GOD and King!
　O guide us by Light, that we
　The Way may find, and still to Thee
　　　Our Hearts, our All for Tribute bring.

2　JESU, the pure, the spotless Lamb,
　Who to the Temple humbly came,
　　　Duteous the Legal Rights to pay:
　O make our proud, our stubborn Will,
　All thy wife, gracious Laws fulfil,
　　　Whate'er rebellious Nature say.

3　JESU, who on the fatal Wood
　Pour'dst out thy Life's last Drop of Blood,
　　　Nail'd to th'accursed shameful Cross:
　O may we bless thy Love, and be
　Ready, dear LORD, to bear for Thee
　　　All Shame, all Grief, all Pain, all Loss.

4　JESU, who by Thine own Love slain,
　By Thine own Pow'r took'st Life again,
　　　And Conqueror from the Grave didst rise:
　O may thy Death our Souls revive,
　And ev'n on Earth a new Life give,
　　　A glorious Life that never dies.

5　JESU, who to thy Heav'n again
　Return'dst in Triumph, there to reign
　　　Of Men and Angels Sov'reign King:
　O may our parting Souls take Flight
　Up to that Land of Joy and Light,
　　　And there for ever grateful sing.

6 All

6 All Glory to the sacred Three,
One undivided Deity,
    All Honour, Pow'r, and Love and Praise;
Still may thy blessed Name shine bright
In Beams of uncreated Light,
    Crown'd with its own eternal Rays.

On the CRUCIFIXION.

1 BEHOLD the SAVIOUR of Mankind
    Nail'd to the shameful Tree!
How vast the Love that Him inclin'd
    To bleed and die for Thee!

2 Hark how he groans! while Nature shakes,
    And Earth's strong Pillars bend!
The Temple's Veil in sunder breaks,
    The solid Marbles rend.

3 'Tis done! the precious Ransom's paid;
    Receive my Soul, he cries;
See where he bows his sacred Head!
    He bows his Head and dies.

4 But soon He'll break Death's envious Chain,
    And in full Glory shine!
O Lamb of GOD, was ever Pain,
    Was ever Love like Thine!

The MAGNIFICAT.

1 MY Soul extols the mighty LORD,
    In GOD the SAVIOUR joys my Heart:
Thou hast not my low State abhorr'd;
    Now know I, Thou my SAVIOUR art.

2 Sorrow and Sighs are fled away,
    Peace now I feel, and Joy and Reft:
Renew'd, I hail the Feftal Day,
    Henceforth by endlefs Ages bleft.

3 Great are the Things which Thou haft done,
    How holy is thy Name, O LORD!
How wondrous is thy Mercy fhewn
    To all that tremble at thy Word!

4 Thy conqu'ring Arm with Terror crown'd,
    Appear'd the Humble to fuftain:
And all the Sons of Pride have found
    Their boafted Wifdom void and vain.

5 The Mighty from their native Sky
    Caft down, Thou haft in Darknefs bound:
And rais'd the Worms of Earth on high,
    With Majefty and Glory crown'd.

6 The Rich have pin'd amidft their Store,
    Nor e'er the Way of Peace have trod;
Mean while the hungry Souls thy Pow'r
    Fill'd with the Fulnefs of their G O D.

7 Come, SAVIOUR, come, of old decreed!
    Faithful and true be Thou confeft:
By all Earth's Tribes in *Abraham*'s Seed
    Henceforth thro' endlefs Ages bleft.

Truft in PROVIDENCE.

From the German.

1 COMMIT thou all thy Griefs
    And Ways into his Hands;
To his fure Truth and tender Care,
    Who Earth and Heav'n commands.

2   Who points the Clouds their Courſe,
    Whom Winds and Seas obey;
  He ſhall direct thy wand'ring Feet,
    He ſhall prepare thy Way.

3   Thou on the Lord rely,
    So ſafe ſhalt thou go on;
  Fix on his Work thy ſtedfaſt Eye,
    So ſhall thy Work be done.

4   No Profit canſt thou gain
    By ſelf-conſuming Care;
  To Him commend thy Cauſe, his Ear
    Attends the ſofteſt Pray'r.

5   Thy Everlaſting Truth,
    Father, thy ceaſeleſs Love
  Sees all thy Children's Wants, and knows
    What beſt for each will prove.

6   And whatſoe'er Thou will'ſt,
    Thou doſt, O King of Kings;
  What thy unerring Wiſdom choſe,
    Thy Pow'r to Being brings.

7   Thou ev'ry where haſt Way,
    And all Things ſerve thy Might;
  Thy ev'ry Act pure Bleſſing is,
    Thy Path unſully'd Light.

8   When Thou ariſeſt, Lord,
    What ſhall thy Work withſtand?
  When all thy Children want Thou giv'ſt,
    Who, who ſhall ſtay thy Hand?

9   Give to the Winds thy Fears;
    Hope, and be undiſmay'd;
  GOD hears thy Sighs, and counts thy Tears,
    GOD ſhall lift up thy Head.

         10 Thro'

10 Thro' Waves, and Clouds, and Storms
 He gently clears thy Way;
Wait Thou his Time, so shall this Night
 Soon end in joyous Day.

11 Still heavy is thy Heart?
 Still sink thy Spirits down?
Cast off the Weight, let Fear depart,
 And ev'ry Care be gone.

12 What tho' Thou rulest not?
 Yet Heav'n, and Earth, and Hell
Proclaim, GOD sitteth on the Throne,
 And ruleth all Things well!

13 Leave to his Sov'reign Sway
 To choose, and to command;
So shalt thou wondring own, his Way
 How wise, how strong his Hand.

14 Far, far above thy Thought
 His Counsel shall appear,
When fully He the Work hath wrought,
 That caus'd thy needless Fear.

15 Thou seest our Weakness, LORD,
 Our Hearts are known to Thee;
O lift Thou up the sinking Hand,
 Confirm the feeble Knee!

16 Let us in Life, in Death,
 Thy stedfast Truth declare,
And publish with our latest Breath
 Thy Love and Guardian Care!

In AFFLICTION.

1 ETERNAL Beam of Light Divine,
    Fountain of unexhausted Love,
In whom the FATHER's Glories shine,
    Thro' Earth beneath, and Heav'n above;

2 JESU! the weary Wand'rer's Rest;
    Give me thy easy Yoke to bear,
With stedfast Patience arm my Breast,
    With spotless Love, and lowly Fear.

3 Thankful I take the Cup from Thee,
    Prepar'd and mingled by thy Skill:
Tho' bitter to the Taste it be,
    Pow'rful the wounded Soul to heal.

4 Be Thou, O Rock of Ages nigh:
    So shall each murm'ring Thought be gone,
And Grief, and Fear, and Care shall fly
    As Clouds before the Mid-day Sun.

5 Speak to my warring Passions, " Peace;
    Say to my trembling Heart, " Be still:
Thy Pow'r my Strength and Fortress is,
    For all Things serve thy Sov'reign Will.

6 O Death, where is thy Sting? Where now
    Thy boasted Victory, O Grave?
Who shall contend with GOD: Or, Who
    Can hurt whom GOD delights to save?

In AFFLICTION, or PAIN.

From the German:

1 THou Lamb of GOD, Thou Prince of Peace,
 For Thee my thirsty Soul doth pine!
My longing Soul implores thy Grace,
 O make me in thy Likeness shine.

2 With fraudless, even, humble Mind,
 Thy Will in all Things may I see:
In love be ev'ry Wish resign'd,
 And hallow'd my whole Heart to Thee.

3 When Pain o'er my weak Flesh prevails,
 With Lamb-like Patience arm my Breast;
When Grief my wounded Soul assails,
 In lowly Meekness may I rest.

4 Close by thy Side still may I keep,
 Howe'er Life's various Current flow;
With stedfast Eye mark ev'ry Step,
 And follow Thee where'er Thou go.

5 Thou, LORD, the dreadful Fight hast won;
 Alone Thou hast the Wine-press trod:
In me thy strengthening Grace be shewn,
 O may I conquer thro' thy Blood!

6 So when on *Sion* Thou shalt stand,
 And all Heav'ns Host adore their King,
Shall I be found at thy Right Hand,
 And free from Pain thy Glories sing.

ANOTHER.

From the same.

1 ALL Glory to th'Eternal Three,
  Of Light and Love th'unfathom'd Sea!
Whose boundless Pow'r, whose saving Grace,
Reliev'd me in my deep Distress.

2 Still, LORD, from thy exhaustless Store,
  Pure Blessing, and Salvation show'r;
  'Till Earth I leave, and soar away
  To Regions of unclouded Day.

3 My Heart from all Pollution clean,
  O purge it, tho' with Grief and Pain:
  To Thee lo! I my All resign,
  Thine be my Will, my Soul be Thine.

4 O guide me, lead me in thy Ways:
  'Tis Thine the sinking Hand to raise!
  O may I ever lean on Thee:
  'Tis Thine to prop the feeble Knee.

5 O Father, sanctify this Pain,
  Nor let one Tear be shed in vain!
  Soften, yet arm my Breast: No Fear,
  No Wrath, but Love alone be there.

6 O leave not, cast me not away
  In fierce Temptation's dreadful Day:
  Speak but the Word; instant shall cease
  The Storm, and all my Soul be Peace!

In DESERTION *or* TEMPTATION.

1 AH! my dear LORD, whose changeless Love
  To Me, nor Earth nor Hell can part;
When shall my Feet forget to rove?
 Ah, what shall fix this faithless Heart?

2 Why do these Cares my Soul divide,
  If Thou indeed hast set me free?
Why am I thus, if GOD hath dy'd;
  If GOD hath dy'd to ransom Me?

3 Around me Clouds of Darkness roll,
  In deepest Night I still walk on;
Heavily moves my fainting Soul,
  My Comfort and my GOD are gone.

4 Chearless and all forlorn I droop;
  In vain I lift my weary Eye;
No Gleam of Light, no Ray of Hope
  Appears throughout the darken'd Sky.

5 My feeble Knees I bend again,
  My drooping Hands again I rear:
Vain is the Task, the Effort vain,
  My Heart abhors the irksome Pray'r.

6 Oft with thy Saints my Voice I raise,
  And seem to join the tasteless Song:
Faintly ascends th'imperfect Praise,
  Or dies upon my thoughtless Tongue.

7 Cold, weary, languid, heartless, dead,
  To thy dread Courts I oft repair;
By Conscience drag'd, or Custom led
  I come; nor know that GOD is there!

I 2   8 Nigh

8 Nigh with my Lips to Thee I draw,
   Unconscious at thy Altar found;
 Far off my Heart: Nor touch'd with Awe,
   Nor mov'd – tho' Angels tremble round.

9 In All I do, Myself I feel,
   And groan beneath the wonted Load,
Still unrenew'd, and carnal still,
   Naked of CHRIST, and void of GOD.

10 Nor yet the Earthly *Adam* dies,
   But lives, and moves, and fights again,
Still the fierce Gusts of Passion rise,
   'And rebel Nature strives to reign.

11 Fondly my foolish Heart essays
   T'augment the Source of perfect Bliss,
Love's All-sufficient Sea to raise
   With Drops of Creature-Happiness.

12 O Love! thy Sov'reign Aid impart,
   And guard the Gifts thyself hast giv'n:
My Portion Thou, my Treasure art,
   And Life, and Happiness, and Heav'n.

13 Would ought with Thee my Wishes share,
   Tho' dear as Life the Idol be,
The Idol from my Breast I'll tear,
   Resolv'd to seek my All from Thee.

14 Whate'er I fondly counted Mine,
   To Thee, my LORD, I here restore:
 Gladly I all for Thee resign:
   Give me Thyself, I ask no more!

ANOTHER

ANOTHER.

1 MY GOD (if I may call Thee Mine.
    From Heav'n and Thee remov'd fo far)
Draw nigh; thy pitying Ear incline,
    And caft not out my languid Pray'r.
Gently the Weak Thou lov'ft to lead,
    Thou lov'ft to prop the feeble Knee,
O break not then a bruifed Reed,
    Nor quench the fmoaking Flax in me.

2 Buried in Sin, thy Voice I hear,
    And burft the Barriers of my Tomb,
In all the Marks of Death appear,
    Forth at thy Call, tho' bound, I come,
Give me, O give me fully, LORD,
    Thy Refurrection's Pow'r to know;
Free me indeed; repeat the Word,
    And loofe my Bands, and let me go.

3 Fain would I go to Thee, my GOD,
    Thy Mercies, and my Wants to tell:
I feel my Pardon feal'd in Blood;
    SAVIOUR, thy Love I wait to feel.
Freed from the Pow'r of cancel'd Sin;
    When fhall my Soul triumphant prove?
Why breaks not out the Fire within
    In Flames of Joy, and Praife, and Love?

4 When fhall my Eye affect my Heart,
    Sweetly diffolv'd in gracious Tears?
Ah, LORD, the Stone to Flefh convert!
    And 'till thy lovely Face appears,
Still may I at thy Footftool keep,
    And watch the Smile of op'ning Heav'n:
Much would I pray, and love, and weep;
    I would; for I have much forgiv'n.

5 Yet O! ten Thousand Lusts remain,
    And vex my Soul, absolv'd from Sin,
Still rebel Nature strives to reign,
    Still am I all unclean, unclean!
Assail'd by Pride, allur'd by Sense,
    On Earth the Creatures court my Stay;
False flatt'ring Idols, get ye hence,
    Created Good be far away!

6 JESU, to Thee my Soul aspires,
    JESU, to Thee I plight my Vows,
Keep me from Earthly, base Desires,
    My GOD, my SAVIOUR, and my Spouse.
Fountain of all-sufficient Bliss,
    Thou art the Good I seek below;
Fulness of Joys in Thee there is,
    Without 'tis Mis'ry all, and Woe.

7 Take this poor, wandring, worthless Heart,
    Its Wandrings all to Thee are known,
May no false Rival claim a Part,
    Nor Sin disseize Thee of Thine own.
Stir up thy interposing Pow'r,
    Save me from Sin, from Idols save,
Snatch me from fierce Temptation's Hour,
    And hide, O hide me in the Grave!

8 I *know* Thou wilt accept me Now,
    I *know* my Sins are now forgiv'n!
My Head to Death O let me bow,
    Nor keep my Life, to lose my Heav'n.
Far from this Snare my Soul remove,
    This only Cup would I decline,
I deprecate a Creature-Love,
    O take me, to secure me Thine.

9 Or if thy Wiser Will ordain
    The Trial, I would die to shun,
Welcome the Strife, the Grief, the Pain,
    Thy Name be prais'd, thy Will be done!

I from thy Hand the Cup receive,
  Meekly fubmit to thy Decree,
Gladly for Thee confent to live!
  Thou, LORD, haft liv'd, had died for Me!

ISAIAH xliii. 2.

When thou paffeft thro' the Waters,
I will be with thee; and thro'
the Rivers, they fhall not overflow
thee: When thou walkeft thro' the
Fire thou fhalt not be burnt; nei-
fhall the Flame kindle upon thee.

1 PEACE, doubting Heart—my GOD's I am!
  Who form'd me Man forbids my Fear:
The LORD hath call'd me by my Name,
  The LORD protects for ever near:
His Blood for Me did once atone,
And ftill he loves and guards his own.

2 When paffing thro' the Watry Deep,
  I afk in FAITH his promis'd Aïd,
The Waves an awful Diftance keep,
  And fhrink from my devoted Head:
Fearlefs their Violence I dare;
They cannot harm, for GOD is there!

3 To Him my Eye of FAITH I turn,
  And thro' the Fire purfue my Way;
The Fire forgets its Pow'r to burn,
  The lambent Flames around me play:
I own his Pow'r, accept the Sign,
And fhout to prove the SAVIOUR Mine.

4 Still

4 Still nigh me, O my SAVIOUR, ſtand,
   And guard in fierce Temptation's Hour;
Hide in the Hollow of thy Hand,
   Shew forth in me thy Saving Pow'r,
Still be thy Arm my ſure Defence,
Nor Earth, nor Hell ſhall pluck me thence.

5 Since Thou haſt bid me come to Thee,
   (Good as Thou art, and ſtrong to ſave)
I'll walk o'er Life's tempeſtuous Sea,
   Upborn by the unyielding Wave;
Dauntleſs, tho' Rocks of Pride be near,
And yawning Whirlpools of Deſpair.

6 When Darkneſs intercepts the Skies,
   And Sorrow's Waves around me roll,
When high the Storms of Paſſion riſe,
   And half o'erwhelm my ſinking Soul;
My Soul a ſudden Voice ſhall feel,
And hear a Whiſper, " Peace, be ſtill."

7 Tho' in Affliction's Furnace tried,
   Unhurt, on Snares and Deaths I'll tread;
Tho' Sin aſſail, and Hell thrown wide,
   Pour all its Flames upon my Head,
Like *Moſes*' Buſh I'll mount the higher,
And flouriſh, unconſum'd in Fire.

The BELIEVER's SUPPORT.

From the German.

1 O Thou, to whoſe all-ſearching Sight
   The Darkneſs ſhineth as the Light,
Search, prove my Heart; it pants for Thee:
O burſt theſe Bands, and ſet it free.

2 Waſh

2 Wafh out its Stains, refine its Drofs,
  Nail my Affections to the Crofs!
  Hallow each Thought: Let all within
  Be clean, as Thou, my LORD, art clean.

3 If in this darkfome Wild I ftray,
  Be Thou my Light, be Thou my Way:
  No Foes, no Violence I fear,
  No Fraud, while Thou, my G O D, art near.

4 When rifing Floods my Soul o'erflow,
  When finks my Heart in Waves of Woe,
  JESU, thy timely Aid impart,
  And raife my Head, and cheer my Heart.

5 SAVIOUR, where'er thy Steps I fee,
  Dauntlefs, untir'd I follow Thee:
  O let thy Hand fupport me ftill,
  And lead me to thy holy Hill.

6 If rough and thorny be the Way,
  My Strength proportion to my Day:
  'Till Toil, aed Grief, and Pain fhall ceafe,
  Where all is Calm, and Joy, and Peace.

Living by CHRIST.

From the fame.

1 JESU, thy boundlefs Love to me
     No Thought can reach, no Tongue declare:
  O knit my thankful Heart to Thee,
     And reign without a Rival there:
  Thine wholly, Thine alone I am:
  Be Thou alone my conftant Flame.

2 O grant that nothing in my Soul
    May dwell, but thy pure Love alone:
O may thy Love poffefs me whole,
    My Joy, my Treafure, and my Crown.
Strange Fires far from my Soul remove,
My ev'ry Act, Word, Thought, be Love,

3 O Love, how chearing is thy Ray?
    All Pain before thy Prefence flies!
Care, Anguifh, Sorrow melt away,
    Where'er thy healing Streams arife:
O JESU, nothing may I fee,
Nothing hear, feel, or think but Thee!

4 Unwearied may I this purfue,
    Dauntlefs to the High Prize afpire;
Hourly within my Breaft renew
    This holy Flame, this heav'nly Fire;
And Day and Night be all my Care
To guard this facred Treafure there.

5 My SAVIOUR, Thou thy Love to me
    In Want, in Pain, in Shame haft fhow'd;
For me on the accurfed Tree,
    Thou pouredft forth thy guiltlefs Blood:
Thy Wounds upon my Heart imprefs,
Nor ought fhall the lov'd Stamp efface.

6 More hard than Marble is my Heart,
    And foul with Sins of deepeft Stain:
But Thou the mighty SAVIOUR art,
    Nor flow'd thy cleanfing Blood in vain.
Ah! foften, melt this Rock, and may
Thy Blood wafh all thefe Stains away.

7 O that my Heart, which opens ftands,
    May catch each Drop, that torturing Pain,
Arm'd by my Sins, wrung from thy Hands,
    Thy Feet, thy Head, thy ev'ry Vein:

That

That ftill my Breaft may heave with Sighs,
Still Tears of Love o'erflow my Eyes.

8 O that I as a little Child
　May follow Thee, nor ever reft,
'Till fweetly Thou haft pour'd thy mild
　And lowly Mind into my Breaft.
Nor ever may we parted be
'Till I become one Spirit with Thee.

9 O draw me, SAVIOUR, after Thee,
　So fhall I run and never tire:
With gracious Words ftill comfort me;
　Be Thou my Hope, my fole Defire:
Free me from ev'ry Weight: Nor Fear,
Nor Sin can come, if Thou art here.

10 My Health, my Light, my Life, my Crown,
　My Portion, and my Treafure Thou!
O take me, feal me for Thine own;
　To Thee alone my Soul I bow:
Without Thee all is Pain; my Mind
Repofe in nought but Thee can find.

11 Howe'er I rove, where'er I turn,
　In Thee alone is all my Reft:
Be Thou my Flame; within me burn,
　JESU, and I in Thee am bleft.
Thou art the Balm of Life: My Soul
Is faint; O fave, O make it whole!

12 What in thy Love poffefs I not?
　My Star by Night, my Sun by Day;
My Spring of Life when parch'd with Drought,
　My Wine to chear, my Bread to ftay,
My Strength, my Shield, my fafe Abode,
My Robe before the Throne of GOD!

13 Ah Love! Thy Influence withdrawn
    What profits me that I am born?
All my Delight, my Joy is gone,
    Nor know I Peace, 'till Thou return:
Thee may I seek 'till I attain;
And never may we part again.

14 From all Eternity with Love
    Unchangeable Thou haft me view'd;
Ere knew this beating Heart to move,
    Thy tender Mercies me purfu'd:
Ever with me may they abide,
And clofe me in on ev'ry Side.

15 Still let thy Love point out my Way,
    (How wondrous Things thy Love hath wrought!)
Still lead me left I go aftray,
    Direct my Work, infpire my Thought:
And when I fall, foon may I hear
Thy Voice, and know that Love is near.

16 In Suff'ring be thy Love my Peace,
    In Weaknefs be thy Love my Pow'r;
And when the Storms of Life fhall ceafe,
    JESU, in that important Hour,
In Death as Life be Thou my Guide,
And fave me, who for me haft died!

GOD's Love to Mankind.

From the fame.

1 O GOD, of Good th'unfathom'd Sea,
    Who would not give his Heart to Thee!
Who would not love Thee with his Might?
O JESU, Lover of Mankind,
Who would not his whole Soul and Mind
    With all his Strength to Thee unite?

2 Thou

2 Thou shin'st with everlasting Rays;
  Before the unsufferable Blaze
     Angels with both Wings veil their Eyes:
  Yet free as Air thy Bounty streams
  On all thy Works; thy Mercy's Beams
     Diffusive as thy Sun's arise.

3 Astonish'd at thy frowning Brow,
  Earth, Hell, and Heav'ns strong Pillars bow,
     Terrible Majesty is Thine!
  Who then can that vast Love express
  Which bows Thee down to me, who less
     Than nothing am, 'till Thou art mine?

4 High-thron'd on Heav'ns eternal Hill,
  In Number, Weight, and Measure still
     Thou sweetly ord'rest all that is:
  And yet Thou deign'st to come to me,
  And guide my Steps, that I with Thee
     Enthron'd may reign in endless Bliss.

5 Fountain of Good, all Blessing flows
  From Thee; no Want thy Fulness knows:
     What but Thyself canst Thou desire?
  Yes: Self-sufficient as Thou art,
  Thou dost desire my worthless Heart,
     This, only this Thou dost require.

6 Primeval Beauty! in thy Sight
  The first-born, fairest Sons of Light
     See all their brightest Glories fade:
  What then to me thy Eyes could turn,
  In Sin conceiv'd, of Woman born,
     A Worm, a Leaf, a Blast, a Shade?

7 Hell's Armies tremble at thy Nod,
  And trembling own th'Almighty GOD,
     Sov'reign of Earth, Air, Hell and Sky.
        K 2   But

But who is This that comes from far,
Whofe Garments roll'd in Blood appear?
'Tis GOD made Man for Man to die!

8 O GOD of Good th'unfathom'd Sea,
Who would not give his Heart to Thee?
Who would not love Thee with his Might?
O JESU, Lover of Mankind,
Who would not his whole Soul and Mind
With all his Strength to Thee unite?

***

GOD's GREATNESS.

From the fame.

1 O GOD, Thou bottomlefs Abyfs,
Thee to Perfection who can know?
O Height immenfe! what Words fuffice
Thy countlefs Attributes to fhow:
Unfathomable Depths Thou art!
O plunge me in thy Mercy's Sea;
Void of true Wifdom is my Heart,
With Love embrace and cover me.
While Thee All-infinite I fet
By FAITH before my ravifh'd Eye,
My Weaknefs bends beneath the Weight,
O'erpower'd I fink, I faint, I die.

2 Eternity thy Fountain was,
Which, like Thee, no Beginning knew;
Thou waft e'er Time began his Race,
Ere glow'd with Stars th'Etherial Blue:
Greatnefs unfpeakable is Thine,
Greatnefs, whofe undiminifh'd Ray,
When fhort-liv'd Worlds are loft, fhall fhine,
When Earth and Heav'n are fled away.

Unchan-

Unchangeable, all-perfect LORD,
   Essential Life's unbounded Sea,
What lives and moves, lives by thy Word;
   It lives, and moves, and is from Thee.

3 Thy Parent-Hand, thy forming Skill
   Firm fix'd this Universal Chain;
Else empty, barren Darkness still
   Had held his unmolested Reign:
Whate'er in Earth, or Sea, or Sky
   Or shuns, or meets the wandring Thought,
Escapes or strikes the searching Eye,
   By Thee was to Perfection brought.
High is thy Pow'r above all Height:
   Whate'er thy Will decrees is done:
Thy Wisdom equal to thy Might
   Only to Thee, O GOD, is known.

4 Heaven's Glory is thy awful Throne,
   Yet Earth partakes thy gracious Sway;
Vain Man! thy Wisdom Folly own,
   Lost is thy Reason's feeble Ray.
What his dim Eye could never see,
   Is plain and naked to thy Sight;
What thickest Darkness veils, to Thee
   Shines clearly as the Morning Light:
In Light Thou dwell'st: Light that no Shade,
   No Variation ever knew:
And Heav'n and Hell stand all display'd,
   And open to thy piercing View.

5 Thou, true and only GOD, lead'st forth
   Th'immortal Armies of the Sky:
Thou laugh'st to scorn the Gods of Earth;
   Thou thunder'st, and amaz'd they fly.
With down-cast Eye th'Angelick Choir
   Appear before thy awful Face,
Trembling they strike the golden Lyre,
   And thro' Heav'ns Vault resound thy Praise.

        In

In Earth, in Heav'n, in all Thou art:
  The confcious Creature feels thy Nod,
Whofe forming Hand on every Part
  Impreft the Image of its GOD.

6 Thine, LORD, is Wifdom, Thine alone;
  Juftice, and Truth before Thee ftand;
Yet nearer to thy facred Throne
  Mercy with-holds thy lifted Hand.
Each Ev'ning fhews thy tender Love,
  Each rifing Morn thy plenteous Grace;
Thy waken'd Wrath doth flowly move,
  Thy willing Mercy flies apace:
To thy benign, indulgent Care,
  Father, this Light, this Breath we owe,
And all we have, and all we are
  From Thee, great Source of Being flow.

7 Parent of Good, thy bounteous Hand
  Inceffant Bleffings down diftills,
And all in Air, or Sea, or Land
  With plenteous Food and Gladnefs fills.
All Things in Thee live, move, and are,
  Thy Pow'r infus'd doth all fuftain;
Ev'n thofe thy daily Favours fhare
  Who thanklefs fpurn thy eafy Reign.
Thy Sun Thou bidft his genial Ray
  Alike on All impartial pour;
To all who hate or blefs thy Sway
  Thou bidft defcend the fruitful Show'r.

8 Yet while at length, who fcorn'd thy Might
  Shall feel Thee a confuming Fire,
How fweet the Joys, the Crown how bright
  Of thofe who to thy Love afpire!
All Creatures praife th'Eternal Name!
  Ye Hofts that to his Courts belong,
Cherubic Quires, Seraphic Flames,
  Awake th'everlafting Song.

Thrice

Thrice Holy, Thine the Kingdom is,
  The Pow'r omnipotent is Thine,
And when created Nature dies
  Thy never-ceasing Glories shine.

HYMN *on the Titles of* CHRIST.

1   ARISE, my Soul, arise
      Thy SAVIOUR's Sacrifice!
  All the Names that Love could find,
    All the Forms that Love could take
  JESUS in Himself has join'd,
    Thee, my Soul his own to make.

2   Equal with GOD, most High,
        He laid his Glory by:
  He, th'Eternal GOD, was born,
    Man with Men He deign'd t'appear,
  Object of his Creature's Scorn,
    Pleas'd a Servant's Form to wear.

3   Hail everlasting LORD,
        Divine, Incarnate *Word!*
  Thee let all my Pow'rs confess,
    Thee my latest Breath proclaim;
  Help, ye Angel Choirs, to bless,
    Shout the lov'd *Immanuel's* Name.

4   Fruit of a Virgin's Womb
        The promis'd Blessing's come:
  CHRIST the Father's Hope of old,
    CHRIST the *Woman's* conqu'ring *Seed,*
  CHRIST the SAVIOUR! long foretold,
    Born to bruise the Serpent's Head.

5   Refulgent from afar
        See the bright *Morning Star!*

See

See the *Day-spring* from on high
   Late in deepeft Darknefs rife,
Night recedes, the Shadows fly,
   Flame with Day the Op'ning Skies!

6   Our Eyes on Earth furvey
     The Dazling *Shechinah!*
Bright, in endlefs Glory bright,
   Now in Flefh He ftoops to dwell,
GOD of GOD, and Light of Light,
   Image of th' Invifible.

7   He fhines on Earth ador'd
     The *Prefence of the* LORD:
GOD, the mighty GOD and true,
   GOD by higheft Heav'n confeft,
Stands difplay'd to Mortal View,
   GOD Supreme, for ever bleft.

8   JESU! to Thee I bow
     Th' Almighty's *Fellow* Thou!
Thou, the Father's Only Son;
   Pleas'd He ever is in Thee,
Juft and Holy Thou alone,
   Full of Grace and Truth for Me.

9   High above ev'ry Name
     JESUS, the great *I AM!*
Bows to *JESUS* ev'ry Knee,
   Things in Heav'n, and Earth, and Hell,
Saints adore Him, Demons flee,
   Fiends, and Men, and Angels feel.

10   He left his Throne above
     Emptied of all, but Love:
Whom the Heav'ns cannot contain
   GOD vouchfaf'd a Worm t' appear,
LORD of Glory, *Son of Man,*
   Poor, and vile, and abject here.

11   His own on Earth he fought ---- --
       His own receiv'd Him not:
Him, a Sign by All blafphem'd,
     Outcaft and defpis'd of Men,
Him they all a Madman deem'd,
     Bold to fcoff the *Nazarine.*

12   Hail *Galilean* King!
       Thy humble State I fing;
Never fhall my Triumphs' end,
     Hail derided Majefty,
JESUS, hail! the Sinner's Friend,
     Friend of Publicans—and Me!

13   Thine Eye obferv'd my Pain,
       Thou good *Samaritan!*
Spoil'd I lay, and bruis'd by Sin,
     Gafp'd my faint expiring Soul,
Wine and Oil thy Love pour'd in,
     Clos'd my Wounds, and made me whole.

14   Hail the Life-giving LORD,
       Divine, Engrafted Word!
Thee the *Life* my Soul has found,
     Thee the *Refurrection* prov'd:
Dead I heard the Quick'ning Sound,
     Own'd thy Voice; Believ'd, and Lov'd!

15   With Thee gone up on high
       I live, no more to die:
Firft and *Laft,* I feel Thee now,
     Witnefs of thy Empty Tomb,
Alpha and Omega Thou,
     Waft, and Art, and Art to come!

IId *HYMN*

II^d *HYMN to CHRIST.*

1 SAVIOUR, the World's and Mine,
   Was ever Grief like Thine!
Thou my Pain, my Curse haft took,
   All my Sins were laid on Thee;
Help me, LORD; to Thee I look,
   Draw me, SAVIOUR, after Thee.

2 'Tis done! My GOD hath died,
   My Love is Crucify'd!
Break this ftony Heart of mine,
   Pour my Eyes a ceafelefs Flood,
Feel, my Soul, the Pangs Divine,
   Catch, my Heart, the iffuing Blood!

3 When, O my GOD, fhall I
   For Thee fubmit to die?
How the mighty Debt repay,
   Rival of thy Paffion prove?
Lead me in Thyfelf the Way,
   Melt my Hardnefs into Love.

4 To Love is all my Wifh,
   I only live for This:
Grant me, LORD, my Heart's Defire,
   There by FAITH for ever dwell:
This I always will require
   Thee and only Thee to feel.

5 Thy Pow'r I pant to prove
   Rooted and fix'd in Love,
Strengthen'd by thy Spirit's Might,
   Wife to fathom Things Divine,
What the Length, and Breadth, and Height,
   What the Depth of Love like Thine.

6 Ah!

6   Ah! give me This to know
       With all thy Saints below.
Swells my Soul to compaſs Thee,
    Gaſps in Thee to live and move,
Fill'd with All the Deity,
    All immerſt and loſt in Love!

III^d *HYMN to CHRIST.*

1   STILL, O my Soul, prolong
      The never-ceaſing Song!
CHRIST my Théme, my Hópe, my Joy;
    His be all my Happy Days,
Praiſe my ev'ry Hour employ,
    Ev'ry Breath be ſpent in Praiſe.

2   His would I wholly be
      Who liv'd and died for me:
Grief was all his Life below,
    Pain, and Poverty, and Loſs:
Mine the Sins that bruis'd Him ſo,
    Scourg'd, and nail'd him to the Croſs.

3   He bore the Curſe of All,
      A Spotleſs Criminal:
Burthen'd with a World of Guilt,
    Blacken'd with Imputed Sin,
Man to ſave his Blood he ſpilt,
    Died, to make the Sinner clean.

4   Join Earth and Heav'n to bleſs
      The LORD *our Righteouſneſs!*
Myſt'ry of Redemption This,
    This the SAVIOUR's ſtrange Deſign,
Man's Offence was Counted His,
    Ours is Righteouſneſs Divine.

5   Far as our Parent's Fall
       The Gift is come to All:
   Sinn'd we All, and died in one?
      Juſt in One we All are made,
   CHRIST the Law fulfill'd alone,
      Dy'd for All, for All Obey'd.

6   In Him compleat we ſhine,
     . His Death, his Life is Mine.
   Fully am I juſtify'd,
      Free from Sin, and more than free;
   Guiltleſs, ſince for Me He dy'd,
      Righteous, ſince He Liv'd for Me!

7   JESU! to Thee I bow,
      Sav'd to the Utmoſt now.
   O the Depth of Love Divine!
      Who thy Wiſdom's Stores can tell?
   Knowledge infinite is Thine,
      All thy Ways Unſearchable!

Hymn to *CHRIST the King.*

1 JESU, my GOD and King,
      Thy Regal State I ſing.
   Thou, and only Thou art great,
      High thine Everlaſting Throne;
   Thou the Sov'reign Potentate,
      Bleſt, Immortal Thou alone.

2   Eſſay your choiceſt Strains,
      The King *Meſſiah* reigns!
   Tune your Harps, Celeſtial Quire,
      Joyful all, your Voices raiſe,
   CHRIST than Earth-born Monarchs higher,
      Sons of Men and Angels praiſe.

3 Hail your dread LORD and Ours,
   Dominions, Thrones, and Pow'rs!
 Source of Pow'r He rules alone:
  Veil your Eyes, and proftrate fall,
 Caft your Crowns before his Throne,
  Hail the Caufe, the LORD of all!

4 Let Earth's remoteft Bound
   With echoing Joys refound;
 CHRIST to praife let all confpire:
  Praife doth all to CHRIST belong;
 Shout ye firft-born Sons of Fire,
  Earth repeat the Glorious Song.

5 Worthy, O LORD, art Thou
   That 'ev'ry Knee fhould bow,
 Every Tongue to Thee confefs,
  Univerfal Nature join,
 Strong and Mighty Thee to blefs,
  Gracious, Merciful, Benign!

6 Wifdom is due to Thee,
   And Might, and Majefty:
 Thee in Mercy rich we prove;
  Glory, Honour, Praife receive,
 Worthy Thou of all our Love,
  More than all we pant to give.

7 Juftice and Truth maintain
   Thine Everlafting Reign.
 One with Thine Almighty Sire,
  Partner of an Equal Throne,
 King of Hearts, let all confpire,
  Gratefully thy Sway to own.

8 Prince of the Hofts of GOD,
   Difplay thy Pow'r abroad:

Strong and high is thy Right Hand,
 Terrible in Majefty!
Who can in Thine Anger ftand?
 Who the vengeful Bolt can flee?

9 Thee when the Dragon's Pride
  To Battle vain defy'd,
Brighter than the Morning-ftar
 Lucifer, as Lightning fell,
Far from Heav'n, from Glory far,
 Headlong hurl'd to deepeft Hell.

10 Sin felt of old thy Pow'r,
  Thou Patient Conqueror!
Long he vex'd the World below,
 Long they groan'd beneath his Reign;
Thou deftroy'dft the Tyrant Foe,
 Thou redeem'dft the Captive, Man.

11 Trembles the King of Fears
  Whene'er thy Crofs appears.
Once its dreaded Force he found:
 SAVIOUR, cleave again the Sky;
Slain by an Eternal Wound
 Death fhall then for ever die!

II^d *Hymn to CHRIST the King.*

1 JESU, Thou art our King,
  To Me thy Succour bring.
CHRIST the Mighty One art Thou,
 Help for All on Thee is laid:
This the Word; I claim it Now,
 Send me now the Promis'd Aid.

2 High on thy Father's Throne,
  O look with Pity down!

         Held

Help, O help! attend my Call,
  Captive lead Captivity,
King of Glory, Lord of All,
  Christ, be Lord, be King to Me!

3   I pant to feel thy Sway,
        And only Thee t'obey.
Thee my Spirit gasps to meet,
  This my one, my ceaseless Pray'r,
Make, O make my Heart thy Seat,
  O set up thy Kingdom there!

4   Triumph and reign in Me,
        And spread thy Victory:
Hell, and Death, and Sin controul,
  Pride, and Self, and ev'ry Foe,
All subdue; thro' all my Soul
  Conqu'ring and to conquer go.

The Saviour *glorify'd by All.*

From *the* German.

1   THOU, Jesu, art our King,
        Thy ceaseless Praise we sing:
Praise shall our glad Tongue employ,
  Praise o'erflow our grateful Soul,
While we vital Breath enjoy,
  While Eternal Ages roll.

2   Thou art th'Eternal Light,
        That shin'st in deepest Night.
Wondring gaz'd th'Angelic Train,
  While Thou bow'dst the Heav'ns beneath,
GOD with GOD wert Man with Man,
  Man to save from endless Death.

3   Thou for our Pain didſt mourn,
         Thou haſt our Sickneſs born:
All our Sins on Thee were laid;
      Thou with unexampled Grace
All the mighty Debt haſt paid
      Due from *Adam*'s helpleſs Race.

4   Thou haſt o'erthrown the Foe,
         GOD's Kingdom fix'd below.
Conqu'ror of all adverſe Pow'r,
      Thou Heav'n's Gates haſt open'd wide:
Thou Thine own doſt lead ſecure
      In thy Croſs, and by thy Side.

5   Enthron'd above yon Sky
         Thou reign'ſt with G O D moſt high.
Proſtrate at thy Feet we fall:
      Pow'r ſupreme to Thee is giv'n;
Thee, the righteous Judge of all,
      Sons of Earth, and Hoſts of Heav'n.

6   Cherubs with Seraphs join,
         And in thy Praiſe combine:
All their Quires thy Glories ſing:
      Who ſhall dare with Thee to vie?
Mighty LORD, eternal King,
      Sov'reign both of Earth and Sky!

7   Hail venerable Train,
         Patriarchs, firſt-born of Men!
Hail Apoſtles of the Lamb,
      By whoſe Strength ye faithful prov'd:
Join t'extol his ſacred Name
      Whom in Life and Death ye lov'd.

8   The Church thro' all her Bounds
         With thy high Praiſe reſounds.

Confeſ-

Confeſſors undaunted here
   Unaſham'd proclaim their King ;
Children's feebler Voices there
   To thy Name Hoſanna's ſing.

9   'Midſt Danger's blackeſt Frown
   Thee Hoſts of Martyrs own :
Pain and Shame alike they dare,
   Firmly, ſingularly Good ;
Glorying thy Croſs to bear,
   'Till they ſeal their Faith with Blood.

10   Ev'n Heathens feel thy Pow'r,
   Thou ſuff'ring Conqueror !
Thouſand-Virgins, chaſte and clean,
   From Love's pleaſing Witchcraft free;
Fairer than the Sons of Men,
   Conſecrate their Hearts to Thee.

11   Wide Earth's remoteſt Bound
   Full of thy Praiſe is found :
And all Heav'ns eternal Day
   With thy ſtreaming Glory flames :
All thy Foes ſhall melt away
   From th'inſufferable Beams.

12   O Lord, O GOD of Love,
   Let Us thy Mercy prove !
King of all with pitying Eye
   Mark the Toil, the Pains we feel :
'Midſt the Snares of Death we lie,
   'Midſt the banded Pow'rs of Hell.

13   Ariſe, ſtir up thy Pow'r
   Thou deathleſs Conqueror !
Help us to obtain the Prize,
   Help us well to cloſe our Race ;
That with Thee above the Skies
   Endleſs Joys we may poſſeſs

I 3

A MORNING HYMN.

1 " SEE the Day-fpring from afar
    " Ufher'd by the Morning-Star!
Hafte ; to Him who fends the Light,
Hallow the Remains of Night.

2 Souls, put on your glorious Drefs,
Waking into Righteoufnefs:
Cloath'd with CHRIST afpire to fhine,
Radiance He of Light Divine;

3 Beam of the Eternal Beam,
He in GOD, and GOD in Him!
Strive we Him in Us to fee,
Tranfcript of the Deity.

4 Burft we then the Bands of Death,
Rais'd by his all-quickning Breath ;
Long we to be loos'd from Earth,
Struggle into fecond Birth.

5 Spent at length is Nature's Night;
CHRIST attends to give us Light,
CHRIST attends Himfelf to give ;
GOD we now may fee, and live.

6 Tho' the Outward Man decay ;
Form'd within us Day by Day
Still the Inner Man we view,
CHRIST creating all Things New.

7 Turn, O turn us, LORD, again,
Raifer Thou of Fallen Man!
Sin deftroy, and Nature's Boaft,
SAVIOUR Thou of Spirits Loft!

8 Thy great Will in Us be done:
Crucified and dead Our own,
Ours no longer let us be;
Hide us from Ourselves in Thee!

9 Thou the Life, the Truth, the Way,
Suffer us no more to stray;
Give us, LORD, and ever give
Thee to know, in Thee to live!

ANOTHER.   *From the* German.

1 JESU, thy Light again I view,
   Again thy Mercy's Beams I see,
And all within me wakes, anew
   To pant for thy Immensity:
Again my Thoughts to Thee aspire
In fervent Flames of strong Desire.

2 But O! what Offering shall I give
   To Thee, the LORD of Earth and Skies?
My Spirit, Soul, and Flesh receive
   An holy, living Sacrifice:
Small as it is, 'tis all my Store:
More shouldst Thou have if I had more.

3 Now then, my GOD, Thou hast my Soul;
   No longer mine, but Thine I am:
Guard Thou thy own; possess it whole,
   Chear it by Hope, with Love inflame.
Thou hast my Spirit; there display
Thy Glory, to the perfect Day.

4 Thou hast my Flesh; Thine hallow'd Shrine,
   Devoted solely to thy Will:
Here let thy Light for ever shine,
   This House still let thy Presence fill:
O Source of Life, live, dwell, and move
In Me, 'till all my Life be Love.

5 O

5 O never in thefe Veils of Shame,
   Sad Fruits of Sin, my Glorying be!
Cloath with Salvation thro' thy Name
   My Soul, and may I put on Thee!
Be living FAITH my coftly Drefs,
And my beft Robe thy Righteoufnefs!

6 Send down thy Likenefs from above,
   And let this my Adorning be:
Cloath me with Wifdom, Patience, Love,
   With Lowlinefs, and Purity,
Than Gold and Pearls more precious far,
And brighter than the Morning-Star.

7 LORD, arm me with thy Spirit's Might,
   Since I am call'd by thy great Name:
In Thee my wandring Thoughts unite,
   Of all my Works be Thou the Aim.
Thy Love attend me all my Days,
And my fole Bufinefs be thy Praife!

CHRIST *protecting and fanctifying.*

From the fame.

1 O JESU, Source of calm Repofe,
   Thy Like nor Man, nor Angel knows,
     Faireft among ten thoufand fair!
Even thofe whom Death's fad Fetters bound,
Whom thickeft Darknefs compaft round,
     Find Light and Life, if Thou appear.

2 Effulgence of the Light Divine,
Ere rolling Planets knew to fhine,
     Ere Time its ceafelefs Courfe began;
Thou, when th'appointed Hour was come,
Didft not abhor the Virgin's Womb,
     But GOD with GOD wert Man with Man.

3 The

3 The World, Sin, Death oppofe in vain,
Thou by thy dying Death haft flain,
   My great Deliverer, and my GOD!
In vain does the old Dragon rage,
In vain all Hell its Pow'rs engage;
   None can withftand thy conqu'ring Blood.

4 LORD over all, fent to fulfil
Thy gracious Father's fov'reign Will,
   To thy dread Scepter will I bow:
With duteous Rev'rence at thy Feet,
Like humble *Mary*, lo, I fit:
   Speak, LORD, thy Servant heareth now.

5 Renew Thine Image, LORD, in me,
Lowly and gentle may I be;
   No Charms but thefe to Thee are dear:
No Anger mayft Thou ever find,
No Pride in my unruffled Mind,
   But FAITH and heav'n-born Peace be there.

6 A patient, a victorious Mind
That, Life and all Things caft behind,
   Springs forth obedient to thy Call;
An Heart, that no Defire can move,
But ftill t'adore, believe, and love,
   Give me, my LORD, my Life, my All.

Supplication for Grace.

From the fame.

1 O GOD of GOD, in whom combine
The Heights, and Depths of Love Divine,
   With thankful Hearts to Thee we fing:
To Thee our longing Souls afpire
In fervent Flames of ftrong Defire:
   Come, and thy facred Unction bring.

2 All

2 All Things in Earth, and Air, and Sea
   Exift, and live, and move in Thee:
     All Nature trembles at thy Voice:
   With Awe ev'n we thy Children prove
   Thy Pow'r: O let us tafte thy Love;
     So evermore fhall we rejoice.

3 O pow'rful Love, to Thee we bow,
   Object of all our Wifhes Thou,
     (Our Hearts are naked to Thine Eye)
   To Thee, who from th'Eternal Throne
   Cam'ft, empty'd of thy Godhead, down
     For us to groan, to bleed, to die.

4 Grace we implore; when Billows roll
   Grace is the Anchor of the Soul;
     Grace ev'ry Sicknefs knows to heal:
   Grace can fubdue each fond Defire,
   And Patience in all Pain infpire,
     Howe'er rebellious Nature fwell.

5 O Love, our ftubborn Wills fubdue,
   Create our ruin'd Frame anew;
     Difpel our Darknefs by thy Light:
   Into all Truth our Spirit guide,
   But from our Eyes for ever hide
     All Things difpleafing in thy Sight.

6 Be Heav'n ev'n now our Soul's Abode,
   Hid be our Life with CHRIST in GOD,
     Our Spirit, LORD, be One with Thine:
   Let all our Works in Thee be wrought,
   And fill'd with Thee be all our Thought,
     'Till in us thy full Likenefs fhine.

HYMN

HYMN *to the* HOLY GHOST.

1 COME, HOLY GHOST, all-quickning Fire,
    Come, and in me delight to reſt!
Drawn by the Lure of ſtrong Deſire,
    O come, and conſecrate my Breaſt:
The Temple of my Soul prepare,
And fix thy ſacred Preſence there!

2 If now Thine Influence I feel,
    If now in Thee begin to live;
Still to my Heart Thyſelf reveal,
    Give me Thyſelf, for ever give:
A Point my Good, a Drop my Store:
Eager I aſk, and pant for more.

3 Eager for Thee I aſk and pant,
    So ſtrong the Principle Divine
Carries me out with ſweet Conſtraint,
    'Till all my hallow'd Soul be Thine:
Plung'd in the Godhead's deepeſt Sea,
And loſt in Thine Immenſity.

4 My Peace, my Life, my Comfort now,
    My Treaſure, and mine All Thou art!
True Witneſs of my Sonſhip Thou,
    Engraving Pardon on my Heart:
Seal of my Sins in CHRIST forgiv'n,
Earneſt of Love, and Pledge of Heav'n.

5 Come then, my GOD, mark out Thine Heir,
    Of Heav'n a larger Earneſt give,
With clearer Light thy Witneſs bear,
    More ſenſibly within me live:
Let all my Pow'rs Thine Entrance feel,
And deeper ſtamp Thyſelf the Seal.

6 Come

6 Come, HOLY GHOST, all-quick'ning Fire,
   Come, and in me delight to reſt!
Drawn by the Lure of ſtrong Deſire,
   O come, and conſecrate my Breaſt:
The Temple of my Soul prepare,
And fix thy ſacred Preſence there!

Upon the Deſcent of the HOLY GHOST *on the Day of Pentecoſt.*

Alter'd from Dr. H. More.

1 WHEN CHRIST had left his Flock below,
   The Loſs his faithful Flock deplor'd:
Him in the Fleſh no more they know,
   And languiſh for their abſent LORD.

2 Not long—for He gone up on high
   Gifts to receive, and claim his Crown,
Beheld them ſorrowing from his Sky,
   And pour'd the Mighty Bleſſing down.

3 He, for the Preſence of his Fleſh,
   The Spirit's ſeven-fold Gifts imparts,
And living Streams their Souls refreſh,
   And Joy divine o'erflows their Hearts.

4 While all in ſweet Devotion join'd,
   Humbly to wait for GOD, retire,
The promis'd Grace in ruſhing Wind
   Deſcends, and cloven Tongues of Fire.

5 GOD's mighty Spirit fills the Dome,
   The feeble Dome beneath him ſhook,
Trembled the Crowd to feel him come,
   Soon as the Sons of Thunder ſpoke.

Father!

6 Father! if juftly ftill we claim
    To Us and Ours the Promife made,
  To Us be gracioufly the fame,
    And crown with Living Fire our Head.

7 Our Claim admit, and from above
    Of Holinefs the Spirit fhow'r,
  Of wife Difcernment, humble Love,
    And Zeal, and Unity, and Pow'r.

8 The Spirit of convincing Speech
    Of Pow'r demonftrative impart,
  Such as may ev'ry Confcience reach,
    And found the Unbelieving Heart.

9 The Spirit of refining Fire,
    Searching the Inmoft of the Mind,
  To purge all fierce and foul Defire,
    And kindle Life more pure and kind.

10 The Sp'rit of FAITH in this thy Day
    To break the Pow'r of cancel'd Sin,
  Tread down its Strength, o'erturn its Sway,
    And ftill the Conqueft more than win.

11 The Spirit breath of Inward Life
    Which in our Hearts thy Laws may write;
  Then Grief expires, and Pain, and Strife,
    'Tis Nature all, and all Delight.

12 On all the Earth thy Spirit fhow'r,
    The Earth in Righteoufnefs renew;
  Thy Kingdom come, and Hell's o'erpow'r,
    And to thy Scepter all fubdue.

13 Like mighty Wind, or Torrent fierce
    Let it Oppofers all o'er-run,
  And ev'ry Law of Sin reverfe,
    That FAITH and Love may make all one.

M   14 Yea

14 Yea, let thy Spirit in ev'ry Place
    Its Richer Energy declare,
  While lovely Tempers, Fruits of Grace,
    The Kingdom of thy CHRIST prepare.

15 Grant this, O Holy GOD, and True!
    The Antient Seers Thou didſt inſpire:
  To Us perform the Promiſe due,
    Deſcend, and crown us Now with Fire.

PUBLICK WORSHIP.

From the German.

1 LO, GOD is here! let us adore
    And own, how dreadful is this Place!
  Let all within us feel his Pow'r,
    And ſilent bow before his Face.
  Who knows his Pow'r, his Grace who prove,
  Serve him with Awe, with Rev'rence love.

2 Lo, GOD is here! Him Day and Night
    Th'united Quires of Angels ſing:
  To Him enthron'd above all Height
    Heav'n's Hoſt their nobleſt Praiſes bring:
  Diſdain not, LORD, our meaner Song,
  Who praiſe Thee with a ſtamm'ring Tongue.

3 Gladly the Toys of Earth we leave,
    Wealth, Pleaſure, Fame, for Thee alone:
  To Thee our Will, Soul, Fleſh we give;
    O take, O ſeal them for Thine own.
  Thou art the GOD; Thou art the LORD:
  Be Thou by all thy Works ador'd!

4 Being of Beings, may our Praiſe
    Thy Courts with grateful Fragrance fill,
  Still may we ſtand before thy Face,
    Still hear and do thy ſov'reign Will:

To Thee may all our Thoughts arife,
Ceafelefs, accepted Sacrifice!

5 In Thee we move.   All Things of Thee
   Are full, Thou Source and Life of All!
Thou vaft, unfathomable Sea!
   Fall proftrate, loft in Wonder, fall,
Ye Sons of Men; for GOD is Man!
All may we lofe, fo Thee we gain!

6 As Flow'rs their op'ning Leaves difplay,
   And glad drink in the Solar Fire,
So may we catch thy ev'ry Ray,
   So may thy Influence us infpire:
Thou Beam of the Eternal Beam!
Thou purging Fire, Thou quickning Flame!

PRAYER *to* CHRIST *before the* SACRAMENT.

From the fame.

1 O Thou, whom Sinners love, whofe Care
      Doth all our Sicknefs heal,
Thee we approach with Heart fincere,
   Thy Pow'r we joy to feel.
To Thee our humbleft Thanks we pay,
   To Thee our Souls we bow;
Of Hell erewhile the helplefs Prey,
   Heirs of thy Glory now.

2 As Incenfe to thy Throne above
   O let our Pray'rs arife!
O wing with Flames of Holy Love
   Our living Sacrifice.

Stir up thy Strength, O LORD of Might,
  Our willing Breasts inspire:
Fill our whole Souls with heav'nly Light,
  Melt with Seraphick Fire.

3 From thy blest Wounds our Life we draw;
  Thine all-atoning Blood
Daily we drink with trembling Awe;
  Thy Flesh our daily Food.
Come, LORD, thy sov'reign Aid impart,
  Here make thy Likeness shine,
Stamp thy whole Image on our Heart,
  And all our Souls be Thine.

HYMN *after the* SACRAMENT.

1 SONS of GOD, triumphant rise,
  Shout th'accomplish'd Sacrifice!
Shout Your Sins in CHRIST forgiv'n,
Sons of GOD, and Heirs of Heav'n!

2 Ye that round our Altars throng,
  List'ning Angels join the Song:
Sing with Us, ye Heav'nly Pow'rs,
Pardon, Grace, and Glory Ours!

3 Love's Mysterious Work is done!
  Greet we now th'atoning Son,
Heal'd and quicken'd by his Blood,
  Join'd to CHRIST, and one with GOD.

4 CHRIST, of all our Hopes the Seal;
  Peace Divine in CHRIST we feel,
Pardon to our Souls applied:
  Dead for All, for Me he died!

5 Sin shall tyrannize no more,
  Purg'd its Guilt, dissolv'd its Pow'r;

JESUS

JESUS makes our Hearts his Throne,
There He lives, and reigns alone.

6 Grace our ev'ry Thought controuls,
Heav'n is open'd in our Souls,
Everlasting Life is won,
Glory is on Earth begun.

7 CHRIRT in Us; in Him we see
Fulnefs of the Deity:
Beam of the Eternal Beam;
Life Divine we taste in Him!

8 Him we taste; but wait to know
Mightier Happinefs below,
Him when fully Ours we prove,
Ours the Heav'n of perfect Love!

ACTS ii. 41, &c.

1 THE Word pronounc'd, the Gofpel-Word,
The Crowd with various Hearts receiv'd:
In many a Soul the SAVIOUR stir'd,
Three thoufand yielded, and believ'd.

2 Thefe by th'Apoftles' Counfels led,
With them in mighty Pray'rs combin'd,
Broke the Commemorative Bread,
Nor from the Fellowfhip declin'd.

3 GOD from above, with ready Grace
And Deeds of Wonder, guards his Flock,
Trembles the World before their Face,
By JESUS crufh'd, their Conqu'ring Rock.

M 3

4 The

4 The happy Band whom CHRIST redeems,
 One only Will, one Judgment know:
None this contentious Earth esteems,
 Distinctions, or Delights below.

5 The Men of worldly Wealth possest
 Their Selfish Happiness remove,
Sell, and divide it to the rest,
 And buy the Blessedness of Love.

6 Thus in the Presence of their G O D,
 JESUS their Life, and Heav'n their Care,
With single Heart they took their Food
 Heighten'd by Eucharist and Pray'r.

7 G O D in their ev'ry Work was prais'd:
 The People bless'd the Law benign:
Daily the Church, his Arm had rais'd,
 Receiv'd the Sons of Mercy in.

To be sung at Work.

1 S ON of the Carpenter, receive
  This humble Work of mine;
Worth to my meanest Labour give,
 By joining it to Thine.

2 Servant of all, to toil for Man
 Thou wou'dst not, LORD, refuse:
Thy Majesty did not disdain
 To be employ'd for us.

3 Thy bright Example I pursue,
 To Thee in all Things rise,
And all I think, or speak, or do,
 Is one great Sacrifice.

4 Carelefs thro' outward Cares I go,
    From all Diftraction free:
My Hands are but engag'd below,
    My Heart is ftill with Thee.

5 O when wilt Thou my Life appear!
    How gladly would I cry,
'Tis done, the Work Thou gav'ft me here,
    'Tis finifh'd, LORD ---- and die.

ANOTHER.

1 SUMMON'D my Labour to renew,
    And glad to act my Part,
LORD, in thy Name, my Tafk I do,
    And with a fingle Heart.

2 End of my every Action Thou!
    Thyfelf in All I fee:
Accept my hallow'd Labour now;
    I do it unto Thee,

3 Whate'er the Father views as Thine,
    He views with gracious Eyes:
JESUS! this mean Oblation join
    To thy great Sacrifice.

4 Stampt with an Infinite Defert
    My Work he then fhall own;
Well pleas'd in Me, when mine Thou art,
    And I his favourite Son!

GOD *with us.*

From the German.

1 ETERNAL Depth of Love Divine
    In JESUS, GOD-with-Us, difplay'd,
How bright thy beaming Glories fhine!
    How wide thy healing Streams are fpread!

With whom doſt Thou delight to dwell?
  Sinners, a vile, and thankleſs Race:
O GOD! what Tongue aright can tell
  How vaſt thy Love, how great thy Grace!

2 The Dictates of thy Sov'reign Will
  With Joy our grateful Hearts receive:
All thy Delight in us fulfill,
  Lo! all we are to Thee we give.
To thy ſure Love, thy tender Care,
  Our Fleſh, Soul, Spirit we reſign;
O! fix thy ſacred Preſence there,
  And feel th'Abode for ever Thine.

3 O King of Glory, thy rich Grace
  Our ſhort Deſires ſurpaſſes far!
Yea, ev'n our Crimes, tho' numberleſs,
  Leſs num'rous than thy Mercies are.
Still on Thee, Father, may we reſt!
  Still may we pant thy Son to know!
Thy Sp'rit ſtill breath into our Breaſt,
  Fountain of Peace, and Joy below!

4 Oft have we ſeen thy mighty Pow'r,
  Since from the World Thou mad'ſt us free:
Still may we praiſe Thee more and more,
  Our Hearts more firmly knit to Thee;
Still, LORD, thy ſaving Health diſplay,
  And arm our Souls with heav'nly Zeal:
So, fearleſs ſhall we urge our Way
  Thro' all the Pow'rs of Earth and Hell!

G O D *our Portion.*

From the Spaniſh.

1 O GOD, my GOD, my All Thou art:
    Ere ſhines the Dawn of riſing Day,
Thy ſov'reign Light within my Heart,
    Thine all-enliv'ning Pow'r diſplay.

2 For Thee my thirſty Soul does pant,
　　While in this deſert Land I live:
And hungry as I am, and faint,
　　Thy Love alone can Comfort give.

3 In a dry Land behold I place
　　My whole Deſire on Thee, O LORD:
And more I joy to gain thy Grace
　　Than all Earth's Treaſures can afford.

4 In Holineſs within thy Gates
　　Of old oft have I ſought for Thee:
Again my longing Spirit waits
　　That Fulneſs of Delight to ſee.

5 More dear than Life itſelf thy Love
　　My Heart and Tongue ſhall ſtill employ,
And to declare thy Praiſe will prove
　　My Peace, my Glory, and my Joy.

6 In bleſſing Thee with grateful Songs
　　My happy Life ſhall glide away;
The Praiſe that to thy Name belongs
　　Hourly with lifted Hands I'll pay.

7 Abundant Sweetneſs, while I ſing
　　Thy Love, my raviſh'd Soul o'erflows,
Secure in Thee, my G O D and King,
　　Of Glory that no Period knows.

8 Thy Name, O LORD, upon my Bed
　　Dwells on my Lips, and fires my Thought,
With trembling Awe in midnight Shade,
　　I muſe on all Thine Hands have wrought.

9 In all I do I feel Thine Aid;
　　Therefore thy Greatneſs will I ſing,
O G O D, who bidſt my Heart be glad
　　Beneath the Shadow of thy Wing.

10 My

10 My Soul draws nigh, and cleaves to Thee;
   Then let or Earth or Hell affail,
Thy Mighty Hand fhall fet me free,
   For whom Thou fav'ft, He ne'er fhall fail.

Gratitude for our Converfion.

From *the* German.

1 THEE will I love, my Strength, my Tower,
   Thee will I love, my Joy, my Crown,
Thee will I love with all my Power,
   In all my Works and Thee alone!
Thee will I love 'till the pure Fire
Fill my whole Soul with chaft Defire.

2 Ah! why did I fo late Thee know,
   Thee, lovelier than the Sons of Men!
Ah! why did I no fooner go
   To Thee, the only Eafe in Pain!
Afham'd I figh, and inly mourn
That I fo late to Thee did turn.

3 In Darknefs willingly I ftray'd;
   I fought Thee, yet from Thee I rov'd:
For wide my wandring Thoughts were fpread,
   Thy Creatures more than Thee I lov'd:
And now, if more at length I fee,
'Tis thro' thy Light, and comes from Thee.

4 I thank Thee, Uncreated Sun,
   That thy bright Beams on me have fhin'd:
I thank Thee, who haft overthrown
   My Foes, and heal'd my wounded Mind:
I thank Thee, whofe enliv'ning Voice
Bids my freed Heart in Thee rejoice.

5 Uphold

5 Uphold me in the doubtful Race,
  Nor fuffer me again to ftray :
Strengthen my Feet, with fteady Pace
  Still to prefs forward in thy Way :
My Soul, and Flefh, O LORD of Might,
Fill, fatiate with thy heav'nly Light.

6 Give to my Eyes refrefhing Tears,
  Give to my Heart chaft, hallow'd Fires,
Give to my Soul with Filial Fears
  The Love that all Heav'n's Hoft infpires :
That all my Pow'rs with all their Might
In thy fole Glory may unite.

7 Thee will I love, my Joy, my Crown !
  Thee will I love my LORD, my GOD !
Thee will I love, beneath thy Frown
  Or Smile, thy Scepter or thy Rod :
What tho' my Flefh and Heart decay ?
Thee fhall I love in endlefs Day !

BOLDNESS *in the* GOSPEL.

From the fame.

1 SHALL I, for fear of feeble Man,
  Thy Spirit's Courfe in me reftrain ?
Or undifmay'd, in Deed and Word
Be a true Witnefs to my LORD ?

2 Aw'd by a Mortal's Frown, fhall I
Conceal the Word of GOD moft high ?
How then before Thee fhall I dare
To ftand, or how Thine Anger bear ?

3 Shall I, to footh th'unholy Throng,
Soften thy Truths, and fmooth my Tongue ?
To gain Earth's gilded Toys, or flee
The Crofs, endur'd, my GOD, by Thee ?

4 What then is He whofe Scorn I dread?
  Whofe Wrath or Hate makes me afraid?
  A Man! an Heir of Death! a Slave
  To Sin! a Bubble on the Wave!

5 Yea let Man rage! fince Thou wilt fpread
  Thy fhadowing Wings around my Head:
  Since in all Pain thy tender Love
  Will ftill my fweet Refrefhment prove.

6 SAVIOUR of Men! thy fearching Eye
  Doth all mine inmoft Thoughts defcry:
  Doth ought on Earth my Wifhes raife;
  Or the World's Pleafures, or its Praife?

7 The Love of CHRIST doth me conftrain
  To feek the wandring Souls of Men:
  With Cries, Intreaties, Tears, to fave,
  To fnatch them ftom the gaping Grave.

8 For this let Men revile my Name,
  No Crofs I fhun, I fear no Shame:
  All hail, Reproach, and welcome Pain!
  Only thy Terrors, LORD, reftrain.

9 My Life, my Blood, I here prefent;
  If for thy Truth they may be fpent,
  Fulfil thy fov'reign Counfel, LORD!
  Thy Will be done! thy Name ador'd!

10 Give me thy Strength, O GOD of Pow'r!
  Then let Winds blow, or Thunders roar!
  Thy faithful Witnefs will I be;
  'Tis fixt: I can do all thro' Thee!

ANOTHER

ANOTHER.

1 CAPTAIN of my Salvation, hear!
    Stir up thy Strength and bow the Skies;
Be Thou, the GOD of Battles, near;
    In all thy Majefty arife!

2 The Day, the dreadful Day's at hand!
    In Battle cover Thou my Head:
Paft is thy Word: I here demand,
    And confident expect Thine Aid.

3 Now arm me for the threatning Fight,
    Now let thy Power defcend from high,
Triumphant in thy Spirit's Might
    So fhall I every Foe defy.

4 I afk thy Help; by Thee fent forth
    Thy glorious Gofpel to proclaim,
Be Thou my Mouth, and fhake the Earth,
    And fpread by Me Thine awful Name.

5 Steel me to Shame, Reproach, Difgrace,
    Arm me with all Thine Armour now,
Set like a Flint my fteady Face,
    Harden to Adamant my Brow.

6 Bold may I wax, exceeding bold
    My high Commiffion to perform,
Nor fhrink thy harfheft Truths t'unfold,
    But more than meet the gathering Storm.

7 Adverfe to Earth's rebellious Throng,
    Still may I turn my fearlefs Face,
Stand as an Iron Pillar ftrong,
    And ftedfaft as a Wall of Brafs.

N   3 Give

8 Give me thy Might, Thou G O D of Power;
    Then let or Men or Fiends affail,
Strong in thy Strength, I'll ftand a Tower
    Impregnable to Earth or Hell.

Congratulation to a Friend, upon Believing in CHRIST.

1 WHAT Morn on Thee with fweeter Ray,
        Or brighter Luftre e'er hath fhin'd?
Be bleft the Memorable Day
        That gave Thee JESUS CHRIST to find!
Gave Thee to tafte his Pard'ning Grace,
From Death to Life in Him to pafs!

2 O how diverfify'd the Scene,
        Since firft that Heart began to beat!
Evil and few thy Days have been:
        In Suff'ring, and in Comfort, great,
Oft haft Thou groan'd beneath thy Load,
And funk—into the Arms of GOD!

3 Long did all Hell its Pow'rs engage,
        And fill'd thy darken'd Soul with Fears:
Baffled at length the Dragon's Rage,
        At length th'Atoning Blood appears:
Thy Light is come, thy Mourning's o'er,
Look up; for Thou fhalt weep no more.

4 Bleft be the Name that fets Thee free,
        The Name that fure Salvation brings!
The Sun of Rightceufnefs on Thee
        Has rofe with Healing in his Wings:
Away let Grief and Sighing flee;
JESUS has died for Thee—for Thee!

5 And

5 And will He now forsake his own,
  Or lose the Purchase of his Blood?
No! for He looks with Pity down,
  He watches over Thee for Good;
Gracious He eyes Thee from above,
And guards, and feeds Thee with his Love.

6 Since Thou wast precious in his Sight,
  How highly favour'd hast Thou been!
Upborn by FAITH to Glory's Height,
  The SAVIOUR-GOD thine Eyes have seen,
Thy Heart has felt its Sins forgiv'n,
And tastes Anticipated Heav'n.

7 Still may his Love thy Fortress be,
  And make Thee still his darling Care,
Settle, confirm, and stablish Thee,
  On Eagles Wings thy Spirit bear,
Fill Thee with Heavenly Joy, and shed
His choicest Blessings on thy Head.

8 Thus may He comfort Thee below,
  Thus may He all his Graces give:
Him but in part Thou here canst know:
  Yet here by FAITH submit to live;
Help Me to fight my Passage thro',
Nor seize thy Heav'n, 'till I may too.

9 Or if the Sov'reign wise Decree
  First number Thee among the Blest,
(The only Good I'd envy Thee)
  Translating to an earlier Rest;
Near in thy latest Hour may I
Instruct, and learn of Thee, to die.

10 Mixt with the Quires that hover round,
  And all the Adverse Powers controul,
Angel of Peace may I be found
  To animate thy parting Soul,

Point

Point out the Crown, and smooth thy Way
To Regions of Eternal Day.

11 Fir'd with the Thought, I see Thee Now
    Triumphant meet the King of Fears!
Stedfast thy Heart, serene thy Brow;
    Divinely confident appears
Thy mounting Soul, and spreads abroad,
And swells to be dissolv'd in GOD.

12 Is this the Soul so late weigh'd down
    By Cares and Sins, by Griefs and Pains!
Whither are all thy Terrors gone?
    JESUS for Thee the Vict'ry gains;
And Death, and Sin and Satan yield
To Faith's unconquerable Shield.

13 Bless'd be the GOD, that calls Thee home;
    Faithful to Thee his Mercies prove:
Thro' Death's dark Vale he bids Thee come,
    And more than conquer in his Love;
Robes Thee in Righteousness Divine,
And makes the Crown of Glory Thine!

HYMN *for* CHRISTMAS-DAY.

1 HARK how all the Welkin rings
    " Glory to the King of Kings,
" Peace on Earth, and Mercy mild,
" GOD and Sinners reconcil'd!

2 Joyful all ye Nations rise,
Join the Triumph of the Skies,
Universal Nature say
" CHRIST the LORD is born to Day!

3 CHRIST, by highest Heav'n ador'd,
CHRIST, the Everlasting Lord,

Late

Late in Time behold him come,
Offspring of a Virgin's Womb.

4 Veil'd in Flesh, the Godhead see,
Hail th'Incarnate Deity!
Pleas'd as Man with Men t'appear
JESUS our *Immanuel* here!

5 Hail the Heav'nly Prince of Peace!
Hail the Sun of Righteousnefs!
Light and Life to All he brings,
Ris'n with Healing in his Wings.

6 Mild he lays his Glory by;
Born; that Man no more may die,
Born; to raise the Sons of Earth,
Born; to give them Second Birth.

7 Come, Desire of Nations, come,
Fix in Us thy humble Home,
Rise, the Woman's Conqu'ring Seed,
Bruise in Us the Serpent's Head.

8 Now display thy saving Pow'r,
Ruin'd Nature now restore,
Now in Myftic Union join
Thine to Ours, and Ours to Thine.

9 *Adam*'s Likenefs, LORD, efface,
Stamp thy Image in its Place,
Second *Adam* from above,
Reinftate us in thy Love.

10 Let us Thee, tho' loft, regain,
Thee, the Life, the Heav'nly Man:
O! to All Thyfelf impart,
Form'd in each Believing Heart.

N 3

HYMN *for the* EPIPHANY.

1 SONS of Men, behold from far,
  Hail the long-expected Star!
Jacob's Star that gilds the Night,
Guides bewilder'd Nature right.

2 Fear not hence that Ill fhould flow,
Wars or Peftilence below,
Wars it bids and Tumults ceafe,
Ufhering in the Prince of Peace.

3 Mild he fhines on all beneath,
Piercing thro' the Shade of Death,
Scatt'ring Error's wide-fpread Night,
Kindling Darknefs into Light.

4 Nations all, far off and near,
Hafte to fee your GOD appear!
Hafte, for Him your Hearts prepare;
Meet him manifefted there!

5 There behold the Day-fpring rife,
Pouring Eye-fight on your Eyes,
GOD in his own Light furvey,
Shining to the Perfect Day.

6 Sing, ye Morning-ftars, again,
GOD defcends on Earth to reign,
Deigns for Man his Life t'employ;
Shout, ye Sons of GOD, for Joy!

HYMN *for* EASTER-DAY.

1 " CHRIST the LORD is ris'n To-day,"
  Sons of Men and Angels fay,

Raife

Raife your Joys and Triumphs high,
Sing ye Heav'ns, and Earth reply.

2 Love's Redeeming Work is done,
Fought the Fight, the Battle won,
Lo! our Sun's Eclipfe is o'er,
Lo! He fets in Blood no more.

3 Vain the Stone, the Watch, the Seal;
CHRIST hath burft the Gates of Hell!
Death in vain forbids his Rife:
CHRIST hath open'd Paradife!

4 Lives again our glorious King,
Where, O Death, is now thy Sting?
Once He died our Souls to fave,
Where thy Victory, O Grave?

5 Soar we now, where CHRIST has led,
Following our Exalted Head,
Made like Him, like Him we rife:
Ours the Crofs; the Grave; the Skies.

6 What tho' once we perifh'd All,
Partners of our Parent's Fall,
Second Life we All receive,
In our Heav'nly *Adam* live.

7 Ris'n with Him, we upward move,
Still we feek the Things above,
Still purfue, and kifs the Son,
Seated on his Father's Throne;

8 Scarce on Earth a Thought beftow,
Dead to all we leave below,
Heav'n our Aim, and lov'd Abode,
Hid our Life with CHRIST in GOD!

9 Hid;

9 Hid; 'till CHRIST our Life appear,
Glorious in his Members here:
Join'd to Him, we then shall shine
All Immortal, all Divine!

10 Hail the LORD of Earth and Heav'n!
Praise to Thee by both be giv'n:
Thee we greet Triumphant now;
Hail the Resurrection Thou!

11 King of Glory, Soul of Bliss,
Everlasting Life is This,
Thee to know, thy Pow'r to prove,
Thus to sing, and thus to love!

HYMN *for* ASCENSION-DAY.

1 HAIL the Day that sees Him rise,
Ravish'd from our wishful Eyes;
CHRIST awhile to Mortals giv'n,
Re-ascends his native Heav'n!

2 There the pompous Triumph waits,
" Lift your Heads, Eternal Gates,
" Wide unfold the radiant Scene,
" Take the King of Glory in!

3 Circled round with Angel Powers,
Their Triumphant LORD, and Ours,
Conqueror over Death and Sin,
Take the King of Glory in!

4 Him tho' highest Heav'n receives,
Still He loves the Earth He leaves;
Tho' returning to his Throne,
Still He calls Mankind his own.

5 See! He lifts his Hands above,
See! He ſhews the Prints of Love!
Hark! His gracious Lips beſtow
Bleſſings on his Church below!

6 Still for us his Death he pleads;
Prevalent, He intercedes;
Near Himſelf prepares our Place,
Harbinger of human Race.

7 Maſter, (will we ever ſay)
Taken from our Head To-day;
See thy faithful Servants, ſee!
Ever gazing up to Thee.

8 Grant, tho' parted from our Sight,
High above yon azure Height,
Grant our Hearts may thither riſe,
Following Thee beyond the Skies.

9 Ever upward let us move,
Wafted on the Wings of Love,
Looking when our LORD ſhall come,
Longing, gaſping after Home.

10 There we ſhall with Thee remain,
Partners of thy endleſs Reign,
There thy Face unclouded ſee,
Find our Heav'n of Heav'ns in Thee!

HYMN *for* WHITSUNDAY.

1 GRANTED is the SAVIOUR's Prayer,
Sent the gracious Comforter;
Promiſe of our Parting LORD,
JESUS to his Heav'n reſtor'd:

2 CHRIST;

2 CHRIST; who now gone up on high,
  Captive leads Captivity,
  While his Foes from Him receive
  Grace, that GOD with Man may live.

3 GOD, the everlasting GOD,
  Makes with Mortals his Abode,
  Whom the Heavens cannot contain,
  He vouchsafes to dwell with Man.

4 Never will he thence depart,
  Inmate of an humble Heart;
  Carrying on his Work within,
  Striving 'till he cast out Sin.

5 There He helps our feeble Moans,
  Deepens our imperfect Groans;
  Intercedes in Silence there,
  Sighs th'Unutterable Prayer.

6 Come, Divine and peaceful Guest,
  Enter our devoted Breast;
  HOLY GHOST, our Hearts inspire,
  Kindle there the Gospel-Fire.

7 Crown the agonizing Srife,
  Principle, and LORD of Life;
  Life Divine in us renew,
  Thou the Gift and Giver too!

8 Now descend and shake the Earth,
  Wake us into Second Birth;
  Now thy quick'ning Influence give,
  Blow; and these dry Bones shall live!

9 Brood Thou o'er our Nature's Night,
  Darkness kindles into Light;
  Spread Thine overshadowing Wings,
  Order from Confusion springs.

10 Pain

10 Pain and Sin, and Sorrow ceafe,
    Thee we tafte and all is Peace;
    Joy Divine in Thee we prove,
    Light of 'Truth, and Fire of Love.

Grace *before* Meat.

1 PARENT of Good, whofe plenteous Grace
      O'er all thy Creatures flows,
    Humbly we afk thy Pow'r to blefs
    The Food thy Love beftows.

2 Thy Love provides the fober Feaft:
      A Second Gift impart,
    Give us with Joy our Food to tafte
      And with a Single Heart.

3 Let it for Thee new Life afford,
      For Thee our Strength repair,
    Bleft by thine all-fuftaining Word,
      And fanctify'd by Prayer.

4 Thee let us tafte ; nor toil below
      For perifhable Meat:
    The Manna of thy Love beftow,
      Give us thy Flefh to eat.

5 Life of the World, our Souls to feed
      Thyfelf defcend from high !
    Grant us of Thee the Living Bread
      'To eat, and never die !

At MEALS.

1 FATHER, our Eyes we lift to Thee,
    And taste our daily Bread:
'Tis now Thine Open Hand we see,
    And on thy Bounty feed.

2 'Tis now the meaner Creatures join
    Richly thy Grace to prove;
Fulfil thy primitive Design,
    Enjoy'd by thankful Love.

3 Still, while our Mouths are fill'd with Good,
    Our Souls to Thee we raise;
Our Souls partake of nobler Food,
    And banquet on thy Praise.

4 Yet higher still our farthest Aim;
    To mingle with the Blest,
T'attend the Marriage of the Lamb,
    And Heaven's Eternal Feast.

GRACE *after* MEAT.

1 BLEST be the GOD, whose tender Care
    Prevents his Children's Cry,
Whose Pity providently near
    Doth all our Wants supply.

2 Blest be the GOD, whose Bounteous Store
    These chearing Gifts imparts;
Who veils in Bread, the secret Power
    That feeds and glads our Hearts.

3 Fountain of Blessings, Source of Good,
    To Thee this Strength we owe,
Thou art the Virtue of our Food,
    Life of our Life below.

                    When

4 When fhall our Souls regain the Skies,
   Thy Heav'nly Sweetnefs prove;
Where Joys in all their Fulnefs rife,
   And all our Food is Love!

ANOTHER.

1 FOUNTAIN of all the Good we fee
   Streaming from Heav'n above,
Saviour, our Faith we act on Thee,
   And exercife our Love.

2 'Tis not the Outward Food we eat
   Doth this new Strength afford,
'Tis Thou, whofe Prefence makes it Meat,
   Thou the Life-giving Word.

3 Man doth not live by Bread alone:
   Whate'er Thou wilt can feed;
Thy Power converts the Bread to Stone,
   And turns the Stone to Bread.

4 Thou art our Food: We tafte Thee now,
   In Thee we move and breath,
Our Bodies only Life art Thou,
   And all befides is Death!

JOHN xvi. 24.

Afk, and ye fhall receive, that your
Joy may be full.

1 RISE my Soul, with Ardor rife,
   Breathe thy Wifhes to the Skies;
Freely pour out all thy Mind,
Seek, and Thou art fure to find;

O

Ready art Thou to receive?
Readier is thy GOD to give.

2 Heavenly Father, LORD of all,
Hear, and fhew Thou hear'ft my Call;
Let my Cries thy Throne affail
Entering Now within the Veil:
Give the Benefits I claim:
LORD, I afk in JESU's Name!

3 Friend of Sinners, King of Saints,
Anfwer my minuteft Wants,
All my largeft Thoughts require,
Grant me all my Hearts Defire,
Give me, 'till my Cup run o'er,
All, and infinitely more.

4 Meek and lowly be my Mind,
Pure my Heart, my Will refign'd:
Keep me dead to all below,
Only CHRIST refolv'd to know,
Firm, and difengag'd, and free,
Seeking all my Blifs in Thee.

5 Suffer me no more to grieve,
Wanting what Thou long'ft to give,
Shew me all thy Goodnefs, LORD,
Beaming from th'Incarnate Word,
CHRIST, in whom thy Glories fhine,
Efflux of the Light Divine.

6. Since the Son hath made me free,
Let me tafte my Liberty,
Thee behold with open Face,
Triumph in thy Saving Grace,
Thy great Will delight to prove,
Glory in thy perfect Love.

7. Since

7 Since the Son hath bought my Peace,
  Mine I fee, whate'er is His ;
  Mine the Comforter I fee,
  Christ is full of Grace for me :
  Mine (the Purchafe of his Blood)
  All the Plenitude of G O D.

8 Abba, Father! hear thy Child
  Late in Jesus reconcil'd!
  Hear, and all the Graces fhower,
  All the Joy, and Peace, and Power,
  All my Saviour afks above,
  All the Life of Heaven of Love.

9 Lord, I will not let Thee go,
  Till The Blessing Thou beftow :
  Hear my Advocate Divine ;
  Lo ! to His my Suit I join :
  Join'd to His it cannot fail —
  Blefs me, for I *Will* prevail!

10 Stoop from thine Eternal Throne,
  See, thy Promife calls Thee down !
  High and lofty as Thou art,
  Dwell within my worthlefs Heart!
  My poor fainting Soul revive ;
  Here for ever walk and live.

11 Heavenly *Adam,* Life Divine,
  Change my Nature into Thine :
  Move, and fpread throughout my Soul,
  Actuate and fill the whole :
  Be it I no longer now
  Living in the Flefh, but Thou.

12 Holy

12 HOLY GHOST, no more delay,
Come, and in thy Temple ſtay;
Now thine Inward Witneſs bear
Strong, and permanent, and clear;
Spring of Life, Thyſelf impart,
Riſe Eternal in my Heart!

PART

PART

THE

THIRD.

The PREFACE.

1. BY Grace, saith *St.* Paul, *ye are saved thro' Faith.* And it is indeed a great Salvation, which they *have* received, who truly *believe on the Name of the Son of* GOD. It is such as *Eye hath not seen, nor Ear heard, neither hath it enter'd into the Heart of Man to conceive,* until GOD *hath reveal'd it by his Spirit,* which alone sheweth these *Deep Things of* GOD.

2. *Of this Salvation the Prophets enquired diligently, searching what Manner of Time the Spirit which was in them did signify, when it testified before-hand the Sufferings of* CHRIST, *and the Glory that should follow;* even that Glorious Liberty from the Bondage of Corruption, which should then be given to the Children of GOD. Much more doth it behove *us,* diligently to enquire after this *Prize of our high Calling,* and earnestly *to hope for the Grace which is brought unto us by the Revelation of* JESUS CHRIST.

3. Some faint Description of this Gracious Gift of GOD, is attempted in a few of the following Verses. But the greater Part of them relate to the Way, rather than the End; either shewing (so far as has fallen under our Observation) the Successive Conquests of Grace, and the gradual Process of the Work of GOD in the Soul; or pointing out the Chief Hindrances in the Way, at which many have stumbled and fallen.

4. This great Gift of GOD, the Salvation of our Souls, which is begun on Earth, but perfect-

A   ed

The Preface.

ed in Heaven, is no other than the Image of
GOD fresh stamp'd upon our Hearts. It is, a
Renewal in the Spirit of our Minds after the Likeness of him that created us. It is a Salvation from
Sin, and Doubt, and Fear: From Fear; for *being
justified freely they who believe have Peace with
GOD, thro' Jesus Christ our Lord, and rejoice in Hope of the Glory of GOD:* From Doubt;
for the *Spirit of GOD beareth witness with their
Spirit, that they are the Children of GOD:* And
from Sin; for *being* now *made free from Sin, they
are become the Servants of Righteousness.*

5. GOD hath *now laid the Axe to the Root of
the Tree, purifying their Hearts by* FAITH, *and
cleansing* all *the Thoughts of their Hearts, by the
Inspiration of his Holy Spirit.* Having this Hope,
that they shall soon see GOD as he is, they *purify themselves even as he is Pure:* And are *holy as
he which hath called them is Holy in all Manner of
Conversation.* Not that they have *already* at-
tained all they shall attain, either are *already* (in
this Sense) *perfect.* But they daily *go* on *from
Strength to Strength: Beholding now as in a Glass
the Glory of the* Lord, *they are changed into the
same Image, from Glory to Glory, as by the Spirit
of the* Lord.

6 And *where the Spirit of the* Lord *is, there
is Liberty*; such Liberty from the Law of Sin and
Death, as the Children of this World *will not
believe, tho' a Man declare it unto them.* The Son
hath made them free, and they are free indeed: In-
somuch that *St. John* lays it down, as a first Principle among true Believers, *We know that whosoever is born of GOD sinneth not: But he that
is begotten of GOD, keepeth himself, and that
wicked one toucheth him not.* And again, *Whosoever abideth in him* (in Christ) *sinneth not.* And
yet

yet again, *Whosoever is born of GOD, doth not commit Sin. For his Seed remaineth in him, and he cannot sin, because he is born of GOD.*

7. The Son hath made them free, who are *thus born of GOD*, from that great Root of Sin and Bitterness, PRIDE. They feel, that *all their Sufficiency is of* God; that *it is he* alone *who* is in all their Thoughts, and *worketh in them both to will and to do, of his good Pleasure.* They feel, that *it is not they who speak, but the Spirit of their Father which speaketh in them*; and that whatsoever is done by their Hands, *the Father which is with them, he doth the Works.* So that GOD is to them all in all, and they are as nothing in his Sight. They are freed from Self-Will; as desiring nothing, no, not for one Moment (for perfect Love casteth out all Desire) but the Holy and Perfect Will of GOD: Not Supplies in Want; not Ease in Pain; not Life or Death, or any Creature; but continually crying in their inmost Soul, "Father, thy Will be done." They are freed from Evil Thoughts, so that they cannot enter into them; no not for one Instant. Aforetime, when an Evil Thought came in, they looked up, and it vanish'd away. But now it does not come in; there being no Room for this, in a Soul which is full of GOD. They are freed from Wandrings in Prayer. Whensoever they pour out their Hearts, in a more immediate Manner before GOD, they have no Thought of any Thing past, or absent, or to come, but of GOD alone; to whom their whole Souls flow in one even Stream, and in whom they are swallowed up. In Times past, they had wandring Thoughts darted in; which yet fled away like Smoke. But now that Smoke does not rise at all, but they continually see Him which is invisible. They are freed from all Darkness, having no Fear, no Doubt,

either

either as to their State in general; or as to any particular Action: For their *Eye* being *single, their whole Body is full of Light.* Whatſoever is needful, they *are taught of* GOD. They *have an Unction from the Holy One, which abideth in them, and teacheth them every* Hour, what they ſhall do, and what they ſhall ſpeak. Nor have they therefore any Need to *reaſon* concerning it; for they ſee the Way ſtraight before them. The Lamb is their Light, and they ſimply follow Him, whitherſoever He goeth. Hence alſo they are, *in one Senſe,* freed from Temptations; for tho' numberleſs Temptations *fly about them,* yet they wound them not, they trouble them not, they have no Place *in them.* At all Times their Soul is even and calm: Their Heart is ſtedfaſt and unmoveable; their Peace flowing as a River, *paſſeth all Underſtanding,* and they *rejoice with Joy unſpeakable, and full of Glory.* For they are *ſeal'd by the Spirit unto the Day of Redemption;* having the Witneſs in themſelves, That *there is laid up for them a Crown of Righteouſneſs, which the* Lord *ſhall give them in that Day:* And being fully perſuaded thro' the Holy Ghoſt, that *neither Death nor Life, nor Things preſent, nor Things to come, nor Heighth, nor Depth, nor any other Creature, ſhall be able to ſeparate them from the Love of* GOD, *which is in* Christ Jesus, *their* Lord.

8. Not that every one is *a Child of the Devil,* (as ſome have raſhly aſſerted, who know not what they ſpeak, nor whereof they affirm) 'till he is, in this full Senſe, *Born of* GOD. On the contrary, whoſoever he be, who hath a ſure Truſt and Confidence in GOD, that thro' the Merits of Christ *his Sins are forgiven, and he reconcil'd to the Favour of* GOD; he is a Child of GOD, and if he abide in Him, an Heir of all the Great and Precious Promiſes. Neither ought he in any wiſe

to *caft away his Confidence*, or to deny the Faith he hath received, becaufe it is Weak, becaufe hitherto it is only *as a Grain of Muftard-Seed*; or becaufe *it is tried with Fire*, fo that his Soul is *in Heavinefs, through Manifold Temptations.* For tho' *the Heir, as long as he is a Child, differeth nothing from a Servant, yet is he Lord of all.* GOD doth not *defpife the Day of fmall Things*; the Day of Fears, and Doubts, and Clouds, and Darknefs: But *if there be firft a willing Mind,* preffing toward the Mark of the Prize of our High Calling, *it is accepted* (for the prefent) *according to what a Man hath, and not according to what he hath not.*

9. Neither therefore dare we affirm (as fome have done) that this full Salvation is *at once* given to True Believers. There is indeed an *inftantaneous* (as well as a *gradual*) Work of GOD in the Souls of his Children: And there wants not, we know, a Cloud of Witneffes, who have received *in one Moment,* either a clear Senfe of the Forgivenefs of their Sins, or the abiding Witnefs of the Holy Spirit. But we do not know a fingle Inftance, in any Place, of a Perfon's receiving, *in one and the fame Moment,* Remiffion of Sins, the abiding Witnefs of the Spirit, and a New, a Clean Heart.

10. Indeed how GOD *may* work, we cannot tell: But the general Manner wherein he *does* work, is this. Thofe who once trufted in themfelves that they were Righteous, who were *Rich and had need of Nothing,* are, by the Spirit of GOD applying his Word, convinc'd that they are *Poor and Naked.* All the Things that they have done are brought to their Remembrance, and fet in Array before them; fo that they fee the Wrath of GOD hanging over their Heads, and

feel

feel they deserve the Damnation of Hell. In their Trouble they cry unto the LORD, and he shews He hath taken away their Sins, and opens the *Kingdom of Heaven* in their Hearts, even Righteousness, and Peace, and Joy in the Holy Ghost. Fear, and Sorrow, and Pain are fled away, and Sin hath no more Dominion over them. Knowing they are justified freely through Faith in his Blood, they have Peace with GOD thro' JESUS CHRIST; they rejoice in Hope of the Glory of GOD; and the Love of GOD is shed abroad in their Hearts.

11. In this Peace they remain for Days, or Weeks, or Months, and commonly suppose they shall not know War any more, till some of their old Enemies, their Bosom Sins, or, the Sin which did most easily beset them (perhaps Anger or Desire) assault them again, and thrust sore at them, that they may fall. Then arises Fear, that they shall not endure to the End, and often Doubt, whether GOD has not forgotten them, or whether they did not deceive themselves, in thinking their Sins were forgiven, and that they were Children of GOD? Under these Clouds, especially if they reason with the Devil, or are received to Doubtful Disputations, they go *mourning* all the Day long, even as a Father mourneth for his only Son whom he loveth. But it is seldom long before their LORD answers for himself, sending them the Holy Ghost, *to comfort* them, to bear Witness continually with their Spirit, that they are the Children of GOD. And then they are indeed *meek*, and gentle and teachable, even as little Children. Their Stony Heart was broken in Pieces, before they received Remission of Sins: Yet it continued hard; but now it is melted down, it is soft, tender, and susceptible of any Impression. And now first do they see the Ground of their

Heart;

The PREFACE.

Heart; which GOD would not before difclofe unto them, left the Flefh fhould fail before him, and the Spirit which he had made. Now they fee all the hidden Abominations there; the Depths of Pride, and Self, and Hell: Yet having the Witnefs in-themfelves, " Thou art an Heir of " GOD, a Joint Heir with CHRIST; Thou fhalt " *inherit the* New Heavens and the New *Earth,* " wherein dwelleth Righteoufnefs;" Their Spirit rejoiceth in GOD their SAVIOUR, even in the midft of this fiery Trial, which continually heightens both the ftrong Senfe they then have of their Inability to help themfelves, and the inexpreffible *Hunger* they feel *after a* full Renewal in his Image, in *Righteoufnefs,* and all true Holinefs. Then GOD is mindful of the Defire of them that fear him: He remembers his Holy Covenant, and he giveth them a fingle Eye and a clean Heart. He ftamps upon them his own Image and Superfcription: He createth them anew in CHRIST JESUS: He cometh unto them with his Son and his Bleffed Spirit, and fixing his Abode in their Souls, bringeth them into the *Reft which remaineth for the People of GOD.*

HYMNS

HYMNS

AND

SACRED POEMS.

PART III.

The Fifty Fifth Chapter of ISAIAH.

1 O! Every one that thirsts, draw nigh;
(Tis G O D invites the fallen Race)
Mercy and free Salvation buy ;
Buy Wine, and Milk, and Gospel
Grace.

2 Come to the Living Waters, come !
Sinners, obey your Maker's Call;
Return, ye weary Wanderers, home,
And find my Grace is free for All.

3 See, from the Rock a Fountain rise !
For you in healing Streams it rolls:
Money ye need not bring, nor Price,
Ye lab'ring, burthen'd, Sin-sick Souls.

4 Nothing ye in exchange shall give ;
Leave all you have and Are behind,
Frankly the Gift of GOD receive,
Pardon, and Peace in Jesus find.

P

5 Why seek ye That which is not Bread,
    Nor can your hungry Souls sustain?
On Ashes, Husks, and Air ye feed,
    Ye spend your little All in vain.

6 In Search of empty Joys below,
    Ye toil with unavailing Strife:
Whither, ah whither would you go?
    I have the Words of Endless Life.

7 Hearken to me with earnest Care,
    And freely eat substantial Food;
The Sweetness of my Mercy share,
    And taste that I alone am Good.

8 I bid you all my Goodness prove,
    My Promises for All are free:
Come taste the Manna of my Love,
    And let your Soul delight in Me.

9 Your willing Ear and Heart incline,
    My Words believingly receive;
Quicken'd your Soul, by Faith divine,
    An Everlasting Life shall live.

10 You for my own I then shall take,
    Shall surely Seal you for my own,
My Covenant of Mercy make,
    And 'stablish it in *David*'s Son.

11 A Faithful Witness of my Grace,
    Him have I to the People given,
To teach a sinful World my Ways,
    And lead, and train them up for Heaven.

12 Son of my Love, behold, to Thee
    From all Eternity I give
Sinners who to thy Wounds will flee;
    The Soul that chuseth Life shall live.

13 Nations,

13 Nations, wh'om once Thou did'ft not own,
   Thou Thine Inheritance fhalt call;
Nations who knew not Thee fhall run,
   And haif the GOD that died for All.

14 For I, the Holy GOD, and True,
   To glorify thy Name have fworn:
And lo! my Faithfulnefs I fhew;
   And lo! to Thee the *Gentiles* turn.

15 Seek ye the LORD with timely Care,
   Ye Servants of uncancel'd Sin,
While all that feek may find Him near
   With open Arms to take them in.

16 His Evil let the Sinner leave,
   In Bitternefs of Spirit mourn,
Death's Sentence in himfelf receive,
   And to a gracious GOD return.

17 Surely our GOD will bid him live,
   Will with the Arms of Love embrace;
Freely, abundantly forgive,
   And fhew him all his Depths of Grace.

18 For thus the mighty GOD hath faid,
   My Ways, and Thoughts ye cannot fcan;
Ye cannot, whom my Hands have made,
   Your Infinite Creator fpan.

19 Me will ye mete with Reafon's Line?
   Or teach my Grace how far to move?
Fathom my Mercy's deep Defign,
   My Heighth, and Breadth, and Length of Love!

20 Far as the Heavens that Earth furpafs,
   Far as my Throne thofe nether Skies,
My Ways of Love, and Thoughts of Grace
   Beyond your low Conceptions rife.

P 2   21 For

21 For as the Snow from Heaven comes down,
 The firſt and latter Rains diſtill,
The Earth with Fruitfulneſs to crown,
 Man's Heart with Food and Joy to fill:

22 As no Return the Shower can know,
 But falls a thirſty Land to chear,
But executes its Charge below,
 While Plenty decks the ſmiling Year:

23 So ſhall the Word my Lips have ſpoke,
 Accompliſh that which I ordain;
My Word I never will revoke;
 My Word is not gone forth in vain.

24 In My Redeeming Work employ'd,
 And ſent my Pleaſure to fulfil,
Vain it ſhall not return, and void,
 But proſper, and perform my Will.

25 With Me is plenteous Mercy found,
 Redemption free for All to know;
And where your Sin doth moſt abound,
 My more abundant Grace ſhall flow.

26 From Guilt and Pain ye ſhall be freed,
 From the black Dungeon of Deſpair,
Into my Heavenly Kingdom led,
 And reap Eternal Pleaſures there.

27 All ye that in my Word believe,
 Shall ſee my Love in JESU's Face;
The Peace and Joy of FAITH receive,
 And triumph in My Saving Grace.

28 The Trees ſhall clap their Hands and ſing,
 Mountains and Hills their Voices raiſe;
All the new Heavens and Earth ſhall ring
 With JESUS their Creator's Praiſe.

29 Where

29 Where Thorns deform'd the barren Ground,
 Where noisome Weeds the Soul o'erspread,
There shall the Fruits of Grace abound,
 And Second Nature lift her Head.

30 The Trees of GOD shall deck the Soil,
 The Plants of Righteousness arise;
The Lord shall on his Garden smile,
 His late-returning Paradise.

31 The Earth, in Token of his Grace,
 Shall spread the Odour of his Fame,
And everlasting Trophies raise,
 To glorify the Saviour's Name.

The Eleventh Chapter of St. Paul's
Epistle to the Hebrews:

OR, THE

Life *of* FAITH *Exemplified.*

Verse i.

1 AUTHOR of Faith, Eternal Word,
 Whose Spirit breaths the Active Flame,
Faith, like its Finisher and Lord,
 To-day, as Yesterday the same;

2 To Thee our humble Hearts aspire,
 And ask the Gift unspeakable:
Increase in us the kindled Fire,
 In us the Work of Faith fulfil.

3 By Faith we know Thee strong to save,
 (Save us, a Present Saviour Thou!)
Whate'er we hope, by Faith we Have,
 Future and past subsisting Now.

4 To

4 To Him that in thy Name believes,
    Eternal Life with Thee is given,
Into Himſelf He all receives,
    Pardon, and Happineſs, and Heaven.

5 The Things unknown to feeble Senſe,
    Unſeen by Reaſon's glimm'ring Ray,
With ſtrong, commanding Evidence
    Their Heavenly Origine diſplay.

6 FAITH lends its Realizing Light,
    The Clouds diſperſe, the Shadows fly,
Th'Inviſible appears in Sight,
    And G O D is ſeen by Mortal Eye.

V E R S E S ii, iii.

1 By FAITH the Holy Men of old
    Obtain'd a never-dying Name,
The ſacred Leaves their Praiſe unfold,
    And GOD Himſelf records their Fame.

2 Thro' FAITH we know the Worlds were made,
    By his great Word to Being brought:
He ſpake: The Earth and Heaven obey'd;
    The Univerſe ſprang forth from Nought.

3 The Heavens thy glorious Power proclaim,
    If Thou in us thy Power declare;
We know from whom the Fabrick came,
    Our Heart believes, when G O D is there.

4 Thee thro' Thyſelf we underſtand,
    When Thou in us Thyſelf haſt ſhown,
We ſee Thine All creating Hand,
    And *feel* a G O D thro' FAITH alone.

Verse iv.

1 Believing in the Woman's Seed,
    And juftified by Faith alone,
Abel a nobler Offering made,
    And GOD vouchfaf'd his Gifts to own.

2 Witnefs Divine he thus obtain'd,
    The Gift of Righteoufnefs receiv'd;
And now he wears the Crown he gain'd,
    And fees the Christ he once believ'd.

3 Still by his Faith he fpeaks tho' dead,
    He calls us to the Living Way:
We hear; and in his Footfteps tread:
    We *firft* believe, and *then* obey.

Verses v, vi.

1 Exempted from the General Doom,
    The Death which All are born to know,
Enoch obtain'd his Heavenly Home
    By Faith, and difappear'd below.

2 From Earth unpainfully releas'd,
    Tranflated to the Realms of Light,
He found the GOD by Faith he pleas'd,
    His Faith was fweetly loft in Sight.

3 GOD, without Faith, we cannot pleafe:
    For all, who unto GOD would come,
Muft *feelingly* believe He Is,
    And gives to all their righteous Doom.

4 We *feelingly* believe Thou art:
    Behold we ever feek Thee, Lord,
With all our Mind, with all our Heart,
    And find Thee now our Great Reward.

VERSE vii.

1 Divinely warn'd of Judgments near,
    Noah believ'd a threatning GOD,
With humble FAITH, and holy Fear
    He built the Ark, and 'scap'd the Flood.

2 He (while the World that disbeliev'd,
    The careless World of Sinners died,)
The Righteousness of FAITH receiv'd:
    Noah by FAITH was justified.

3 We too by FAITH the World condemn,
    Of Righteousness Divine possest,
Escape the Wrath that covers Them,
    Safe in the Ark of JESUS's Breast.

VERSES viii, ix, x.

1 Obedient to his GOD's Command,
    And influenc'd by FAITH alone,
Abraham left his native Land,
    Went out, and sought a Place unknown.

2 A Place he should possess at last,
    When full Four hundred Years were o'er:
Upon the Word himself he cast,
    He follow'd GOD, and ask'd no more.

3 As in a strange, tho' promis'd, Land,
    (A Land his distant Heirs receiv'd,)
He, and his Sons in Tents remain'd;
    He knew in whom he had believ'd.

4 A better Heritage he sought,
    A City built by GOD on high,
Thither he rais'd his tow'ring Thought,
    He fix'd on Heaven his stedfast Eye.

5 Whose

5 Whofe firm Foundations never move,
  Jerufalem was all his Care,
The New *Jerufalem* above;
  His Treafure, and his Heart was there.

6 And fhall not We the Call obey,
  And hafte where GOD commands, to go?
Defpife thefe Tenements of Clay,
  Thefe Dreams of Happinefs below?

7 Yes, LORD; we hearken to thy Call,
  As Sojourners o'er Earth we rove,
We have for Thee forfaken all,
  And feek the Heaven of perfect Love.

VERSES xi, xii.

1 By FAITH the Handmaid of the LORD,
  Sarah, receiv'd a Power unknown,
She judg'd Him faithful to his Word;
  Barren and old fhe bore a Son.

2 Nature had loft its Genial Power,
  And *Abraham* was old in vain:
Impoffibilities are o'er,
  If FAITH affent, and GOD ordain.

3 He glorified JEHOVAH's Name;
  (GOD fpake the Word, it muft be done)
Father of Nations he became,
  And Multitudes fprang forth from One.

4 From one Old Man the Race did rife,
  A barren Womb the Myriads bore,
Countlefs, as Stars that deck the Skies,
  As Sands that crown the Ocean Shore.

VERSES

VERSES xiii, xiv, xv, xvi.

1 The Worthies These of antient Days,
   By FAITH they lived, in FAITH they died:
Not yet receiv'd the Promis'd Grace,
   But darkly from afar descry'd.

2 Assur'd the SAVIOUR *should* appear
   And confident in CHRIST to come,
Him they embrac'd, tho' distant, near;
   And languish'd for their Heavenly Home.

3 Pilgrims they here themselves confess'd,
   Who no Abiding-place must know,
Strangers on Earth they could not rest,
   Or find their Happiness below.

4 Regardless of the Things behind,
   The Earthly Home from whence they came,
A better Land they long'd to find,
   A promis'd Heaven was all their Aim.

5 Their FAITH the Gracious Father sees,
   And kindly for his Children cares,
He condescends to call them His,
   And suffers them to call Him Theirs:

6 For them his Heaven He hath prepar'd,
   His New *Jerusalem* above;
And LOVE is there their great Reward,
   A whole Eternity of Love.

VERSES xvii, xviii, xix.

1 *Abraham*, when severely tried,
   His FAITH by his Obedience shew'd,
He with the harsh Command complied,
   And gave his *Isaac* back to GOD.

2 His

2 His Son the Father offer'd up,
    Son of his Age, his only Son,
Object of all his Joy and Hope,
    And lefs belov'd than G O D alone.

3 His Seed elect, his Heir foretold,
    Of whom the promis'd CHRIST fhould rife,
He could not from his G O D with-hold
    That beft, that coftlieft Sacrifice.

4 The Father curb'd his fwelling Grief,
    'Twas G O D requir'd, it muft be done;
He ftagger'd not thro' Unbelief,
    He bar'd his Arm to flay his Son.

5 He refted in JEHOVAH's Power,
    The Word muft ftand which GOD hath faid,
He knew th' Almighty could reftore,
    Could raife his *Ifaac* from the Dead.

6 He knew in whom he had believ'd,
    And, trufting in Omnipotence,
His Son as from the Dead receiv'd,
    His ftedfaft FAITH receiv'd him thence.

7 O for a FAITH like His, that We
    The bright Example may purfue,
May gladly give up all to Thee,
    To whom our more than all is due!

8 Now, LORD, for Thee our All we leave,
    Our willing Soul thy Call obeys,
Pleafure, and Wealth, and Fame we give,
    Freedom, and Life to win thy Grace.

9 Is there a Thing than Life more dear,
    A Thing from which we cannot part?
We Can: We now rejoice to tear
    The Idol from our bleeding Heart.

10 JESU

10 JESU accept our Sacrifice,
   All Things for Thee we count but Loſs:
Lo! at thy Word our *Iſaac* dies,
   Dies on the Altar of thy Croſs.

11 Now to Thyſelf the Victim take,
   Nature's laſt Agony is o'er,
Freely thine own we render back,
   We grieve to part with All no more.

12 For what to Thee, O LORD, we give,
   An hundred fold we here obtain,
And ſoon with Thee ſhall all receive,
   And Loſs ſhall be Eternal Gain.

VERSES xx, xxi, xxii.

1 *Iſaac* by FAITH declar'd his Race
   In *Jacob* and in *Eſau* bleſt,
The Younger by peculiar Grace
   A nobler Heritage poſſeſs'd.

2 By FAITH expiring *Jacob* knew
   Diſtinguiſh'd Mercies to pronounce,
His Hands found out the happy Two,
   And bleſs'd his fav'rite *Joſeph*'s Sons.

3 He rais'd himſelf upon the Bed,
   Prop'd on a Staff he own'd his LORD,
The Patriarch bow'd his hoary Head,
   His Body with his Soul ador'd.

4 *Joſeph* by FAITH the Flight foretold
   Of *Iſrael*'s afflicted Race;
GOD their hard Bondage ſhould behold,
   And lead them to the Promis'd Place.

Thither

5 Thither he Will'd his Bones to go,
   And take Poffeffion in their Stead;
His Bones the Promis'd Land fhall fhew,
   He claims his *Canaan*, tho' dead.

VERSES xxiii, xxiv, xxv, xxvi, xxvii, xxviii.

1 *Mofes* by FAITH from Death was fav'd,
   While heedlefs of the Tyrant's Will,
His Parents in their GOD believ'd,
   And dar'd the lovely Babe conceal.

2 By FAITH, when now to Manhood grown,
   A juft Contempt of Earth he fhew'd,
Refus'd a Prince's Name to own,
   And fought but to be great in GOD.

3 In vain its Pomps, Ambition fpreads,
   Glory in vain difplays her Charms,
A brighter Crown its Luftre fheds,
   A purer Flame his Bofom warms.

4 Wifely he chofe the Better Part.
   Suff'rings with GOD's Elect to fhare,
To Pleafures vain he fteel'd his Heart,
   No Room for Them when GOD is there.

5 Fleeting he deem'd them all, and vain,
   His Heart on heavenly Joys beftow'd,
Partaker of his People's Pain,
   Th'afflicted People of his GOD.

6 *Egypt* unfolds her Golden-Blaze,
   Yet all for CHRIST he counts but Lofs;
A richer Treafure he furveys,
   His LORD's anticipated Crofs.

Q

He

7 He triumph'd in His glorious Shame,
    On Pleasure, Fame, and Wealth look'd down,
'Twas Heaven at which his Wishes aim,
    Aspiring to a Starry Crown.

8 By Faith he left the oppressive Land,
    And scorn'd the petty Rage of Kings,
Supported by JEHOVAH's Hand,
    And shadow'd by JEHOVAH's Wings.

9 His steady Way he still pursu'd,
    Nor Hopes nor Fears retard his Pace,
Th'INVISIBLE before him stood,
    And Faith unveil'd the Saviour's Face.

10 By Faith he slew the Typick Lamb,
    And kept the Passover of GOD:
He knew from whom its Virtue came,
    The Saving Power of Sprinkled Blood.

11 With all the Servants of his Lord,
    He (while the first-born Victims died)
Dar'd the Destroying Angel's Sword,
    And, arm'd with Blood, its Point defied!

Verse xxix.

1 While thro' the Sea by Faith they past,
    The Sea retir'd at GOD's Command,
The Waves shrink back with trembling Haste,
    The Waves a Chrystal Barrier stand.

2 Th'*Egyptians* daring to pursue,
    With Horror found a wat'ry Grave,
Too late their Want of Faith they knew,
    And sunk beneath th'o'erwhelming Wave.

VERSES xxx, xxxi, xxxii, xxxiii, xxxiv, xxxv.

1 By FAITH, while *Ifrael*'s Hoft furrounds
    Proud *Jericho*'s devoted Walls,
The Ark ftands ftill, the Trumpet founds,
    The People fhout, the City falls!

2 *Rahab* by FAITH Deliverance found,
    Nor perifh'd with th'accurfed Race:
The Harlot for her FAITH renown'd,
    Amongft the Worthies takes her Place.

3 Worthies, who all recorded ftand,
    And fhine in Everlafting Lays;
And juftly now might Each demand
    The Tribute of diftincter Praife.

4 *Gideon* and *Barak* claim the Song,
    And *David* good, and *Samuel* wife,
And *Jephtha* bold, and *Sampfon* ftrong,
    And all the ancient Prophets rife!

5 The Battles of the LORD they fought
    Thro' FAITH, and mighty States fubdu'd,
And Works of Righteoufnefs they wrought,
    And prov'd the Faithfulnefs of GOD.

6 They ftop'd the Lion's Mouths, the Rage
    Of Fire they quench'd, efcap'd the Sword,
The Weak grew ftrong, and bold t'engage,
    And chafe the Hofts that dar'd their LORD.

7 Women their quicken'd Dead receiv'd,
    Women the Heighth of FAITH difplay'd,
With ftedfaft Confidence believ'd,
    Believ'd their Children from the Dead.

VERSES xxxv, xxxvi, xxxvii.

1 Others, as in a Furnace try'd,
  With Strength of paſſive Grace endu'd,
Tortures, and Deaths, thro' FAITH defy'd,
  Thro' FAITH reſiſted unto Blood.

2 Earth they beheld with gen'rous Scorn,
  On all its proffer'd Goods look'd down,
High on a Fiery Chariot borne,
  They loſt their Life to keep their Crown.

3 Secure a better Life to find,
  The Path of varied Death they trod,
Their Souls triumphantly reſign'd,
  And died into the Arms of GOD.

4 The Prelude of Contempt they found,
  A Spectacle to Fiends and Men;
Cruelly mock'd, and ſcourg'd, and bound,
  'Till Death ſhut up the Bloody Scene.

5 Or ſton'd, they glorified their LORD,
  Or joy'd, aſunder ſawn, t'expire,
Or ruſh'd to meet the ſlaught'ring Sword,
  Or triumph'd in the tort'ring Fire.

VERSES xxxvii, xxxviii.

1 Naked, or in rough Goatſkins clad,
  In ev'ry Place they long confeſs'd
The GOD, for whom o'er Earth they ſtray'd
  Tormented, deſtitute, diſtreſs'd.

2 Of whom the World unworthy was,
  Whom only GOD their Maker knew,
The World they puniſh'd with their Loſs,
  The Holy Anchorites withdrew.

Lone

3 Lone unfrequented Wilds they trod,
　　O'er Mountain-tops the Wanderers ran,
With milder Beasts in Dens abode,
　　And shun'd the Haunts of Savage Man.

VERSES xxxix, xl.

1 Fam'd for their FAITH all these believ'd,
　　By Justifying Grace made whole:
Nor yet the promis'd Grace receiv'd,
　　The CHRIST, the Fulness in their Soul.

2 A better Gift He Us provides,
　　On whom the Gospel-Times are come;
And lo! the Holy Ghost *abides*
In us, and makes our Hearts his Home.

3 We now our Elder Brethren meet,
　　Their FAITH, and Happiness improve,
And soon with Them shall shine compleat
　　In CHRIST, and perfected in Love.

Looking unto *JESUS*.

1 REEGARDLESS now of Things below,
　　JESUS, to Thee my Heart aspires,
Determin'd Thee alone to know,
　　Author, and End of my Desires:
Fill me with Righteousness Divine;
To end, as to begin, is Thine.

2 What is a worthless Worm to Thee?
　　What is in Man thy Grace to move?
That still 'Thou seekest those who flee
　　The Arms of thy pursuing Love?
That still Thine inmost Bowels cry
Why, Sinner, wilt thou perish, why?

3 Ah fhew me, LORD, my Depth of Sin!
    Ah, LORD, thy Depth of Mercy fhew!
End, JESUS, end this War within:
    No Reft my Spirit e'er fhall know,
'Till Thou thy quickning Influence give:
Breathe, LORD, and thele dry Bones fhall live.

4 There, there before the Throne Thou art,
    The Lamb e'er Earth's Foundations flain!
Take Thou, O take this guilty Heart;
    Thy Blood will wafh out every Stain:
No Crofs, no Sufferings I decline;
Only let all my Heart be Thine!

The Same.

1 GOD of Love, incline Thine Ear!
  CHRIST my King, Hafte, and bring
    Thy Salvation near.

2 Thee my reftlefs Soul requires;
    Reftlefs 'till Thou fulfil
  All its large Defires.

3 Only Thou to me be given;
    Thou be mine, I refign
  All in Earth or Heaven.

4 JESUS, come, my Sicknefs cure;
    Shew Thine Art, Cleanfe an Heart
  Full of Thoughts impure.

5 Painfully it now afpires
    To be free, Full of Thee,
  Full of hallow'd Fires.

6 Lo, I tread on Deaths and Snares,
    Sinking ftill Into Ill,
  Plung'd in Griefs and Cares.   When,

7 When, O when wilt Thou appear?
  O draw nigh! Say, " 'Tis I;
 And I will not fear.

8 Haften, haften the glad Hour,
  Come and be Unto me
 Health, and Love, and Power.

9 CHRIST my Life, my Inward Heaven,
  Thro' the whole Of my Soul
 Spread thy Little Leaven.

10 Make me to the End endure;
  Let me feel Love the Seal:
 Love fhall make it fure.

11 Love, thine Image Love reftore;
  Let me love, Hence remove,
 And be feen no more.

A *Morning* HYMN.

1 CHRIST, whofe Glory fills the Skies,
  CHRIST, the true, the only Light,
Sun of Righteoufnefs, arife,
  Triumph o'er the Shades of Night:
Day-fpring from on High, be near:
Day-ftar, in my Heart appear.

2 Dark and Chearlefs is the Morn
  Unaccompanied by Thee,
Joylefs is the Day's Return,
  Till thy Mercy's Beams I fee;
Till they Inward Light impart,
Glad my Eyes, and warm my Heart.

Vifit

3 Visit then this Soul of mine,
   Pierce the Gloom of Sin and Grief,
Fill me, Radiancy Divine,
   Scatter all my Unbelief,
More and more thyself display,
Shining to the Perfect Day.

ANOTHER.

1 JESUS the all-restoring Word,
   My fallen Spirit's Hope,
After thy lovely Likeness, LORD,
   O when shall I wake up!

2 Thou, O my GOD, Thou only art
   The Life, the Truth, the Way:
Quicken my Soul, instruct my Heart,
   My sinking Footsteps stay.

3 Of all Thou hast in Earth below
   In Heaven above to give,
Give me thine only Self to know,
   In Thee to walk, and live.

4 Fill me with all the Life of Love,
   In mystick Union join
Me to Thyself, and let me prove
   The Fellowship Divine.

5 Open the Intercourse between
   My longing Soul and Thee,
Never to be broke off again
   Thro' all Eternity.

6 Grant this, O LORD; for thou hast died
   That I might be forgiven,
Thou hast THE RIGHTEOUSNESS supplied,
   For which I merit Heaven.

An

An Evening HYMN.

1 JESUS, the all-atoning Lamb,
    Lover of loſt Mankind,
Salvation in whoſe only Name
    A Sinful World can find:

2 I aſk thy Grace to make me clean,
    I come to Thee, my GOD:
Open, O LORD, for this Day's Sin
    The Fountain of thy Blood.

3 Hither my ſpotted Soul be brought,
    And every idle Word,
And every Work, and every Thought
    That hath not pleas'd my LORD.

4 Hither my Actions righteous deem'd
    By Man, and counted good,
As filthy Rags by GOD eſteem'd,
    'Till ſprinkled with thy Blood.

5 No! my beſt Actions cannot ſave,
    But Thou muſt purge ev'n Them:
And (for in Thee I now believe)
    My worſt cannot condemn.

6 To Thee then, O vouchſafe me Power
    For Pardon ſtill to flee,
And every Day, and every Hour
    To waſh myſelf in Thee.

To the Rev. Mr. WHITEFIELD.

1 BROTHER in CHRIST, and well-belov'd,
    Attend, and add thy Pray'r to mine,
As *Aaron* call'd, and *inly mov'd,*
    To minister in Things Divine!

2 Faithful, and often own'd of GOD,
    Vessel of Grace, by JESUS us'd;
Stir up the Gift on thee bestow'd,
    The Gift, thro' *Hallow'd Hands* transfus'd.

3 Fully thy heavenly Mission prove,
    And make thine own Election sure;
Rooted in FAITH, and Hope, and Love,
    Active to work, and firm t'endure.

4 Scorn to contend with Flesh and Blood,
    And trample on so mean a Foe;
By stronger Fiends in vain withstood,
    Dauntless to nobler Conquests go.

5 Go where the darkest Tempest low'rs,
    Thy Foes, triumphant Wrestler, foil;
Thrones, Principalities, and Powers,
    Engage, o'ercome, and take the Spoil.

6 The Weapons of thy Warfare take,
    With Truth and Meekness arm'd ride on;
Mighty, thro' GOD, Hell's Kingdom shake,
    Satan's strong Holds, thro' GOD, pull down.

7 Humble each vain aspiring Boast,
    Intensely for GOD's Glory burn;
Strongly declare the Sinner lost,
    SELF-RIGHTEOUSNESS o'erturn, o'erturn.

Tear

8 Tear the bright Idol from his Shrine,
    Nor fuffer him on Earth to dwell;
T'ufurp the Place of Blood Divine,
    But chafe him to his native Hell.

9 Be all into Subjection brought,
    The Pride of Man let FAITH abafe;
And captivate his every Thought,
    And force him *to be fav'd by Grace.*

To the fame, before his Voyage.

1 SERVANT of GOD, the Summons hear,
    Thy Mafter calls, arife, obey!
The Tokens of his Will appear,
    His Providence points out thy Way.

2 Lo! we commend thee to his Grace!
    In Confidence go forth! be ftrong!
Thy Meat his Will, thy Boaft his Praife,
    His Righteoufnefs be all thy Song.

3 Strong in the LORD's Almighty Power,
    And arm'd in Panoply Divine,
Firm may'ft thou ftand in Danger's Hour,
    And prove the Strength of JESUS Thine.

4 Thy Breaft-Plate be his Righteoufnefs,
    His facred Truth thy Loins furround;
Shod be thy beauteous Feet with Peace,
    Spring forth, and fpread the Gofpel Sound.

5 Fight the good Fight, and ftand fecure
    In FAITH's impenetrable Shield;
Hell's Prince fhall tremble at its Power,
    With all his fiery Darts repell'd.

Prevent

6 Prevent thy Foes, nor wait their Charge,
  But call their ling'ring Battle on,
But strongly grasp thy Seven-fold Targe,
  And bear the World and Satan down.

7 The Helmet of Salvation take,
  The LORD's, the Spirit's conqu'ring Sword,
Speak from the Word; in Lightning speak;
  Cry out, and Thunder from the Word.

8 Champion of GOD, thy LORD proclaim,
  JESUS alone resolv'd to know;
Tread down thy Foes in JESU's Name:
  Go; conqu'ring, and to conquer go.

9 Thro' Racks and Fires pursue thy Way,
  Be mindful of a dying GOD;
Finish thy Course, and win the Day:
  Look up; and seal the Truth with Blood.

A Hymn, to be sung at Sea.

1 LORD of the wide-extended Main,
    Whose Power the Winds and Seas controuls,
Whose Hand doth Earth and Heaven sustain,
    Whose Spirit leads believing Souls;

2 For Thee we leave our Native Shore,
    (We, whom thy Love delights to keep)
In other Worlds thy Works explore,
    And see thy Wonders in the Deep,

3 Tis here thine unknown Paths we trace,
    Which dark to human Eyes appear,
While through the mighty Waves we pass,
    FAITH only sees that GOD is here.

Through-

4 Throughout the Deep thy Footſteps ſhine,
    We own thy Way is in the Sea,
O'er-aw'd by Majeſty Divine,
    And loſt in thy Immenſity!

5 Thy Wiſdom here we learn t'adore,
    Thine Everlaſting Truth we prove,
Amazing Heights of boundleſs Power,
    Unfathomable Depths of Love.

6 Infinite G O D, thy Greatneſs ſpann'd
    Theſe Heavens, and meted out the Skies,
Lo! in the Hollow of thy Hand,
    The meaſur'd Waters ſink and riſe!

7 Thee to Perfection who can tell?
    Earth, and her Sons beneath Thee lie,
Lighter than Duſt within thy Scale,
    ——leſs than Nothing in Thine Eye.

8 Yet in thy Son Divinely Great,
    We claim thy Providential Care:
Boldly we ſtand before thy Seat,
    Our Advocate hath plac'd us there.

9 With Him we are gone up on high,
    Since He is ours, and we are His;
With him we reign above the Sky,
    Yet walk upon our ſubject Seas.

10 We boaſt of our recover'd Pow'rs,
    Lords are we of the Lands, and Floods,
And Earth, and Heaven, and All is ours,
    And we are CHRIST's, and CHRIST is GOD's!

R   *In*

In a Storm.

1 GLORY to Thee, whose powerful Word,
    Bids the Tempestuous Wind arise,
Glory to Thee, the Sovereign LORD
    Of Air, and Earth, and Seas, and Skies!

2 Let Air, and Earth, and Skies obey,
    And Seas Thine awful Will perform:
From them we learn to own thy Sway,
    And shout to meet the gathering Storm.

3 What tho' the Floods lift up their Voice,
    Thou hearest, LORD, our louder Cry;
They cannot damp thy Children's Joys,
    Or shake the Soul when GOD is nigh.

4 Headlong we cleave the yawning Deep,
    And back to highest Heaven are born,
Unmov'd, tho' rapid Whirlwinds sweep,
    And all the watry World upturn.

5 Roar on, ye Waves! our Souls defy
    Your roaring to disturb our Rest,
In vain t'impair the Calm ye try,
    The Calm in a Believer's Breast.

6 Rage, while our FAITH the SAVIOUR tries,
    Thou Sea, the Servant of his Will:
Rise, while our GOD permits thee, rise;
    But fall, when He shall say, *Be still!*

ZECH.

ZECH. xii. 10.

They shall look upon Me whom they have pierced.

From the German.

1 EXTENDED on a curfed Tree,
    Befmear'd with Duft, and Sweat, and Blood,
See here, the King of Glory fee!
Sinks, and expires the Son of GOD!

2 Who, Who, my SAVIOUR, this hath done;
    Who could thy facred Body wound?
No Guilt thy fpotlefs Heart hath known;
    No Guile hath in thy Lips been found.

3 I, I alone have done the Deed!
    'Tis I thy facred Flefh have torn:
My Sins have caus'd Thee, LORD, to bleed:
    Pointed the Nail, and fixt the Thorn.

4 The Burthen for me to fuftain
    Too great, on Thee, my LORD, was laid:
To heal me, Thou haft born my Pain;
    To blefs me, Thou a Curfe waft made.

5 In the devouring Lion's Teeth
    Torn, and forfook of all, I lay:
Thou fpring'ft into the Jaws of Death,
    From Death to fave the helplefs Prey.

6 My SAVIOUR, how fhall I proclaim,
    How pay the mighty Debt I owe?
Let all I have, and all I am
    Ceafelefs to All thy Glory fhew.

R 2

7 Too much to Thee I cannot give,
   Too much I cannot do for Thee:
   Let all thy Love, and all thy Grief
   Grav'n on my Heart for ever be!

8 The meek, the ftill, the lowly Mind
   O may I learn from Thee, my GOD
   And Love with fofteft Pity join'd
   For thofe that trample on thy Blood.

9 Still let thy Tears, thy Groans, thy Sighs
   O'erflow my Eyes, and heave my Breaft,
   'Till loofe from Flefh, and Earth I rife,
   And ever in thy Bofom reft.

The Means *of* Grace.

1 LONG have I feem'd to ferve Thee, Lord,
      With unavailing Pain;
   Fafted, and pray'd, and read thy Word,
      And heard it preach'd, in vain.

2 Oft did I with th'Affembly join,
      And near Thine Altar drew;
   A Form of Godlinefs was mine.
      The Pow'r I never knew.

3 To pleafe Thee, thus (at laft I fee)
      In vain I hop'd, and ftrove:
   For what are Outward Things to Thee,
      Unlefs they fpring from Love?

4 I fee the perfect Law requires
      Truth in the Inward Parts,
   Our full Confent, our whole Defires,
      Our Undivided Hearts.

5 But

5 But I of *Means* have made my Boast,
    Of *Means* an Idol made,
  The Spirit in the Letter loft,
    The Subftance in the Shade.

6 I refted in the Outward Law,
    Nor knew its deep Defign;
  The Length, and Breadth, I never faw,
    And Heighth of Love Divine.

7 Where am I now, or what my Hope?
    What can my Weaknefs do?
  JESU! to Thee my Soul looks up,
    'Tis Thou muft make it new.

8 Thine is the Work, and Thine alone:
    But fhall I idly ftand?
  Shall I the written Rule difown,
    And flight my GOD's Command?

9 Wildly fhall I from Thine turn back,
    A better Path to find;
  Thine Holy Ordinance forfake,
    And caft thy Words behind?

10 Forbid it, gracious LORD, that I
    Should ever learn Thee fo!
  No---let me with thy Word comply,
    If I thy Love would know.

11 Suffice for me, that Thou, my LORD,
    Haft bid me faft, and pray:
  Thy Will be done, thy Name ador'd;
    'Tis only mine t'obey.

12 Thou bidft me fearch the facred Leaves,
    And tafte the Hallow'd Bread:
  The kind Commands my Soul receives,
    And icr_s on Thee to feed.

13 Still for thy Loving Kindnefs, LORD,
    I in thy Temple wait;
I look to find Thee in thy Word,
    Or at thy Table meet.

14 Here, *in Thine own appointed Ways,*
    I wait to learn thy Will:
Silent I ftand before thy Face,
    And hear Thee fay, " *Be ftill!*

15 *Be ftill--and know that I am GOD!*
    'Tis all I live to know,
To feel the Virtue of thy Blood,
    And fpread its Praife below.

16 I wait my Vigour to renew,
    Thine Image to retrieve,
The Veil of outward Things pafs thro',
    And gafp in Thee to live.

17 I work; and own the Labour vain:
    And *thus* from Works I ceafe:
I ftrive, and fee my fruitlefs Pain,
    'Till GOD create my Peace.

18 Fruitlefs, 'till Thou Thyfelf impart,
    Muft all my Efforts prove:
They cannot change a finful Heart,
    They cannot purchafe Love.

19 I do the Thing thy Laws enjoin,
    And *then* the Strife give o'er:
To Thee I *then* the whole refign,
    I *truft* in Means no more.

20 I truft in Him who ftands between
    The Father's Wrath and me:
JESU! Thou great Eternal Mean,
    I look for all from Thee.

21 Thy Mercy pleads, thy Truth requires,
     Thy Promiſe calls Thee down:
   Not for the Sake of my Deſires-------
     But Oh! regard Thine own!

22 I ſeek no Motive out of Thee:
     Thine own Deſires fulfil:
   If now thy Bowels yearn on me,
     On me perform thy Will.

23 Doom, if Thou canſt, to endleſs Pains,
     And drive me from thy Face:
   But if thy ſtronger Love conſtrains,
     Let me be *ſav'd by Grace.*

Waiting for CHRIST.

1 UNCHANGEABLE, Almighty LORD,
     The True, and Merciful, and Juſt,
   Be mindful of thy gracious Word,
     Wherein Thou cauſeſt me to truſt.

2 My weary Eyes look out in vain,
     And long thy ſaving Health to ſee:
   But known to Thee is all my Pain:
     When wilt Thou come, and comfort me!

3 Priſoner of Hope, to Thee I turn,
     Thee my ſtrong Hold, and only Stay:
   Harden'd in Grief, I ever mourn:
     Why do thy Chariot-wheels delay?

4 But ſhall thy Creature aſk Thee why?
     No; I retract the eager Prayer:
   LORD, as Thou wilt, and not as I;
     I cannot chuſe: Thou canſt not err.

5 To Thee, the only Wife, and True,
  See then at laft I all refign ;
Make me in CHRIST a Creature new,
  The Manner, and the Time be Thine.

6 Only preferve my Soul from Sin,
  Nor let me faint for want of Thee :
I'll wait till Thou appear *within*,
  And plant thy Heaven of Love in me.

Before Reading the Scriptures.

1 FATHER of All, in whom alone
  We live, and move, and breathe,
One bright celeftial Ray dart down,
  And chear thy Sons beneath.

2 While in thy Word we fearch for Thee,
  (We fearch with trembling Awe)
Open our Eyes, and let us fee
  The Wonders of thy Law.

3 Now let our Darknefs comprehend
  The Light that fhines fo clear :
Now the Revealing Spirit fend,
  And give us Ears to hear.

4 Before us make thy Goodnefs pafs,
  Which here by FAITH we know ;
Let us in JESUS fee thy Face,
  And die to all below.

ANOTHER.

1 TEACHER Divine, we afk thy Grace,
  Thefe facred Leaves t'unfold :
Here in the Cryftal cleareft Glafs,
  Let us thy Face behold

           2 Shew

2 Shew us thy Sire; for known to Thee
    The Father's Glories are:
The dread Paternal Majefty
    Thou only canft declare.

3 Open the Scriptures now; reveal
    All which *for us* Thou art:
Talk with us, LORD, and let us feel
    The Kindling in our Heart.

4 In Thee we languifh to be found;
    To catch thy Words we bow;
We liften for the quick'ning Sound ·
    Speak, LORD; we hear Thee now.

ANOTHER.

1 COME, HOLY GHOST, our Hearts infpire,
    Let us Thine Influence prove;
Source of the old Prophetick Fire,
    Fountain of Life, and Love.

2 Come, HOLY GHOST, (for, mov'd by Thee,
    Thy Prophets wrote and fpoke:)
Unlock the Truth, Thyfelf the Key,
    Unfeal the Sacred Book.

3 Expand thy Wings celeftial Dove,
    Brood o'er our Nature's Night;
On our diforder'd Spirits move,
    And let there now be Light.

4 GOD thro' Himfelf we then fhall know,
    If Thou *within* us fhine,
And found, with all thy Saints below,
    The Depths of Love Divine.

Before

Before Preaching.

1 FORTH in thy Strength, O Lord, I go,
   Thy Gospel to proclaim,
Thine only Righteousness to shew,
   And glorify thy Name.

2 Ordain'd I am, and sent by Thee,
   As by the Father Thou:
And lo! Thou always art with me!
   I plead the Promise Now.

3 O give me now to speak thy Word
   In this appointed Hour;
Attend it with thy Spirit, Lord,
   And let it come with Power.

4 Open the Hearts of All that hear,
   To make their Saviour Room,
Now let them find Redemption near,
   Let Faith by Hearing come.

5 Give them to hear the Word as Thine,
   And (while they thus receive)
Prove it the Saving Power Divine,
   To Sinners that believe.

After Preaching.

1 GLORY, and Praise, and Love to Thee,
   For this effectual Door,
Jesu! who publishest by me
   The Gospel to the Poor.

Glory

2 Glory to thy great Name alone,
  That Life and Power imparts:
Now, Lord, thy genuine Gospel own,
  And graft it on their Hearts.

3 Now let them feel the Tidings true,
  Grant to thy Word Success;
Water it with thy Heavenly Dew,
  And give the wish'd Increase.

4 Savour of Life, O let it prove,
  And shew their Sins forgiven;
Work in them FAITH, which works by Love,
  And surely leads to Heaven.

HYMN *to* GOD *the Sanctifier.*

1 COME, Holy Ghost, all-quickning Fire,
    Come, and my hallow'd Heart inspire,
  Sprinkled with the Atoning Blood:
Now to my Soul Thyself reveal;
Thy mighty Working let me feel,
  And know that I am born of GOD.

2 Thy Witness with my Spirit bear,
That GOD, *my* GOD inhabits there;
  Thou, with the FATHER and the SON,
Eternal Light's coeval Beam,
Be CHRIST in me, and I in Him,
  'Till perfect we are made in One.

3 When wilt Thou my whole Heart subdue?
Come, Lord, and form my Soul anew,
  Emptied of Pride, and Self, and Hell:
Less than the least of all thy Store
Of Mercies, I myself abhor:
  All, all my Vileness may I feel.

4 Humble,

4 Humble, and teachable, and mild,
O may I, as a little Child,
   My lowly Mafter's Steps purfue :
Be Anger to my Soul unknown ;
Hate, Envy, Jealoufy, be gone !
   In Love create Thou all Things new.

5 Let Earth no more my Heart divide,
With CHRIST may I be crucified,
   To Thee with my whole Soul afpire ;
Dead to the World, and all its Toys,
Its idle Pomp, and fading Joys,
   Be Thou alone my One Defire.

6 Be Thou my Joy, be Thou my Dread ;
In Battle cover Thou my Head,
   Nor Earth, nor Hell fo fhall I fear :
So fhall I turn my fteady Face ;
Want, Pain defy, enjoy Difgrace,
   Glory in Diffolution near.

7 My Will be fwallow'd up in Thee :
Light in thy Light ftill may I fee,
   Beholding Thee with open Face :
Call'd the full Power of FAITH to prove,
Let all my hallow'd Heart be Love,
   And all my finlefs Life be Praife.

8 Come, HOLY GHOST, all-quickning Fire,
My confecrated Heart infpire,
   Sprinkled with the Atoning Blood :
Still to my Soul Thyfelf reveal ;
Thy mighty Working may I feel,
   And know that I am one with GOD !

Written

Written in Sickness.

1 WHILE Sickness shakes the House of Clay,
  And sap'd by Pain's continued Course,
My Nature hastens to decay,
  And waits the Fever's friendly Force:

2 Whither should my glad Soul aspire,
  But Heav'nward to my SAVIOUR's Breast?
Wafted on Wings of warm Desire,
  To gain her Everlasting Rest.

3 O when shall I no longer call
  This Earthly Tabernacle mine?
When shall the shatter'd Mansion fall,
  And rise rebuilt by Hands Divine?

4 Burthen'd beneath this fleshly Load,
  Earnestly here for Ease I groan,
Athirst for Thee, the Living GOD,
  And ever struggling to be gone.

5 Where Thou, and only Thou art lov'd,
  Far from the World's insidious Art,
Beyond the Range of Fiends remov'd,
  And safe from my deceitful Heart;

6 There let me rest, and sin no more:
  Come quickly, LORD, and end the Strife,
Hasten my last, my mortal Hour,
  Swallow me up in Endless Life.

7 Ah let it not my LORD displease,
  That eager thus for Death I sue,
T'ward the high Prize impatient press,
  And snatch the Crown to Conquest due.

8 Mafter, thy Greatnefs wants not me :
    O how fhall I thy Caufe defend !
Captain, releafe, and fet me free ;
    Here let my ufelefs Warfare end.

9 'Tis not the Pain I feek to fhun,
    The deftin'd Crofs, and purging Fire ;
Sin do I fear, and Sin alone,
    Thee, only Thee do I defire.

10 For Thee, within myfelf, for Thee
    I groan, and for th'Adoption wait,
When Death fhall fet my Spirit free,
    And make my Happinefs compleat.

11 No longer then, my LORD, defer,
    From Earth and Sin to take me Home ;
Now let my Eyes behold Thee near ;
    Come quickly, O my SAVIOUR, come.

Upon parting with his Friends.

1 CEASE, foolifh Heart, thy fond Complaints,
    Nor heave with unavailing Sighs,
Equal is GOD to all thy Wants,
    The hungry Soul Himfelf fupplies :
Gladly thy every Wifh refign ;
Thou canft not want, if GOD is thine.

2 Stop this full Current of thy Tears,
    Or pour for Sin th'ennobled Flood :
Look up, my Soul, fhake off thy Fears,
    Or fear to lofe a gracious GOD.
To Him, thine only Reft, return ;
In vain for Him thou canft not mourn.

3 Still vex'd and troubled is my Heart?
   Still wails my Soul the Penal Lofs?
Ling'ring I groan with all to part,
   I groan to bear the grievous Crofs;
The grievous Crofs I fain would fly,
Or fink beneath its Weight, and die.

4 Sad foothing Thought! to lofe my Cares,
   And filently refign my Breath!
Cut off a Length of wretched Years,
   And fteal an unfufpected Death;
Now to lay down my weary Head,
And lift it — free among the Dead!

5 When will the dear Deliv'rance come,
   Period of all my Pain and Strife!
O that my Soul, which gafps for Home,
   Which ftruggles in the Toils of Life,
Eafe, and a Refting Place could find,
And leave this World of Woe behind!

6 O that the Bitternefs were paft,
   The Pain of Life's long ling'ring Hour!
While fnatch'd from Paffion's furious Blaft,
   And fav'd from Sorrow's baleful Pow'r,
I mock the Storm, out-ride the Wave,
And gain the Harbour of the Grave.

7 Blefs'd, peaceful State! Where lull'd to Sleep,
   The Suff'rer's Woes fhall all be o'er!
There plaintive Grief no more fhall weep,
   Remembrance there fhall vex no more;
Nor fond Excefs, nor pining Care,
Nor Lofs, nor Parting fhall be there!

II.

1 O Holy, Holy, Holy Lord!
 Righteous in all thy Ways art Thou!
I yield, and tremble at thy Word,
 Beneath thy mighty Hand I bow,
I own, while humbled in the Duſt,
I own the Puniſhment is juſt.

2 Joy of my Eyes the Creature was;
 Deſired; but O! deſired for Thee!
Why feel I then th'imbitter'd Loſs?
 Late in thy Judgment's Light, I ſee
Whom now thy Stroke hath far remov'd,
I lov'd—alas! too dearly lov'd!

3 And can I ſee my Comfort gone,
 (My All of Comfort here below)
And not allow a parting Groan,
 And not permit my Tears to flow?
Can I forbear to mourn and cry?
No---let me rather weep, and die.

4 Dear, lovely, gracious Souls, to me
 Pleaſant your Friendlineſs has been;
So ſtrange your Love, from Droſs ſo free,
 The Fountain in the Stream was ſeen;
From Heaven the pure Affection flow'd,
And led, from whom it ſprang, to GOD.

5 To Him thro' Earth-born Cares ye paſs,
 To Him your looſen'd Souls aſpire:
Glory to GOD's victorious Grace!
 O could I catch the ſacred Fire,
Your ſhining Steps from far purſue,
And love, and weep, and part like you.

6 Partners

6 Partners of all my Griefs and Joys,
    Help me to caſt on GOD my Care,
To make his Will my only Choice,
    Away the dear Right Eye to tear,
The wiſe Decree with you t'adore,
To truſt, ſubmit, and grieve no more.

7 O let your Prayers the Saviour move,
    In Love my Spirit to renew!
O could I taſte the Saviour's Love,
    Gladly I then ſhould part with you;
My All triumphantly reſign,
And lodge you in the Arms divine.

III.

1 Why ſhould a ſinful Man complain,
    When mildly chaſten'd for his Good?
Start from the ſalutary Pain,
    And tremble at a Father's Rod?
Why ſhould I grieve his Hand t'endure,
Or murmur to accept my Cure?

2 Beneath th'afflictive Stroke I fall;
    And ſtruggle to give up my Will;
Weeping I own 'tis Mercy all;
    Mercy purſues and holds me ſtill,
Kindly refuſes to depart,
And ſtrongly vindicates my Heart.

3 Humbly I now the Rod revere,
    And Mercy in the Judgment find,
'Tis GOD afflicts; I own Him near;
    'Tis He, 'tis He ſeverely kind,
Watches my Soul with jealous Care,
Diſdainful of a Rival there.

4 'Tis

4 'Tis hence my ravifh'd Friends I mourn,
 And Grief weighs down my weary Head,
Far from my bleeding Bofom torn,
 The dear-lov'd, dangerous Joys are fled,
Hence my Complaining never ends:
Oh! I have loft my Friends, my Friends!

5 Long my reluctant Folly held,
 Nor gave them to my GOD's Command;
Hardly at length conftrain'd to yield;
 For oh! the Angel feiz'd my Hand,
Broke off my Grafp, forbad my Stay,
And forc'd my ling'ring Soul away.

6 Yes; the Divorce at laft is made,
 My Soul is crufh'd beneath the Blow;
The Judgment falls, fo long delay'd,
 And lays my ftubborn Spirit low,
My Hope expires, my Comfort ends,
Oh! I have loft my Friends, my Friends!

IV.

1 How fhall I lift my guilty Eyes,
 Or dare appear before thy Face?
When deaf to Mercy's loudeft Cries,
 I long have wearied out thy Grace,
Withftood thy Power, and crofs'd Thine Art,
Nor heard, *My Son, give Me thy Heart?*

2 How could I, LORD, hold out fo long,
 So long thy ftriving Spirit grieve!
Forgive me the defpiteful Wrong:
 Behold, my All for Thee I leave,
The whole, the whole I here reftore,
And fondly keep back Part no more.

3 Lo! I cut off the dear Right Hand,
    Afham'd I fhould fo late obey,
Pluck out mine Eye at thy Command,
    And caft the bleeding Orb away;
Lo, with my laft Referve I part,
I give, I give Thee All my Heart.

4 My Heart, my Will I here refign,
    My Life, my more than Life for Thee:
Take back my Friends, no longer mine;
    Blefs'd be the Love that lent them me:
Blefs'd be the kind revoking Word,
Thy Will be done, thy Name ador'd!

5 Henceforth Thine only Will I chufe,
    To CHRIST I die, to CHRIST I live;
Had I a Thoufand Lives to lofe,
    Had I a Thoufand Friends to give,
All, all I would to Thee reftore,
And grieve that I could give no more.

V.

1 JESU, in whom the weary find
    Their late and permanent Repofe;
Phyfician of the Sin-fick Mind,
    Relieve my Wants, affuage my Woes;
And let my Soul on Thee be caft,
'Till Life's fierce Tyranny be paft.

2 Loos'd from my GOD, and far remov'd,
    Long have I wander'd to and fro,
O'er Earth in endlefs Circles rov'd,
    Nor found whereon to reft below;
Back to my GOD at laft I fly,
For O! the Waters ftill are high.

3 Selfish Purfuits, and Nature's Maze,
 The Things of Earth for Thee I leave,
Put forth thine Hand, thine Hand of Grace,
 Into the Ark of Love receive;
Take this poor flutt'ring Soul to Reft,
And lodge it, SAVIOUR, in thy Breaft.

4 Fill with inviolable Peace,
 'Stablifh, and keep my fettled Heart;
In Thee may all my Wand'rings ceafe,
 From Thee no more may I depart,
Thy utmoft Goodnefs call'd to prove,
Lov'd with an everlafting Love.

Mourning.

1 WHEN, gracious LORD, ah tell me when
  Shall I into myfelf retire?
To Thee difcover all my Pain,
 And fhew my troubled Heart's Defire?

2 I long to pour out all my Soul,
 Sorrow, and Sin's juft Weight to feel,
To fmart, till Thou haft made me whole,
 To mourn till Thou haft faid, *Be ftill.*

3 Sick of Defire for Thee I cry,
 And, weary of forbearing, groan:
Horror, and Sin are ever nigh,
 My Comfort, and my GOD are gone.

4 Trembling in dread Sufpence I ftand;
 Sinking, and falling into Sin,
Till Thou reach out thy mighty Hand,
 And fnatch me from this Hell within.

5 Fain

5 Fain would I rife, and get me hence,
   From every fond Engagement free,
Pleafure, and Praife, and Self, and Senfe,
   And all that holds me back from Thee.

6 O that the mild and peaceful Dove,
   Would lend his Wings to aid my Flight!
Soon would I then far off remove,
   And hide me from this hateful Light

7 Where none but the All-feeing Eye
   Could mark, or interrupt my Grief,
No human Comforter be nigh,
   To torture me with vain Relief.

8 Far in fome lonely defert Place,
   For ever, ever would I fit,
Languifh to fee the Saviour's Face,
   And perifh, weeping at his Feet.

9 O what is Life without my GOD!
   A Burthen more than I can bear:
I ftruggle to throw off the Load,
   Me from myfelf I ftrive to tear.

10 I ever gafp in Christ to live:
   O that to me the Grace be given!
Had I thy Heaven and Earth to give,
   I'd buy Thee with thy Earth and Heaven.

11 If Sufferings could thy Love obtain,
   I'd fuffer all Things for thy Love:
Send me to Hell, I'd there remain:
   But let me there thy Favour prove.

12 Let me thy righteous Doom applaud,
   Thine everlafting Truth declare,
And vindicate the Way of GOD,
   And glorify thy Juftice there.

13 Let me—I know not how to pray ;
My Anguish cannot be exprest :
Jesu, Thou feest what I would fay ;
O let thy Bowels fpeak the reft!

ROMANS vii. 24, 25.

1 FATHER of Mercies, GOD of Love,
Whofe Bowels of Compaffion move
To finful Worms ; whofe Arms embrace,
And ftrain to hold a ftruggling Race !

2 With me ftill let thy Spirit ftrive,
Have Patience, till my Heart I give ;
Affift me to obey thy Call,
And give me Power to pay Thee all.

3 If now my Nature's Weight I feel,
And groan to render up my Will,
Not long the kind Relentings ftay,
The Morning Vapour fleets away.

4 A Monfter to myfelf I am,
Afham'd to feel no deeper Shame ;
Pain'd that my Pain fo foon is o'er,
And griev'd, that I can grieve no more.

5 O who fhall fave the Man of Sin ?
O when fhall end this War within ?
How fhall my Captive Soul break thro'?
Who fhall attempt my Refcue ? Who?

6 A Wretch from Sin and Death fet free ?--
Anfwer, O anfwer, CHRIST, for me,
The Grace of an accepting GOD,
The Virtue of a SAVIOUR's Blood.

Who

Who shall deliver me from the Body of this Death?

1 THOU Son of GOD, Thou Son of Man,
    Whose Eyes are as a Flame of Fire,
With kind Concern regard my Pain,
    And mark my lab'ring Heart's Desire!

2 Its inmost Folds are known to Thee,
    Its secret Plague I need not tell:
Nor can I hide, nor can I flee
    The Sin I ever groan to feel.

3 My Soul it easily besets,
    About my Bed, about my Way,
My Soul at every Turn it meets,
    And half persuades me to obey.

4 Nothing I am, and nothing have,
    Nothing my Helplesness can do;
But Thou art Good, and strong to save,
    And all that seek may find Thee true.

5 How shall I ask, and ask aright?
    My Lips refuse my Heart t'obey:
But all my Wants are in thy Sight;
    My Wants, my Fears, my Sorrows pray.

6 I want thy Love, I fear thy Frown,
    My own foul Sin I grieve to see:
T'escape its Force would Now sink down,
    And die, if Death could set me free.

7 Yet O I cannot burst my Chain,
    Or fly the Body of this Death:
Immur'd in Flesh I still remain,
    And gasp a purer Air to breathe.

8 I groan to break my Prison-Walls,
   And quit the Tenement of Clay;
Nor yet the shatter'd Mansion falls,
   Nor yet my Soul escapes away.

9 Ah LORD! wouldst Thou *within me* live,
   No longer then should I complain,
Nor sighing wish, nor weeping grieve
   For CHRIST my Life, or Death my Gain.

10 From Grief and Sin I then should cease;
   My loosen'd Tongue should then declare
Comfort, and Love, and Joy, and Peace,
   Fill all the Soul when CHRIST is there!

My Soul gaspeth for Thee as a thirsty Land.

1 LORD, how long, how long shall I
   Lift my weary Eyes in Pain?
Seek, but never find Thee nigh,
   Ask thy Love, but ask in vain,
Crush'd beneath my Nature's Load,
Darkly feeling after GOD!

2 O disclose thy lovely Face,
   Quicken all my drooping Powers!
Gasps my fainting Soul for Grace,
   As a thirsty Land for Showers:
Haste, my LORD, no longer stay,
Come, my JESUS, come away!

3 Well Thou know'st I cannot rest,
   'Till I fully rest in Thee,
'Till I am of Thee possest,
   'Till from Sin and Self set free,
All the Life of FAITH I prove,
All the Joy and Heaven of Love.

4 But my fad inconftant State,
   Give me, LORD, this Root within:
Trembling for thy Love I wait,
   Still relapfing into Sin,
Falling, 'till thy Love I feel,
Ever finking into Hell.

5 With me O continue, LORD,
   Keep me, or from Thee I fly:
Strength and Comfort from thy Word
   Imperceptibly fupply ;
Hold me 'till I apprehend,
Make me Faithful to the End.

Longing after CHRIST.

1 JESU, the Strength of all that faint,
   When wilt Thou hear my fad Complaint?
JESU, the weary Wanderer's Reft,
When wilt Thou take me to thy Breaft?

2 My Spirit mourns, by Thee forgot,
   And droops my Heart, where Thou art not:
My Soul is all an aching Void,
And pines, and thirfts, and gafps for GOD.

3 The Pain of Abfence ftill I prove,
   Sick of Defire, but not of Love:
Weary of Life I ever groan,
I long to lay the Burthen down.

4 'Tis Burthen all, and Pain, and Strife:
   O give me Love, and take my Life!
JESU, my only Want fupply,
O let me tafte thy Love, and die!

T

In TEMPTATION.

1 SINKING underneath my Load,
    Darkly feeling after Thee,
Let me afk, my GOD, my GOD,
    Why haft Thou forfaken me!
Why, O why am I forgot!
LORD, I feek, but find Thee not.

2 Still I afk, nor yet receive,
    Knock at the unopen'd Door;
Still I ftruggle to believe,
    Hope, tho' urg'd to hope no more,
Bearing what I cannot bear,
Yielding, fighting with Defpair.

3 Hear in Mercy my Complaint,
    Hear, and haften to my Aid,
Help, or utterly I faint,
    Fails the Spirit Thou haft made;
Save me, or my Foe prevails,
Save me, or thy Promife fails.

4 Struggling in the Fowler's Snare,
    Lo! I ever look to Thee:
Tempted more than I can bear----
    No, my Soul, it cannot be;
True and faithful is the Word,
Sure the Coming of thy LORD.

5 Come then, O my SAVIOUR, come,
    GOD of Truth no longer ftay,
GOD of Love, difpel the Gloom,
    Point me out the promis'd Way,
Let me from the Trial fly,
Sink into thine Arms, and die!

6 Waft

6 Waft me to that happy Shore,
  Port of Eafe, and End of Care;
All thy Storms fhall there be o'er,
  Sin fhall never reach me there,
Surely of my GOD poffeft,
Safe in my Redeemer's Breaft!

MATTHEW v. 3, 4, 6.

1 JESU, if ftill the fame Thou art,
    If all thy Promifes are fure,
Set up thy Kingdom in my Heart,
    And make me rich, for I am poor:
To me be all thy Treafures given,
The Kingdom of an Inward Heaven.

2 Thou haft pronounc'd the Mourner bleft,
    And lo! for Thee I ever mourn:
I cannot; no, I will not reft,
    'Till Thou my only Reft return,
'Till Thou, the Prince of Peace, appear,
And I receive the Comforter.

3 Where is the Bleffednefs beftow'd
    On all that hunger after Thee?
I hunger now, I thirft for GOD!
    See, the poor, fainting Sinner, fee,
And fatisfy with endlefs Peace,
And fill me with thy Righteoufnefs.

4 Ah LORD!----if Thou art in that Sigh,
    Then hear Thyfelf within me pray:
Hear in my Heart thy Spirit's Cry,
    Mark what my lab'ring Soul *would* fay,
Anfwer the deep, unutter'd Groan,
And fhew that Thou and I are One.

5 Shine on thy Work, difperfe the Gloom,
 Light in thy Light I then fhall fee:
Say to my Soul, " Thy Light is come,
 " Glory Divine is ris'n on thee,
" Thy Warfare's paft, thy Mourning's o'er:
" Look up, for thou fhalt weep no more."

6 LORD, I believe the Promife fure,
 And truft Thou wilt not long delay;
Hungry, and forrowful, and poor,
 Upon thy Word myfelf I ftay;
Into thine Hands my All refign,
And wait---'till All Thou art is mine!

In TEMPTATION.

1 JESU, Lover of my Soul,
 Let me to thy Bofom fly,
While the nearer Waters roll,
 While the Tempeft ftill is high:
Hide me, O my SAVIOUR, hide,
 Till the Storm of Life is paft:
Safe into the Haven guide;
 O receive my Soul at laft.

2 Other Refuge have I none,
 Hangs my helplefs Soul on Thee:
Leave, ah! leave me not alone,
 Still fupport, and comfort me.
All my Truft on Thee is ftay'd;
 All my Help from Thee I bring;
Cover my defencelefs Head
 With the Shadow of thy Wing.

3 Wilt Thou not regard my Call?
 Wilt Thou not accept my Prayer?
Lo! I fink, I faint, I fall----
 Lo! on Thee I caft my Care:

Reach

Reach me out thy gracious Hand!
　　While I of thy Strength receive,
Hoping against Hope I stand,
　　Dying, and behold I live!

4. Thou, O CHRIST, art all I want,
　　More than all in Thee I find:
Raise the Fallen, chear the Faint,
　　Heal the Sick, and lead the Blind.
Just, and Holy is thy Name,
　　I am all Unrighteousness,
False, and full of Sin I am,
　　Thou art full of Truth, and Grace.

5. Plenteous Grace with Thee is found,
　　Grace to cover all my Sin:
Let the healing Streams abound,
　　Make, and keep me pure within:
Thou of Life the Fountain art:
　　Freely let me take of Thee,
Spring Thou up within my Heart,
　　Rise to all Eternity!

He *shall save his People from their Sins.*

1. JESUS, in whom the Godhead's Rays
　　Beam forth with milder Majesty,
I see Thee full of Truth and Grace,
　　And come for all I want to Thee.

2. Wrathful, impure, and proud I am,
　　Nor Constancy, nor Strength I have:
But thou, O Lord, art still the same,
　　And hast not lost thy Power to save.

3 Save me from Pride, the Plague expell;
   Jesu, thine humble Self impart;
O let thy Mind within me dwell;
   O give me Lowliness of Heart.

4 Enter Thyself, and cast out Sin;
   Thy Spotless Purity bestow;
Touch me, and make the Leper clean:
   Wash me, and I am white as Snow.

5 Fury is not in Thee, my GOD:
   O why shou'd it be found in Thine!
Sprinkle me, SAVIOUR, with thy Blood,
   And all thy Gentleness is mine.

6 Pour but thy Blood upon the Flame,
   Meek, and dispassionate, and mild,
The Leopard sinks into a Lamb,
   And I become a little Child.

Desiring CHRIST.

1 WHERE shall I lay my weary Head?
   Where shall I hide me from my Shame?
From all I feel, and all I dread,
   And all I have, and all I am!
Swift to outstrip the stormy Wind,
And leave this cursed *Self* behind!

2 O the intolerable Load
   Of Nature waken'd to pursue,
The Footsteps of a distant GOD,
   'Till FAITH hath form'd the Soul anew!
'Tis Death, 'tis more than Death to bear:
I cannot live, 'till GOD is here.

3 Give me thy Wings, Celeftial Dove,
    And help me from myfelf to fly;
Then fhall my Soul far off remove,
    The Tempeft's idle Rage defy,
From Sin, from Sorrow, and from Strife
Efcap'd, and hid in CHRIST, my Life.

4 Stranger on Earth, I fojourn here:
    Yet, O! on Earth I cannot reft,
'Till Thou my hidden Life appear,
    And fweetly take me to thy Breaft:
To Thee my Wifhes all afpire,
And fighs for Thee my whole Defire.

5 Search, and try out my panting Heart:
    Surely, my LORD, it pants for Thee,
Jealous left Earth fhould claim a Part:
    Thine, wholly Thine I gafp to be:
Thou know'ft 'tis all I live to prove;
Thou know'ft I only want thy Love.

Thefe Things were written for our Inftruction.

1 JESU, if ftill Thou art To-day
    As Yefterday the fame,
Prefent to heal, in me difplay
    The Virtue of thy Name.

2 If ftill Thou go'ft about, to do
    Thy needy Creatures Good,
On me, that I thy Praife may fhew,
    Be all thy Wonders fhew'd.

3 Now, LORD, to whom for Help I call,
    Thy Miracles repeat;
With pitying Eyes behold me fall
    A Leper at thy Feet.

                        4 Loath-

Loathfome, and foul, and felf-abhor'd,
    I fink beneath my Sin;
But if Thou wilt, a gracious Word
    Of Thine can make me clean.

Thou fee'ft me deaf to thy Commands,
    Open, O LORD, my Ear;
Bid me ftretch out my wither'd Hands,
    And lift them up in Prayer.

Silent, (alas! Thou know'ft how long)
    My Voice I cannot raife;
But O! when Thou fhalt loofe my Tongue,
    The Dumb fhall fing thy Praife.

Lame at the Pool I ftill am found:
    Give; and my Strength employ;
Light as a Hart I then fhall bound,
    The Lame fhall leap for Joy.

Blind from my Birth to Guilt, and Thee,
    And dark I am within,
The Love of GOD I cannot fee,
    The Sinfulnefs of Sin.

But Thou, they fay, art paffing by;
    O let me find Thee near:
JESUS, in Mercy hear my Cry!
    Thou Son of *David* hear!

Long have I waited in the Way
    For Thee the Heavenly Light;
Command me to be brought, and fay,
    Sinner, receive thy Sight.

While dead in Trefpaffes I lie,
    The quick'ning Spirit give;
Call me, Thou Son of GOD, that I
    May hear thy Voice, and live.

12 While full of Anguifh and Difeafe,
    My weak, diftemper'd Soul
Thy Love compaffionately fees,
    O let it make me whole.

13 While torn by Hellifh Pride, I cry,
    By Legion Luft poffeft,
Son of the Living God, draw nigh,
    And fpeak me into Reft.

14 Caft out thy Foes, and let them ftill
    To Jesu's Name fubmit;
Cloath with thy Righteoufnefs, and heal,
    And place me at thy Feet.

15 To Jesu's Name if all Things now
    A trembling Homage pay,
O let my ftubborn Spirit bow,
    My Stiff-neck'd Will obey.

16 Impotent, dumb, and deaf, and blind,
    And fick, and poor I am;
But fure a Remedy to find
    For all in Jesu's Name.

17 I know in Thee all Fulnefs dwells,
    And all for wretched Man;
Fill every Want my Spirit feels,
    And break off every Chain.

18 If Thou impart Thyfelf to me,
    No other Good I need;
If Thou the Son fhalt make me free,
    I fhall be free indeed.

19 I cannot reft, till in thy Blood
    I full Redemption have;
But Thou, thro' whom I come to God,
    Canft to the utmoft fave.   20 From

20 From Sin, the Guilt, the Power, the Pain,
    Thou wilt redeem my Soul:
  LORD, I believe; and not in vain:
    My FAITH ſhall make me whole.

21 I too with Thee ſhall walk in White,
    With all thy Saints ſhall prove,
  What is the Length, and Breadth, and Height,
    And Depth of Perfeƈt Love.

From *the* German.

1 I Thirſt, Thou wounded Lamb of GOD,
    To waſh me in thy cleanſing Blood,
  To dwell within thy Wounds; then Pain
  Is ſweet, and Life or Death is Gain.

2 Take my poor Heart, and let it be
  For ever cloſ'd to all but Thee!
  Seal Thou my Breaſt, and let me wear
  That Pledge of Love for ever there.

3 How bleſt are they, who ſtill abide
  Cloſe ſhelter'd in thy bleeding Side!
  Who Life, and Strength from thence derive,
  And by Thee move, and in Thee live!

4 What are our Works but Sin and Death,
  'Till Thou thy quick'ning Spirit breathe!
  Thou giv'ſt the Power thy Grace to move--
  O wond'rous Grace! O boundleſs Love!

5 How can it be, Thou Heavenly King,
  That Thou ſhould'ſt us to Glory bring?
  Make Slaves the Partners of thy Throne,
  Deck'd with a never-fading Crown.

6 Hence

6 Hence our Hearts melt, our Eyes o'erflow,
Our Words are loft: Nor will we know,
Nor will we think of ought, befide
" My Lord, my Love is crucified."

7 Ah Lord! enlarge our fcanty Thought,
To know the Wonders Thou haft wrought!
Unloofe our ftamm'ring Tongue, to tell
Thy Love, immenfe, unfearchable!

8 Firft-born of many Brethren Thou!
To Thee, lo! all our Souls we bow,
To Thee our Hearts and Hands we give:
Thine may we die, Thine may we live.

The RESIGNATION.

1 AND wilt Thou yet be found?
And may I ftill draw near?
Then liften to the plaintive Sound
Of a poor Sinner's Prayer.

Jesu, Thine Aid afford,
If ftill the fame Thou art;
To Thee I look, to Thee, my Lord,
Lift up an helplefs Heart.

2 Thou feeft my tortur'd Breaft,
The Strugglings of my Will,
The Foes that interrupt my Reft,
The Agonies I feel:

The Daily Death I prove,
Saviour, to Thee is known;
'Tis worfe than Death, my God to love,
And not my GOD Alone.

3   My peevish Paffions chide,
       Who only canft controul,
Canft turn the Stream of Nature's Tide,
       And calm my troubled Soul.

       O my offended LORD,
       Reftore my inward Peace:
I know Thou canft: Pronounce the Word,
       And bid the Tempeft ceafe.

4   Abate the Purging Fire,
       And *draw* me to my Good;
Allay the Fever of Defire,
       By fprinkling me with Blood.

       I long to fee thy Face,
       Thy Spirit I implore,
The Living Water of thy Grace,
       That I may thirft no more.

5   When fhall thy Love conftrain
       And force me to thy Breaft?
When fhall my Soul return again
       To her Eternal Reft?

       Ah! what avails my Strife,
       My wand'ring to and fro?
Thou haft the Words of endlefs Life,
       Ah! whither fhould I go?

6   Thy condefcending Grace
       To me did freely move:
It calls me ftill to feek thy Face,
       And ftoops to afk my Love.

       LORD, at thy Feet I fall,
       I groan to be fet free,
I fain would now obey the Call,
       And give up All for Thee.

7   To refcue me from Woe,
   Thou didft with all Things part,
Didft lead a fuffering Life below,
   To gain my worthlefs Heart:

   My worthlefs Heart to gain,
   The GOD of All that breathe
Was found in Fafhion as a Man,
   And died a curfed Death.

8   And can I yet delay.
   My little All to give,
To tear my Soul from Earth away,
   For JESUS to receive?

   Nay, but I yield, I yield!
   I can hold out no more,
I fink by dying Love compell'd,
   And own Thee Conqueror.

9   Tho' late I all forfake,
   My Friends, my Life refign,
Gracious Redeemer, take, O take
   And feal me ever Thine.

   Come, and poffefs me whole,
   Nor hence again remove,
Settle, and fix my wav'ring Soul,
   With all thy Weight of Love.

10   My One Defire be This,
   Thy only Love to know,
To feek and tafte no other Blifs,
   No other Good below.

   My Life, my Portion Thou,
   Thou All-fufficient art,
My Hope, my Heavenly Treafure, now
   Enter, and keep my Heart.

11 Rather than let it burn
  For Earth, O quench its Heat,
 Then, when it would to Earth return,
  O let it ceafe to beat.

  Snatch me from Ill to come,
  When I from Thee would fly,
 O take my wand'ring Spirit Home,
  And grant me Then to die!

A PRAYER *againſt the Power of Sin.*

1 O That Thou would'ſt the Heavens rent,
  In Majeſty come down,
 Stretch out thine Arm Omnipotent,
  And ſeize me for Thine own!

2 Deſcend, and let thy Lightning burn
  The Stubble of thy Foe;
 My Sins o'erturn, o'erturn, o'erturn,
  And let the Mountains flow.

3 Thou my impetuous Spirit guide,
  And curb my headſtrong Will:
 Thou only canſt drive back the Tide,
  And bid the Sun ſtand ſtill.

4 What tho' I cannot break my Chain,
  Or e'er throw off my Load,
 The Things impoſſible to Men,
  Are poſſible to GOD.

5 Is any Thing too hard for Thee,
  Almighty LORD of all,
 Whoſe threatning Looks dry up the Sea,
  And make the Mountains fall?

6 Who,

6 Who, who shall in thy Presence stand;
   And match Omnipotence,
Ungrasp the Hold of thy Right-Hand,
   Or pluck the Sinner thence?

7 Sworn to destroy let Earth assail,
   Nearer to save Thou art,
Stronger than all the Powers of Hell,
   And greater than my Heart.

8 Lo! to the Hills I lift mine Eye,
   Thy promis'd Aid I claim,
Father of Mercies, glorify
   Thy fav'rite Jesu's Name.

9 Salvation in that Name is found,
   Balm of my Grief, and Care,
A Med'cine for my every Wound,
   All, all I want is There.

10 Jesu! Redeemer, Saviour, Lord,
   The weary Sinner's Friend,
Come to my Help, pronounce the Word,
   And bid my Troubles end.

11 Deliverance to my Soul proclaim,
   And Life, and Liberty,
Shed forth the Virtue of thy Name,
   And Jesus prove to me.

12 Faith to be heal'd Thou know'st I have,
   For Thou that Faith hast given:
Thou canst, Thou Canst the Sinner save,
   And make me meet for Heaven.

13 Thou canst o'ercome this Heart of mine;
   Thou wilt victorious prove,
For Everlasting Strength is Thine,
   And Everlasting Love.

U 2
14 Thy

14 Thy Powerful Spirit fhall fubdue
    Unconquerable Sin;
  Cleanfe this foul Heart, and make it new,
    And write thy Law within.

15 Bound down with twice ten thoufand Ties,
    Yet let me hear thy Call,
  My Soul in Confidence fhall rife,
    Shall rife, and break thro' all.

16 Speak, and the Deaf fhall hear thy Voice,
    The Blind his Sight receive,
  The Dumb in Songs of Praife rejoice,
    The Heart of Stone believe.

17 The *Ethiop* then fhall change his Skin,
    The Dead fhall feel thy Power,
  The loathfome Leper fhall be clean,
    And I fhall fin no more!

After a Relapfe into Sin.

1 DEPTH of Mercy! Can there be
    Mercy ftill referv'd for me!
Can my GOD his Wrath forbear,
Me, the Chief of Sinners fpare!

2 I have long withftood his Grace,
Long provok'd Him to his Face,
Would not hearken to his Calls,
Griev'd Him by a thoufand Falls.

3 I my Mafter have denied,
I afrefh have crucified,
Oft profan'd his Hallow'd Name,
Put Him to an open Shame.

4 I have fpilt his precious Blood,
Trampled on the Son of GOD,

Fill'd with Pangs unfpeakable,
I who yet *am not in Hell.*

5 Lo! I cumber ftill the Ground!
Lo! an Advocate is found,
" Haften not to cut him down,
" Let this barren Soul alone.

6 JESUS fpeaks, and pleads his Blood,
He difarms the Wrath of GOD,
Now my Father's Bowels move,
Juftice lingers into Love.

7 Kindled his Relentings are,
Me he now delights to fpare,
Cries, " *How fhall I give thee up?*"
Lets the lifted Thunder drop.

8 Whence to *me* this wafte of Love?
Afk my Advocate above,
See the Caufe in JESU's Face,
Now before the Throne of Grace.

9 There for me the SAVIOUR ftands,
Shews his Wounds, and fpreads his Hands,
GOD is LOVE: I know, I feel,
JESUS weeps! and loves mc ftill!

10 JESUS! anfwer from above,
Is not all thy Nature Love!
Wilt Thou not the Wrong forget,
Suffer me to kifs thy Feet?

11 If I rightly read thy Heart,
If Thou all Compaffion art,
Bow Thine Ear, in Mercy bow,
Pardon, and accept me now.

12 Pity from Thine Eye let fall ;
By a Look my Soul recall,

Now

Now the Stone to Flesh convert,
Cast a Look and break my Heart.

13 Now incline me to repent,
Let me now my Fall lament;
Now my foul Revolt deplore,
Weep, believe, and sin no more.

Written in Stress of Temptation.

1 I AM the Man, who long have known
  The Fierceness of Temptation's Rage!
And still to GOD for Help I groan:
  When shall my Groans his Help engage?

2 Out of the Deep on CHRIST I call,
  In Bitterness of Spirit cry;
Broken upon that Stone I fall;
  I fall; the Chief of Sinners I!

3 SAVIOUR of Men, my sad Complaint
  Let me into thy Bosom pour:
Beneath my Load of Sin I faint,
  And Hell is ready to devour.

4 A Devil to myself I am,
  Yet cannot 'scape the Flesh I tear,
Beast, Fiend, and Legion is my Name,
  My Lot the Blackness of Despair.

5 Why then in this unequal Strife,
  To Tophet's utmost Margin driven,
Still gasps my parting Soul for Life,
  Nor quite gives up her Claim to Heaven?

6 Why hopes for Help my drooping Heart,
  (Hopes against Hope) when none is nigh?
I cannot from my LORD depart,
  But kiss the Feet at which I die.

7 My

7 My LORD, (I ftill will call Thee mine,
    Till fentenc'd to Eternal Pain;)
    Thou wouldeft not thy Cup decline,
    The Vengeance due to guilty Man.

8 My Sufferings all to Thee are known,
    Tempted in every Point like me:
    Regard my Griefs, regard thine own:
    JESU, remember *Calvary!*

9 O call to Mind thine earneft Prayers,
    Thine Agony and Sweat of Blood,
    Thy ftrong and bitter Cries and Tears,
    Thy mortal Groan, MY GOD, MY GOD?

10 For whom didft Thou the Crofs endure?
    Who nail'd thy Body to the Tree?
    Did not thy Death my Life procure?
    O let thy Bowels anfwer me!

11 Art Thou not touch'd with Human Woe?
    Hath Pity left the Son of Man?
    Doft Thou not all our Sorrow know,
    And claim a Share in all our Pain?

12 Canft Thou forget thy Days of Flefh?
    Canft Thou *my* Miferies not feel?
    Thy tender Heart it bleeds afrefh!
    It bleeds! and Thou art JESUS ftill!

13 I feel, I feel Thee now the fame,
    Kindled thy kind Relentings are;
    Thefe Meltings from thy Bowels came,
    Thy Spirit groan'd this inward Prayer.

14 Thy Prayer is heard, thy Will is done!
    Light in thy Light at length I fee;
    Thou wilt preferve my Soul Thine own,
    And fhew forth all thy Power in me.

15 My Peace returns, my Fears retire,
 I find Thee lifting up my Head,
Trembling I now to Heaven aspire,
 And hear the Voice that wakes the Dead.

16 Have I not heard, have I not known,
 That Thou the Everlasting LORD,
Whom Earth and Heaven their Maker own,
 Art always faithful to thy Word?

17 Thou wilt not break a bruised Reed,
 Or quench the faintest Spark of Grace,
'Till thro' the Soul thy Power is spread,
 Thine All-victorious Righteousness.

18 With Labour faint Thou wilt not fail,
 Or wearied give the Sinner o'er,
'Till in this Earth thy Judgment dwell,
 And born of GOD I sin no more.

19 The Day of small and feeble Things
 I know Thou never wilt despise;
I know, with Healing in his Wings,
 The Sun of Righteousness shall rise.

20 My Heart Thou wilt anew create,
 The Fulness of thy Spirit give:
In stedfast Hope for this I wait,
 And confident in CHRIST believe.

MICAH vi. 6, &c.

1 WHEREWITH, O GOD, shall I draw near,
 And bow my self before thy Face?
How in thy purer Eyes appear?
 What shall I bring to gain thy Grace?

2 Will Gifts delight the LORD most High ?
   Will multiplied Oblations please ?
Thousands of Rams His Favour buy,
   Or slaughter'd Hecatombs appease ?

3 Can these assuage the Wrath of GOD ?
   Can these wash out my guilty Stain ?
Rivers of Oil and Seas of Blood !
   Alas ! they all must flow in vain.

4 Shall I my darling *Isaac* give,
   What e'er is dearest in my Eyes ?
Wilt Thou my Soul and Flesh receive
   An Holy, Living Sacrifice ?

5 Who e'er to Thee themselves approve,
   Must take the Path thy Word has shew'd,
Justice pursue, and Mercy love,
   And humbly walk by FAITH with GOD.

6 But tho' my Life henceforth be Thine,
   Future for Past can ne'er atone ;
Tho' I to Thee the whole resign,
   I only give Thee back thine own.

7 My Hand performs, my Heart aspires :
   But Thou my Works hast wrought in me ;
I render Thee thine own Desires,
   I breathe what first were breath'd from Thee.

8 What have I then wherein to trust ?
   I nothing have, I nothing am :
Excluded is my every Boast,
   My Glory swallow'd up in Shame.

9 Guilty I stand before thy Face ;
   I feel on me thy Wrath abide :
?Tis just the Sentence should take Place :
   ?Tis just—but O ! thy Son hath died !

10 JESUS

10 JESUS, the Lamb of GOD, hath bled,
    He bore our Sins upon the Tree,
Beneath our Curfe He bow'd his Head,
    'TIS FINISH'D! He hath died for me!

11 For me, I now believe he died:
    He made my every Crime his own,
Fully for me He fatisfied:
    Father, well pleas'd behold thy Son!

12 See where before thy Throne He ftands,
    And pours the All-prevailing Prayer,
Points to his Side, and lifts his Hands,
    And fhews that I am graven there.

13 He ever lives for me to pray;
    He prays, that I with Him may reign:
Amen to what my LORD doth fay!
    JESU, Thou canft not pray in vain.

HYMNS

HYMNS
AND
SACRED POEMS.
PART IV.

REDEMPTION *found.*

From the German.

1 Ow I have found the Ground, wherein
   Sure my Soul's Anchor may remain,
   The Wounds of JESUS, for my Sin
   Before the World's Foundation slain:
   Whose Mercy shall unshaken stay,
   When Heaven and Earth are fled away.

2 Father, Thine Everlasting Grace
   Our scanty Thought surpasses far:
   Thy Heart still melts with Tenderness,
   Thy Arms of Love still open are
   Returning Sinners to receive,
   That Mercy they may taste, and live.

3 O Love, thou bottomless Abyss!
   My Sins are swallow'd up in Thee:
   Cover'd is my Unrighteousness,
   Nor Spot of Guilt remains in me,
   While JESU's Blood thro' Earth and Skies,
   Mercy, free, boundless Mercy cries!

4 With

4 With Faith I plunge me in this Sea;
   Here is my Hope, my Joy, my Reſt!
Hither, when Hell aſſails, I flee,
   I look into my SAVIOUR's Breaſt;
Away, ſad Doubt, and anxious Fear!
Mercy is all that's written there.

5 Tho' Waves and Storms go o'er my Head,
   Tho' Strength, and Health, and Friends be gone,
Tho' Joys be wither'd all, and dead,
   Tho' every Comfort be withdrawn,
On this my ſtedfaſt Soul relies,
Father, thy Mercy never dies.

6 Fix'd on this Ground will I remain,
   Tho' my Heart fail, and Fleſh decay:
This Anchor ſhall my Soul ſuſtain,
   When Earth's Foundations melt away;
Mercy's full Power I then ſhall prove,
Lov'd with an Everlaſting Love.

From the ſame.

1 HOLY Lamb, who Thee receive,
   Who in Thee begin to live,
Day and Night they cry to Thee,
As Thou art, ſo let us be.

2 JESU, ſee my panting Breaſt;
   See, I pant in Thee to reſt!
Gladly wou'd I now be clean:
Cleanſe me now from every Sin.

3 Fix, O fix my wavering Mind;
   To thy Croſs my Spirit bind;
Earthly Paſſions far remove:
Swallow up our Souls in Love.

4 Duft and Afhes tho' we be,
Full of Guilt and Mifery,
Thine we are, Thou Son of GOD:
Take the Purchafe of thy Blood.

5 Who in Heart on Thee believes,
He th' Atonement now receives:
He with Joy beholds thy Face,
Triumphs in thy pard'ning Grace.

6 See, ye Sinners, fee the Flame
Rifing from the flaughter'd Lamb,
Marks the new, the living Way,
Leading to Eternal Day!

7 JESU, when this Light we fee,
All our Soul's athirft for Thee:
When thy quick'ning Power we prove,
All our Heart diffolves in Love.

8 Boundlefs Wifdom, Power Divine,
Love unfpeakable are Thine:
Praife by All to Thee be given,
Sons of Earth and Hofts of Heaven!

CHRIST *our Wifdom.*

1 MADE unto me, O LORD, my GOD,
Wifdom Divine Thou art:
Thy Light, which firft my Darknefs fhew'd,
Still fearches out my Heart.

2 Thy Spirit, breathing in the Word,
 Gave me myself to fee,
Fallen, till by thy Grace reftor'd,
 And Loft, till found in Thee.

3 JESUS, of all my Hopes the Ground,
 Thro' Thee thy Name I know,
The only Name where Health is found,
 Whence Life and Bleffings flow.

4 'Tis now by Faith's enlighten'd Eye
 I fee thy ftrange Defign,
See the GOD-Man come down to die,
 That GOD may All be mine!

5 Thou art the Truth : I now receive
 Thy Unction from above,
Divinely taught in Thee believe,
 And learn the Lore of Love.

6 Still with thy Grace anoint mine Eyes,
 Throughout my Darknefs fhine ;
O make me to Salvation wife :
 My All be ever Mine !

CHRIST *our Righteoufnefs.*

1 JESU, Thou art my Righteoufnefs,
 For all my Sins were Thine :
Thy Death hath bought of GOD my Peace,
 Thy Life hath made Him mine.

2 Spotlefs, and Juft in Thee I am ;
 I Feel my Sins forgiven ;
I tafte Salvation in thy Name,
 And antedate my Heaven.

3 For ever here my Reſt ſhall be,
    Cloſe to thy bleeding Side;
This all my Hope and all my Plea,
    For *me* the SAVIOUR died!

4 My Dying SAVIOUR, and my GOD,
    Fountain for Guilt, and Sin,
Sprinkle me ever with thy Blood,
    And cleanſe, and keep me clean,

5 Waſh me, and make me thus Thine own:
    Waſh me, and mine Thou art;
Waſh me, but not my Feet alone,
    My Hands, my Head, my Heart.

6 Th' Atonement of thy Blood apply,
    Till Faith to Sight improve,
Till Hope ſhall in Fruition die,
    And all my Soul be Love.

CHRIST *our Sanctification.*

1 JESU, my Life, Thyſelf apply,
    Thy Holy Spirit breathe,
My vile Affections crucify,
    Conform me to thy Death.

2 Conqu'ror of Hell, and Earth, and Sin,
    Still with thy Rebel ſtrive,
Enter my Soul, and work within,
    And kill, and make alive.

3 More of thy Life, and more I have,
    As the old *Adam* dies:
Bury me, SAVIOUR, in thy Grave,
    That I with Thee may riſe.

W 2   4 Reign

4 Reign in me, LORD, Thy Foes controul,
    Who would not own thy Sway;
Diffuse thine Image thro' my Soul;
    Shine to the Perfect Day.

5 Scatter the laſt Remains of Sin,
    And ſeal me Thine Abode;
O make me Glorious all within,
    A Temple built by GOD.

6 My Inward Holineſs Thou art,
    For Faith hath made Thee mine:
With all thy Fulneſs fill my Heart,
    Till all I am is Thine!

CHRIST *our Redemption.*

1 THEE, O my great Deliverer, Thee
    My Ranſom I adore,
Thy Death from Hell hath ſet me free,
    And I am damn'd no more.

2 In Thee I ſure Redemption have,
    The Pardon of my Sin;
Thy Blood I find mighty to ſave;
    Thy Blood hath made me clean.

3 I feel the Power of JESU's Name,
    It breaks the Captive's Chain;
And Men oppoſe, and Fiends exclaim,
    And Sin ſubſiſts in vain.

4 Redeem'd from Sin, its Guilt and Power
    My Soul in Faith defies:
But O! I wait the welcome Hour,
    When this frail Body dies.

5 Come

5 Come Thou, my dear Redeemer, come,
. Let me my Life refign,
O take thy Ranfom'd Servant home,
  And make me wholly Thine.

6. Fully redeem'd I fain would rife
  In Soul and Body free,
And mount to meet Thee in the Skies,
  And ever reign with Thee.

---

*It is very meet, right, and our boun-
den Duty, that we fhould at all
Times, and in all Places, give
Thanks unto Thee, O* LORD, *Holy
Father, Almighty, Everlafting*
GOD.

1 MEET and right it is to fing
  Glory to our GOD and King,
Meet in every Time, and Place,
Right to fhew forth all thy Praife.

2 Sing we now in Duty bound,
Eccho the triumphant Sound,
Publifh it thro' Earth abroad,
Praife the Everlafting GOD.

3 Praifes *here* to Thee we give,
Here our *open* Thanks receive,
Holy Father, fovereign LORD,
Always, every where ador'd.

4 Sons of *Belial*, hear the Cry,
Loud as ye our GOD defy;
You can fhout in Satan's Name,
Shall not We our GOD proclaim?

W   You

5 You can brave th' Eternal Laws,
Zealous in *your* Master's Cause ;
JESU, shall Thy Servants be
Less resolv'd and bold for Thee ?

6 No, tho' Men and Fiends exclaim,
Sing we still in JESU's Name ;
JESUS will we ever bless,
Thee before thy Foes confess.

7 Silent have we been too long,
Aw'd by Earth's rebellious Throng ;
Shou'd we still to sing deny,
LORD, the very Stones wou'd cry !

HYMN *to the* TRINITY.

FOUNTAIN of Deity,
 Father, all hail to Thee!
Ever equally ador'd,
 Hail the Spirit, and the Son,
Holy, holy, holy LORD,
 One in Three, and Three in One.

ANOTHER.

SING we to our GOD above
 Praise, Eternal as His Love :
Praise Him, all ye Heavenly Host,
FATHER, SON, and HOLY GHOST.

ANOTHER.

FATHER live, by all Things fear'd ;
 Live the Son, alike rever'd ;

Equally

Equally be Thou ador'd,
HOLY GHOST, Eternal LORD.

Three in Perfon, One in Power,
Thee we worfhip evermore:
Praife by All to Thee be given,
Endlefs Theme of Earth and Heaven.

ANOTHER.

1 PRAISE be to the Father given;
    CHRIST He gave Us to fave,
Now the Heirs of Heaven.

2 Pay we equal Adoration
    To the Son: He alone
Wrought out our Salvation.

3 Glory to th' Eternal Spirit!
    Us He feals, CHRIST reveals,
And applies His Merit.

4 Worfhip, Honour, Thanks and Bleffing,
    One and Three, Give we Thee,
Never, never ceafing.

ANOTHER.

TO GOD, who reigns enthron'd on high,
    To his dear Son, who deign'd to die
Our Guilt and Mifery to remove,
To that bleft Spi'rit who Life imparts,
Who rules in all Believing Hearts,
    Be endlefs Glory, Praife, and Love.

ANOTHER.

ANOTHER.

1 LET Heaven and Earth agree
    The Father's Praise to sing,
Who draws us to the Son, that He
    May us to Glory bring.

2   Honour and endless Love,
    Let GOD the Son receive,
Who saves us here, and prays above,
    That we with Him may live.

3   Be everlasting Praise
    To GOD the Spirit given,
Who now attests us Sons of Grace,
    And seals us Heirs of Heaven.

4   Drawn, and redeem'd, and seal'd,
    We'll sing the One and Three,
With Father, Son, and Spirit fill'd
    To all Eternity.

ANOTHER.

1 FATHER of Mankind, Be ever ador'd:
    Thy Mercy we find, In sending our LORD
To ransom and bless us: Thy Goodness we praise,
For sending in JESUS Salvation by Grace.

2 O Son of his Love, Who deignedst to die,
Our Curse to remove, Our Pardon to buy;
Accept our Thanksgiving, Almighty to save,
Who openest Heaven, To All that believe.

3 O Spirit of Love, Of Health, and of Power,
Thy Working we prove, Thy Grace we adore;
                             Whose

[Blood,
Whofe inward Revealing Applies our LORD's
Attefting, and fealing Us Children of GOD.

HYMN *for the* Kingfwood *Colliers.*

1 GLORY to GOD, whofe fovereign Grace
    Hath animated fenfelefs Stones,
Call'd us to ftand before his Face,
    And rais'd us into *Abraham's* Sons.

2 The People that in Darknefs lay,
    In Sin and Error's deadly Shade,
Have feen a glorious Gofpel Day,
    In JESU's lovely Face difplay'd.

3 Thou only, LORD, the Work haft done,
    And bar'd Thine Arm in all our Sight,
Haft made the Reprobates thine own,
    And claim'd the Outcafts as thy Right.

4 Thy Single Arm, Almighty LORD,
    To us the great Salvation brought,
Thy Word, thine All-creating Word,
    That fpake at firft the World from Nought.

5 For this the Saints lift up their Voice,
    And ceafelefs praife to Thee is given,
For this the Hofts above rejoyce :
    We raife the Happinefs of Heaven.

6 For this, no longer Sons of Night,
    To Thee our Thanks and Hearts we give :
To Thee who call'd us into Light,
    To Thee we die, to Thee we live.

7 Suffice,

7 Suffice, that for the Season paſt,
　Hell's horrid Language fill'd our Tongues,
We all thy Words behind us caſt,
　And lewdly ſang the Drunkard's Songs.

8 But O the Power of Grace Divine!
　In Hyms we now our Voices raiſe,
Loudly in ſtrange Hoſannahs join,
　And Blaſphemies are turn'd to Praiſe!

9 Praiſe GOD, from whom all Bleſſings flow,
Praiſe Him all Creatures here below,
Praiſe Him above, ye Heavenly Hoſt,
Praiſe FATHER, SON, and HOLY GHOST.

To be ſung while at Work.

1 GIVE we to the LORD above
　Bleſſing, Honour, Praiſe, and Love,
To the GOD that loos'd our Tongue
Sing we an unwonted Song.

2 He to us hath come unſought,
Us hath out of Darkneſs brought,
Darkneſs ſuch as Devils feel,
Iſſuing from the Pit of Hell.

3 Had He not in Mercy ſpar'd,
Hell had been our ſure Reward;
There we had receiv'd our Hire,
Fewel of Eternal Fire.

4 But we now extol his Name,
Pluck'd as Firebrands from the Flame,
Proofs of his unbounded Grace,
Monuments of endleſs Praiſe.

5 We are now in JESUS found,
  With his Praise let Earth resound,
  Tell it out thro' all her Caves,
  JESU's Name the Sinner saves!

6 With his Blood He us hath bought,
  His we Are, who once were not;
  Far, as Hell from Heaven, remov'd,
  He hath call'd us His Belov'd.

7 Sing we then with one accord
  Praises to our loving LORD,
  Who the Stone to Flesh converts,
  Let us give Him all our Hearts.

8 Harder were they than the Rock,
  Till they felt his Mercy's Stroke,
  Gushing Streams did then arise
  From the Fountains of our Eyes.

9 Never let them cease to flow,
  Since we now our JESUS know,
  Let us, 'till we meet above,
  Sing, and pray, and weep, and love.

ISAIAH XXXV.

1 HEAVENLY Father, Sovereign LORD,
  Ever faithful to thy Word,
  Humbly we our Seal set to,
  Testify that Thou art True.

2 Lo! for us the Wilds are glad,
  All in chearful Green array'd,
  Opening Sweets they all disclose;
  Bud, and blossom as the Rose.

3 Hark!

3 Hark! the Waftes have found a Voice,
  Lonely Defarts now rejoice,
  Gladfom Hallelujahs fing,
  All around with Praifes ring.

4 Lo, abundantly they bloom,
  Lebanon is hither come,
  Carmel's Stores the Heavens difpenfe,
  Sharon's fertile Excellence.

5 See thefe barren Souls of ours
  Bloom, and put forth Fruits and Flowers,
  Flowers of *Eden*, Fruits of Grace,
  Peace, and Joy, and Righteoufnefs.

6 We behold (the Abjects We)
  CHRIST th' Incarnate Deity,
  CHRIST in whom thy Glories fhine,
  Excellence of Strength Divine.

7 Ye that tremble at his Frown,
  He fhall lift your Hands caft down;
  CHRIST who all your Weaknefs fees,
  He fhall prop your feeble Knees.

8 Ye of fearful Hearts be ftrong,
  JESUS will not tarry long;
  Fear not, left his Truth fhould fail,
  JESUS is unchangeable.

9 GOD, your GOD fhall furely come,
  Quell your Foes, and feal their Doom,
  He fhall come, and fave you too:
  We, O LORD, have found Thee true.

10 Blind we were, but now we fee:
   Deaf; we hearken now to Thee:
   Dumb; for Thee our Tongues employ:
   Lame; and lo, we leap for Joy!

11 Faint

11 Faint we were, and parch'd with Drought,
   Water at thy Word gush'd out,
   Streams of Grace our Thirst refresh,
   Starting from the Wilderness.

12 Still we gasp thy Grace to know;
   Here for ever let it flow,
   Make the thirsty Land a Pool,
   Fix the Spirit in our Soul.

13 Where the ancient Dragon lay,
   Open for Thyself a Way,
   There let holy Tempers rise,
   All the Fruits of Paradise.

14 Lead us in the Way of Peace,
   In the Path of Righteousness,
   Never by the Sinner trod,
   Till he feels thy cleansing Blood.

15 There the Simple cannot stray,
   Babes, tho' blind, may find the Way,
   Find, nor ever thence depart,
   Safe in Lowliness of Heart.

16 Far from Fear, from Danger far,
   No devouring Beast is there;
   There the Humble walk secure,
   GOD hath made their Footsteps sure.

17 JESU, mighty to redeem,
   Let our Lot be cast with Them,
   Far from Earth our Souls remove,
   Ransom'd by thy dying Love.

18 Leave us not below to mourn,
   Fain we would to Thee return,
   Crown'd with Righteousness arise,
   Far above these nether Skies.

X   19 Come,

19 Come, and all our Sorrows chace,
Wipe the Tears from every Face,
Gladnefs let us now obtain,
Partners of thine endlefs Reign.

20 Death the lateft Foe deftroy ;
Sorrow then fhall yeid to Joy,
Gloomy Grief fhall flee away ;
Swallow'd up in endlefs Day.

***

For a MINISTER.

1 AH ! my dear Mafter ! Can it be
That I fhould lofe by ferving Thee ?
In feeking Souls fhould lofe my own,
And others fave, my felf undone ?

2 Yet am I loft (fhould'ft Thou depart)
Betray'd by this Deceitful Heart,
Deftroy'd, if Thou my Labour blefs,
And ruin'd by my own Succefs.

3 Hide me ! if Thou refufe to hide,
I fall a Sacrifice to Pride:
I cannot fhun the Fowler's Snare,
The Fiery Teft I cannot bear.

4 Helplefs to Thee for Aid I cry,
Unable to refift, or fly :
I muft not, LORD, the Tafk decline,
For All I have, and Am is Thine.

5 And well Thou know'ft I did not feek,
Uncall'd of GOD, for GOD to fpeak,
The dreadful Charge I fought to flee,
" Send whom Thou wilt, but fend not me."

6 Long

6 Long did my Coward Flesh delay,
  And still I tremble to obey,
  Thy Will be done, I faintly cry,
  But rather — suffer me to die.

7 Ah! rescue me from Earth and Sin,
  Fightings without, and Fears within,
  More, more than Hell myself I dread,
  Ah! cover my defenceless Head!

8 Surely Thou wilt. Thou canst not send,
  And not my helpless Soul defend,
  Call me to stand in Danger's Hour,
  And not support me with thy Power

9 Lord, I believe the Promise true,
  Behold, I always am with you;
  Always if Thou with me remain,
  Hell, Earth, and Sin shall rage in vain.

10 Give me thine All-sufficient Grace —
   Then hurl your Fiery Darts of Praise,
   Jesus and me you ne'er shall part,
   For GOD is greater than my Heart.

At setting out to preach the Gospel.

1 ANGEL of GOD, whate'er betide,
     Thy Summons I obey;
  Jesus, I take Thee for my Guide,
     And walk in Thee my Way.

2 Secure from Danger and from Dread,
     Nor Earth nor Hell shall move,
  Since over me thine Hand hath spread
     The Banner of thy Love.

3 To leave my Captain I difdain,
   Behind I will not ſtay,
Tho' Shame, and Loſs, and Bonds, and Pain,
   And Death obſtruct the Way.

4 Me to thy Suffering Self conform,
   And arm me with thy Power,
Then burſt the Cloud, deſcend the Storm,
   And come the Fiery Hour !

5 Then ſhall I bear thine utmoſt Will,
   When firſt the Strength is given ——
Come, fooliſh World, my Body kill,
   And drive my Soul to Heaven !

ACTS iv. 24, &c.

1 ALMIGHTY, Univerſal LORD,
   Maker of Heaven and Earth art Thou,
All Things ſprang forth t'obey thy Word,
   Thy powerful Word upholds them now.

2 Why then with unavailing Rage
   Did Heathens with thy People joyn,
And impotently fierce engage
   To execute their vain Deſign ?

3 Indignant Kings ſtood up t' oppoſe
   The LORD, and his Meſſiah's Reign,
And Earth's confed'rate Rulers roſe
   Againſt their GOD in Council vain.

4 Surely againſt thy Holy Son,
   (Son of thy Love, and ſent by Thee,
One with th' Anoiting Spirit, One
   With thy Coequal Majeſty)

5 *Herod* and *Pilate* both combin'd
   Thy sovereign Purpose to fulfill ;
Gentiles and *Jews* unconscious joyn'd
   T' accomplish thine Eternal Will.

6 And now their idle Fury view,
   And now behold their Threatnings, LORD ;
Behold thy faithful Servants too,
   And strengthen us to speak thy Word.

7 Embolden by thine out-stretch'd Arm,
   Fill us with Confidence Divine,
With Heavenly Zeal our Bosoms warm,
   That all may own, the Work is Thine ;

8 May see the Tokens of thine Hand,
   Its Sovereign Grace, its Healing Power,
No more their Happiness withstand,
   And fight against their GOD no more.

9 Now let their Opposition cease,
   Now let them catch the quick'ning Flame,
And forc'd to yield, the Signs increase,
   The Wonders wrought by JESU's Name.

To be sung in a Tumult.

1 EARTH rejoyce, the LORD is King !
   Sons of Men, his Praises sing ;
Sing ye in triumphant Strains,
JESUS our Messiah reigns !

2 Power is all to JESUS given,
   LORD of Hell, and Earth and Heaven,
Every Knee to Him shall bow :
Satan hear, and tremble Now !

3 Roar-

3 Roaring Lion, own his Power:
 Us Thou never canft devour,
 Pluck'd we are out of thy Teeth,
 Sav'd by CHRIST from Hell and Death.

4 Tho' Thou bruife in us his Heel,
 Sorer Vengeance fhalt Thou feel:
 CHRIST, the Woman's conqu'ring Seed,
 CHRIST in us fhall bruife thy Head.

5 Tho' the Floods lift up their Voice,
 Calm we hear thy Children's Noife:
 Horribly they rage in vain;
 GOD is mightier than Man.

6 JESUS Greater we proclaim,
 Him in us, than Thee in Them:
 Thee their God He overpowers;
 Thou art Theirs, and CHRIST is Ours.

7 Strong in CHRIST we thee defy,
 Dare thee all thy Force to try,
 Work in Them, the Slaves of Sin,
 Stir up all thy Hell within:

8 All thy Hofts to Battle bring:
 Shouts in us a ftronger King,
 Lifts our Hearts and Voices high——
 Hark, the Morning-Stars reply!

9 Angels and Archangels join,
 All triumphantly combine,
 All in JESU's Praife agree,
 Carrying on His Victory.

10 Tho' the Sons of Night blafpheme,
 More there are with Us than Them,
 GOD with us, we cannot fear.
 Fear, ye Fiend., for CHRIST is here!

11 Lo!

11 Lo! to Faith's inlightned Sight
   All the mountain flames with Light!
   Hell is nigh, but GOD is nigher,
   Circling us with Hosts of Fire.

12 Our Messias is come down,
   Points us to the Victor's Crown,
   Bids us take our Seats above,
   More than Conqu'rors in His Love.

13 Yes; the Future Work is done,
   CHRIST the SAVIOUR reigns alone,
   Forces *Satan* to submit,
   Bruises him beneath our Feet.

14 We the evil Angels Doom
   Antedate the Joys to come,
   See the dear Redeemer's Face,
   Sav'd, already sav'd by Grace!

Little Children, love one another.

1 GIVER of Concord, Prince of Peace,
     Meek, Lamb-like Son of GOD,
   Bid our unruly Passions cease,
     Extinguish'd with thy Blood.

2 Rebuke the Seas, the Tempest chide,
     Our stubborn Wills controul,
   Beat down our Wrath, root out our Pride,
     And calm our troubled Soul.

3 Subdue in us the Carnal Mind,
     Its Enmity destroy,
   With Cords of Love th'old *Adam* bind,
     And melt him into Joy.

4 Us into clofest Union draw,
    And in our inward Parts
Let Kindnefs fweetly write her Law,
    Let Love command our Hearts.

5 O let *Thy* Love our Hearts conftrain !
    JESUS the Crucified,
What haft thou done our Hearts to gain,
    Languifh'd, and groan'd, and died !

6 Who would not now purfue the Way
    Where JESU's Footfteps fhine ?
Who would not own the pleafing Sway
    Of Charity Divine ?

7 SAVIOUR, look down with pitying Eyes,
    Our jarring Wills controul ;
Let cordial, kind Affections rife,
    And harmonize the Soul.

8 Thee let us feel benignly near,
    With all thy quick'ning Powers,
The founding of thy Bowels hear,
    And anfwer Thee with Ours.

9 O let us find the ancient Way
    Our wond'ring Foes to move,
And force the Heathen World to fay,
    " See how thefe Chriftians love ! "

For the Anniverfary Day of One's Converfion.

1 GLORY to GOD, and Praife, and Love
    Be ever, ever given ;
By Saints below, and Saints above,
    The Church in Earth and Heaven.

2 On this glad Day the glorious Sun
    Of Righteousness arose,
  On my benighted Soul he shone,
    And fill'd it with Repose.

3 Sudden expir'd the Legal Strife,
    'Twas then I ceas'd to grieve,
  My Second, Real, Living Life
    I then began to live.

4 Then with my *Heart* I First believ'd,
    Believ'd with Faith Divine,
  Power with the Holy Ghost receiv'd
    To call the SAVIOUR *Mine.*

5 I felt my LORD's Atoning Blood
    Close to *my* Soul applied;
  Me, me he lov'd——the Son of GOD
    For *me,* for *me* He died!

6 I found, and own'd his Promise true,
    Ascertain'd of *my* Part,
  My Pardon pass'd in Heaven I *knew,*
    When written on my Heart.

7 O for a thousand Tongues to sing
    My dear Redeemer's Praise!
  The Glories of my GOD and King,
    The Triumphs of his Grace.

8 My gracious Master, and my GOD,
    Assist me to proclaim,
  To spread thro' all the Earth abroad
    The Honours of Thy Name.

9 JESUS the Name that charms our Fears,
    That bids our Sorrows cease;
  'Tis Musick in the Sinner's Ears,
    'Tis Life, and Health, and Peace!

10 He breaks the Power of cancell'd Sin,
    He sets the Prisoner free :
His Blood can make the Foulest clean ;
    His Blood avail'd for me.

11 He speaks ; and listening to his Voice,
    New Life the Dead receive,
The mournful, broken Hearts rejoyce,
    The humble Poor *beleive*.

12 Hear Him ye Deaf, His Praise ye Dumb,
    Your loosen'd Tongues employ,
Ye Blind, behold your Saviour come,
    And leap, ye Lame, for Joy.

13 Look unto Him, ye Nations, own
    Your GOD, ye fallen Race !
Look and be sav'd, thro' Faith alone ;
    Be justified by Grace !

14 See all your Sins on JESUS laid ;
    The Lamb of GOD was slain,
His Soul was once an Offering made
    For *every Soul* of Man.

15 Harlots, and Publicans, and Thieves
    In holy Triumph joyn !
Sav'd is the Sinner that believes
    From Crimes as great as Mine.

16 Murtherers, and all ye hellish Crew,
    Ye Sons of Lust and Pride,
Believe the SAVIOUR died for you ;
    For me the SAVIOUR died.

17 Awake from guilty Nature's Sleep,
    And CHRIST shall give you Light,
Cast all your Sins into the Deep,
    And wash the *Ethiop* white.

18 With me, your Chief, you then shall *know*,
    Shall feel your Sins forgiven ;
Anticipate your Heaven below,
    And own that Love is Heaven.

---

1 JOHN ii. 3.

1 FATHER, if I have sinn'd, with Thee
    An Advocate I have :
JESUS the Just shall plead for me,
    The Sinner CHRIST shall save.

2 Pardon and Peace in Him I find ;
    But not for me alone
The Lamb was slain ; for all Mankind
    His Blood did once atone.

3 My Soul is on thy Promise cast,
    And lo ! I claim my Part :
The Universal Pardon's past ;
    O seal it on my Heart.

4 Thou canst not now thy Grace deny ;
    Thou canst not but forgive :
LORD, if thy Justice asks me why —
    In JESUS I believe !

To be sung at Meals.

1 COME let us lengthen out the Feast,
    To Thankfulness improve,
GOD in his Gifts delight to taste,
    And pay them back in Love.

2 His Providence supplies our Needs,
  And Life and Strength imparts;
His open Hand our Bodies feeds,
  And fills with Joy our Hearts.

3 But will He not our Souls substain,
  And nourish with His Grace?
Yes: for Thou wilt not say, in vain
  My People seek my Face.

4 See then we take Thee at thy Word,
  With Confidence draw nigh,
We claim, and of thy Spirit, LORD,
  Expect a fresh Supply.

5 The Sinner, when he comes to Thee,
  His fond Pursuit gives o'er,
From Nature's sickly Cravings free,
  He pines for Earth no more.

6 LORD, we believe; and taste Thee Good,
  Thee All-sufficient own,
And hunger after Heavenly Food,
  And thirst for GOD Alone.

Before a Journey.

1 FORTH at thy Call, O LORD, I go,
  Thy Counsel to fulfill:
'Tis all my Business here below,
  Father, to do thy Will.

2 To do thy Will, while here I make
  My short, unfixt Abode,
An everlasting Home I seek,
  A City built by GOD.

3 O when shall I my *Canaan* gain,
 The Land of Promis'd Ease,
And leave this World of Sin and Pain,
 This howling Wilderness!

4 Come to my Help, come quickly, Lord,
 For whom alone I sigh,
O let me hear the gracious Word,
 And get me up, and die.

Another.

1 ANGELS attend ('tis GOD commands)
 And make me Now your Care:
Hover around, and in your Hands
 My Soul securely bear.

2 With outstretch'd Wings my Temples shade;
 To you the Charge is given:
Are ye not all sent forth to aid
 Th' Anointed Heirs of Heaven?

3 Servants of GOD, both yours and mine,
 Your Fellow-Servant guard:
Sweet is the Task, if He enjoin,
 His Service your Reward.

4 Then let us join our GOD to bless,
 Our Master's Praise to sing,
The Lord of Hosts, the Prince of Peace,
 Our Father, and our King.

5 At Him my mounting Spirit aims,
 My kindling Thoughts aspire,
(Assist, ye ministerial Flames,
 And raise my Raptures higher!)
 Y 6 Upward

6 Upward on Wings of Love I fly,
 Where all his Glories blaze,
Like you behold with Eagle's Eye
 My Heavenly Father's Face.

On a Journey.

1 SAVIOUR, who ready art to hear,
  (Readier than I to pray)
Answer my scarcely utter'd Prayer,
 And meet me on the Way.

2 Talk with me, LORD: Thyself reveal,
 While here o'er Earth I rove;
Speak to my Heart, and let it feel
 The kindling of thy Love:

3 With Thee conversing I forget
 All Time, and Toil, and Care:
Labour is Rest, and Pain is Sweet,
 If Thou, my GOD, art here.

4 Here then, my GOD, vouchsafe to stay,
 And make my Heart rejoyce;
My bounding Heart shall own thy Sway,
 And eccho to thy Voice.

5 Thou callest me to seek thy Face—
 'Tis all I wish to seek,
T' attend the Whispers of thy Grace,
 And hear Thee inly speak.

6 Let this my every Hour employ,
 Till I thy Glory see,
Enter into my Master's Joy,
 And find my Heaven in Thee.

After a Journey.

1 THOU, LORD, haſt bleſt my going out,
   O bleſs my coming in,
Compaſs my Weakneſs round about,
   And keep me ſafe from Sin.

2 Still hide me in thy ſecret Place,
   Thy Tabernacle ſpread,
Shelter me with preſerving Grace,
   And guard my naked Head.

3 To Thee for Refuge may I run,
   From Sin's alluring Snare,
Ready its firſt Approach to ſhun,
   And watching unto Prayer.

4 O that I never, never more
   Might from thy Ways depart!
Here let me give my Wand'rings o'er,
   By giving Thee my Heart.

5 Fix my New Heart on Things above,
   And then from Earth releaſe :
I ask not Life ; but let me love,
   And lay me down in Peace.

At lying down.

1 HOW do thy Mercies cloſe me round
   For ever be thy Name ador'd !
I bluſh in all Things to abound ;
   The Servant is above his LORD.

2 Enur'd to Poverty and Pain,
   A Suffering Life my Maſter led,
The Son of GOD, the Son of Man,
   He had not where to lay his Head.

3 But

3 But lo ! a Place He hath prepar'd
    For me, whom watchful Angels keep,
Nay, He Himself becomes my Guard,
    He smooths my Bed, and gives me Sleep.

4 JESUS protects ; my Fears be gone !
    What can the Rock of Ages move ?
Safe in thine Arms I lay me down,
    Thine everlasting Arms of Love !

5 While Thou art Intimately nigh,
    Who, who shall violate my Rest ?
Sin, Earth, and Hell I now defy,
    I lean upon my Saviour's Breast.

6 I rest beneath th' Almighty's Shade ;
    My Griefs expire, my Troubles cease ;
Thou, LORD, on whom my Soul is staid,
    Wilt keep me still in perfect Peace.

7 Me for Thine own Thou lov'st to take,
    In Time and in Eternity ;
Thou never, never wilt forsake
    An helpless Worm that trusts in Thee.

8 Wherefore in Confidence I close
    My Eyes, for Thine are open still ;
My Spirit lull'd in calm Repose,
    Waits for the Counsels of thy Will.

9 After thy Likeness let me rise,
    If here Thou will'st my longer Stay,
Or close in mortal Sleep mine Eyes,
    To open them in endless Day.

10 Still let me run, or end my Race ;
    I cannot chuse, I all resign ;
Contract or lengthen out my Days ;
    Come Life, come Death; for CHRIST is mine.
                                    Groaning

Groaning for the Spirit of Adoption.

1 FATHER, if Thou my Father art,
 Send forth the Spirit of thy Son,
Breath Him into my panting Heart,
 And make me know, as I am known:
Make me thy confcious Child, that I
May Father, Abba, Father cry.

2 I want the Sp'rit of Power within,
 Of Love, and of an Healthful Mind;
Of Power, to conquer inbred Sin,
 Of Love to Thee, and all Mankind,
Of Health, that Pain and Death defies,
Moft vig'rous, when the Body dies.

3 When fhall I hear the inward Voice,
 Which only Faithful Souls can hear!
Pardon, and Peace, and Heavenly Joys
 Attend the Promis'd Comforter:
He comes! and Righteoufnefs Divine,
And CHRIST, and All with CHRIST is mine!

4 O that the Comforter would come,
 Nor yifit, as a tranfient Gueft,
But fix in me his Conftant Home,
 And take Pofeffion of my Breaft,
And make my Soul his lov'd Abode,
The Temple of indwelling GOD.

5 Come, Holy Ghoft, my Heart infpire,
 Atteft that I am born again!
Come, and baptize me now with Fire,
 Or all thy former Gifts are vain:
I cannot reft in Sins Forgiven;
Where is the Earneft of my Heaven!

6 Where

6 Where thy Indubitable Seal
   That afcertains the Kingdom mine,
The Powerful Stamp I long to feel,
   The Signature of Love Divine :
O fhed it in my Heart abroad,
Fulnefs of Love, of Heaven, of GOD!

HYMN *to* CHRIST *the Prophet.*

1 PROPHET, on Earth beftow'd,
   A Teacher, fent from GOD,
Thee we welcome from above,
   Sent the Father to reveal,
Sent to manifeft His Love,
   Sent to teach His perfect Will.

2   Thee all the Seers of Old
     Prefigur'd and foretold ;
Mofes Thee the Prophet fhew'd,
   Meek and lowly as Thou art,
Abraham, the Friend of GOD,
   David, after his own Heart.

3   The leffer Stars that fhone
     Till Thy great Courfe begun,
With imparted Lufter bright,
   Render'd back their borrow'd Ray,
Pointing to thy glorious Light,
   Ufhering in thy perfect Day.

4   Light of the World below,
     Thee all Mankind may know ;
Thou, the Univerfal Friend,
   Into every Soul haft fhone :
O that All *would* comprehend,
   All adore the rifing Sun.

5
Thy chearing Beams we bless,
Bright Sun of Righteousness :
Life and Immortality
Thou alone to Light hast brought,
Bid the New Creation be,
Call'd the World of Grace from Nought.

6
Image of GOD most High
Display'd to Mortal Eye,
Thee the Patriarchs beheld,
Thee the Angel they ador'd,
Oft in diverse Ways reveal'd,
CHRIST the Everlasting LORD.

7
Thy Godhead we revere,
Wonderful Counsellor !
Thou the Father's Wisdom art,
Great Apostle, Thee we praise,
Chose thy People to convert,
Jacob's fallen Tribes to raise.

8
The *Gentiles* too may see
Their Covenant in Thee,
Opener of Their blinded Eyes,
Thee the Gracious Father gave :
Rise on All, in Glory rise,
Save a World Thou cam'st to save.

9
For This the Heavenly Dove
Descended from above,
He, immeasurably shed,
CHRIST the Prophet mark'd and seal'd,
Pour'd upon thy Sacred Head,
Thee th' Anointing Spirit fill'd.

10
Ah! give us, LORD to know
Thine Office here below :

Preach

Preach Deliverance to the Poor,
Sent for This, O Christ, Thou art,
Jesu, all our Sickness cure;
Bind Thou up the Broken Heart.

11   Publish the Joyful Year
Of GOD's Acceptance near,
Preach Glad Tidings to the Meek,
Liberty to Spirits bound,
General free Redemption speak,
Spread thro' Earth the Gospel-Sound.

12   Humbly behold we sit,
And listen at thy Feet;
Never will we hence remove;
Lo! to Thee our Souls we bow,
Tell us of the Father's Love;
Speak; for, Lord, we hear Thee now.

13   Master, to us reveal
His acceptable Will;
Ever for thy Law we wait,
Write it in our inward Parts,
Our dark Minds illuminate,
Grave thy Kindness on our Hearts.

14   Thine be the choicest Store
Of Blessings evermore!
Thee we hear, on Thee we gaze,
Fairer than the Sons of Men,
Who can see that lovely Face,
Who can hear those Words in vain?

15   Spirit they are, and Life,
They end the Sinner's Strife:
GOD they shew benign and mild;
Glory be to GOD on High!
Now we know Him reconcil'd;
Now we Abba Father cry!

16 Thou

6   Thou art the Truth, the Way,
      O teach us how to pray ;
Worship Spiritual and True
    Still inftruct us how to give,
Let us pay the Service due,
    Let us to GOD's Glory live.

7   Holy and True, the Key
      Of *David* refts on Thee.
Come, Meffias, all Things tell,
    Make us to Salvation wife,
Shut the Gates of Death and Hell,
    Open, open Paradife.

8   Servant of GOD, confefs
      His Truth and Faithfulnefs ;
GOD the gracious GOD proclaim,
    Publifh Him thro' Earth abroad ;
Let the *Gentsles* know thy Name,
    Let us all be taught of GOD.

9   Witnefs, within us place
      The Spirit of his Grace ;
Teach us inwardly, and guide
    By an Unction from above,
Let it in our Hearts abide,
    Source of Light, and Life, and Love.

o   Pronounce our Happy Doom,
      And fhew us Things to come :
All the Depths of LOVE difplay,
    All the Myftery unfold,
Speak us feal'd to thy Great Day,
    In the Book of Life inroll'd.

2   Shepherd, fecurely keep
      Thy little Flock of Sheep ;

Call'd and gather'd into One,
    Feed us, in green Paſtures feed,
Make us quietly lie down,
    By the Streams of Comfort lead.

22   Thou, even Thou art He,
    Whom Pain and Sorrow flee :
Comforter of all that mourn,
    Let us by thy Guidance come,
Crown'd with endleſs Joy return
    To our Everlaſting Home.

Father, I have ſinned againſt Heaven,
   and before Thee, and am no more
   worthy to be called thy Son.

1 WHEN I was a little Child,
    O what Sweetneſs did I prove
Then on me my Father ſmil'd,
    Claſp'd me in the Arms of Love ;
Bore me all my Infant Days,
    Gently by his Spirit led,
Dandled me upon his Knees,
    Made me on his Promiſe feed.

2 But alas ! I ſoon rebell'd,
    Would not caſt on Him my Care,
Swell'd with Pride, with Paſſion ſwell'd,
    I could neither fall, nor err.
I was ſtrong and able grown,
    I could for my ſelf provide,
I had Wiſdom of my own,
    Let the Weaker ſeek a Guide.

3 When

3 When to Him I would not look,
   Griev'd and hardly forc'd away,
Me my Guide at length forsook,
   Me my Father left to stray;
Angrily He hid his Face:
   Careless of his Smile or Frown,
I pursued my Evil Ways,
   Frowardly in Sin went on.

4 Back recall'd, I know not how,———————
   Father, I my Folly mourn :
If Thou art my Father now,
   Now assist me to return,
Freely my Backslidings heal,
   Once again become my Guide,
Save me from my wayward Will,
   Empty me of Self and Pride.

5 Thou who all my Ways hast seen,
   Since I would from Thee depart,
Suffer me no more to lean
   To my own deceitful Heart.
O repair my grievous Loss,
   Comfort to my Soul restore :
Once a little Child I was :
   Lift me up to fall no more.

6 Give me back my Innocence,
   Give me back my Filial Fears,
Humble, loving Confidence,
   Praying Sighs, and speaking Tears :
Weak and helpless may I be,
   To thine only Will resign'd,
Ever hanging upon Thee,
   Simple, ignorant and blind.

Abba

7 Abba Father! hear my Cry,
  Look upon thy weeping Child,
Weeping at thy Feet I lie,
  Kiſs me, and be reconcil'd:
Take me up into thine Arms,
  Let me hang upon thy Breaſt,
Hide me there ſecure from Harms,
  Lull my Sorrowing Soul to Reſt.

At the Approach of Temptation.

1 GOD of my Life, whoſe Gracious Power
      Thro' various Deaths my Soul hath led,
  Or turn'd aſide the Fatal Hour,
      Or lifted up my ſinking Head :

2 In all my Ways thy Hand I own,
      Thy ruling Providence I ſee :
  O help me ſtill my Courſe to run,
      And ſtill direct my Paths to Thee.

3 On Thee my helpleſs Soul is caſt,
      And looks again thy Grace to prove :
  I call to Mind the Wonders paſt,
      The countleſs Wonders of thy Love

4 Thou, LORD, my Spirit oft haſt ſtaid,
      Haſt ſnatch'd me from the gaping Tomb,
  A Monument of thy Mercy made,
      And reſcued me from Wrath to come.

5 Oft hath the Sea confeſs'd thy Power,
      And gave me back to thy Command :
  It could not, LORD, my Life devour,
      Safe in the Hollow of thine Hand.

6 Oft

6 Oft from the Margin of the Grave
   Thou, LORD, haſt lifted up my Head:
Sudden I found Thee near to ſave;
   The Fever own'd thy Touch, and fled.

7 But O! the mightier Work of Grace,
   That ſtill the Life of Faith I live,
That ſtill I pant to ſing thy Praiſe,
   That ſtill my All I gaſp to give!

8 Pluck'd from the roaring Lion's Teeth,
   Caught up from the Eternal Fire,
Snatch'd from the Gates of Hell I breathe,
   And lo! to Heaven I ſtill aſpire!

9 Whither, O whither ſhould I fly,
   But to my loving SAVIOUR's Breaſt;
Secure within thine Arms to lie,
   And ſafe beneath thy Wings to reſt.

10 I ſee the Fiery Trial near,
   But Thou, my GOD, art ſtill the ſame;
Hell, Earth, and Sin I ſcorn to fear,
   Divinely arm'd with JESU's Name.

11 I have no Skill the Snare to ſhun,
   But Thou, O CHRIST, my Wiſdom art:
I ever into Ruin run,
   But Thou art greater than my Heart.

12 I have no Might t' oppoſe the Foe,
   But Everlaſting Strength is Thine.
Shew me the Way that I ſhould go,
   Shew me the Path I ſhould decline.

13 Which ſhall I leave, and which purſue?
   Thou only mine Adviſer be;
My GOD, I know not what to do;
   But Oh! mine Eyes are fix'd on Thee.

Z   14 Fooliſh

14 Foolish, and impotent, and blind,
  Lead me a Way I have not known,
Bring me where I my Heaven may find,
  The Heaven of loving Thee alone.

15 Enlarge my Heart to make Thee Room,
  Enter, and in me ever stay;
The Crooked then shall Strait become,
  The Darkness shall be lost in Day!

In TEMPTATION.

1 WHERE, my Soul, is now thy Boast?
    Where the Sense of Sin forgiven?
Destitute, tormented, lost,
  Down the Stream of Nature driven,
Crush'd by Sin's redoubled Load;
Where, my Soul, is now thy GOD!

2 Far from me my GOD is gone,
  All my Joys with Him are fled,
Every Comfort is withdrawn,
  Peace is lost, and Hope is dead;
Sin, and only Sin I feel,
Pride, and Lust, and Self, and Hell.

3 Did I then my Soul deceive?
  Rashly claim a Part in Thee?
Did I, LORD, in vain believe,
  Falsely hope Thou diedst for me?
Must I back my Hopes restore,
Trust Thou diedst for me no more?

4 No; I never will resign
  What of Thee by Faith I know;
Never cease to call Thee mine,
  Never will I let Thee go;
Be it I my Soul deceive,
Yet I will, I will believe.

5 Tho'

5 Tho' I groan beneath thy Frown,
　　Hence I will not, cannot fly;
Tho' thy Justice cast me down,
　　At thy Mercy-Seat I lye;
Let me here my Sentence meet,
Let me perish at thy Feet!

J o b xxiii. 8, 9, 10.

1　FORWARD I now in Duties go,
　　　But O! my Saviour is not there!
Heavy He makes me drive, and flow,
　　Without the Chariot-Wheels of Prayer.

2 I look to former Times, and strain
　　The Footsteps of my GOD to trace;
Backward I go (but still in vain)
　　To find the Tokens of his Grace.

3 Surrounded by his Power I stand,
　　His Work on other Souls I see,
He deals his Gifts on either Hand,
　　But still He hides Himself from me.

4 Groaning I languish at his Stay,
　　But He regards my every Groan;
Dark and disconsolate my Way;
　　But still my Way to Him is known.

5 When fully He my Faith hath tried,
　　Like Gold I in the Fire shall shine,
Come forth when seven times purified,
　　And strongly bear the Stamp Divine.

After

After a Relapse into Sin.

1 MY GOD, my GOD, on Thee I call,
  Thee only would I know:
One Drop of Blood on me let fall,
  And wash me white as Snow.

2 Touch me, and make the Leper clean,
  Purge my Iniquity:
Unless Thou wash my Soul from Sin,
  I have no Part with Thee.

3 But art Thou not already mine?
  Answer, if mine Thou art!
Whisper within, Thou LOVE Divine,
  And chear my doubting Heart.

4 Tell me again, my Peace is made,
  And bid the Sinner live,
The Debt's discharg'd, the Ransom's paid,
  My Father must forgive.

5 Father, forgive thy froward Child,
  I ask in JESU's Name,
I languish to be reconcil'd:
  And reconcil'd I am.

6 Behold for me the Victim bleeds,
  His Wounds are open'd wide,
For me the Blood of Sprinkling pleads,
  And speaks me Justified.

7 O why did I my SAVIOUR leave,
  So soon unfaithful prove?
How could I thy good Spirit grieve,
  And sin against thy LOVE?

8 I forc'd

8 I forc'd Thee firſt to diſappear,
    I turn'd thy Face aſide:
Ah! LORD, if Thou hadſt ſtill been here,
    Thy Servant had not died.

9 But O! how ſoon thy Wrath is o'er,
    And pard'ning Love takes place!
Aſſiſt me, SAVIOUR, to adore
    The Riches of thy Grace.

10 O could I loſe myſelf in Thee!
    Thy Depth of Mercy prove,
Thou vaſt unfathomable Sea
    Of unexhauſted LOVE!

11 My humbled Soul, when Thou art near,
    In Duſt and Aſhes lyes:
How ſhall a ſinful Worm appear,
    Or meet thy purer Eyes!

12 I loath my ſelf, when GOD I ſee,
    And into Nothing fall,
Content, if Thou exalted be,
    And CHRIST be All in All.

Againſt Hope, believing in Hope.

1 MY GOD! I know, I feel Thee mine,
    And will not quit my Claim,
Till all I have be loſt in Thine,
    And all renew'd I am.

2 I hold Thee with a trembling Hand,
    But will not let Thee go,
Till ſtedfaſtly by Faith I ſtand,
    And all thy Goodneſs know.

3 When

3 When shall I see the welcome Hour
    That plants my GOD in me!
  Spirit of Health, and Life, and Power,
    And perfect Liberty!

4 JESU, thine all-victorious Love
    Shed in my Heart abroad;
  Then shall my Feet no longer rove
    Rooted and fixt in GOD.

5 Love only can the Conquest win,
    The Strength of Sin subdue,
  (Mine own unconquerable Sin)
    And form my Soul anew.

6 Love can bow down the stubborn Neck,
    The Stone to Flesh convert,
  Soften, and melt, and pierce, and break
    An Adamantine Heart.

7 O that in me the Sacred Fire
    Might now begin to glow;
  Burn up the Drofs of bafe Defire,
    And make the Mountains flow!

8 O that it now from Heaven might fall,
    And all my Sins confume!
  Come, Holy Ghoft, for Thee I call,
    Spirit of Burning come!

9 Refining Fire, go through my Heart,
    Illuminate my Soul,
  Scatter thy Life through every Part,
    And fanctify the whole.

0 Sorrow and Self shall then expire,
    While entred into Reft,
  I only live my GOD t'admire,
    My GOD for ever bleft.

11 No longer then my Heart fhall mourn,
    While purified by Grace,
 I only for his Glory burn,
    And always fee his Face.

12 My ftedfaft Soul, from falling free,
    Can now no longer move;
 JESUS is all the World to me,
    And all my Heart is Love.

Bleffed are They that mourn.

1 GRACIOUS Soul, to whom are given
    Holy Hungrings after Heaven,
 Reftlefs Breathings, earneft Moans,
 Deep, unutterable Groans,
 Agonies of Strong Defire,
 Love's fuppreft, *unconfcious* Fire.

2 Turn again to GOD thy Reft,
 JESUS hath pronounc'd Thee bleft:
 Humbly to thy JESUS turn
 Comforter of All that mourn:
 Happy Mourner, hear, and fee,
 Claim the Promife made to thee.

3 Lift to Him thy weeping Eye,
 Heaven behind the Cloud defcry:
 If with CHRIST thou fuffer here,
 When his Glory fhall appear,
 CHRIST His Suffering Son fhall own;
 Thine the Crofs, and Thine the Crown.

4 Juft thro' Him; behold thy Way
 Shining to the perfect Day:
 Dying thus to All beneath,
 Fafhion'd to thy SAVIOUR's Death,
 Him the Refurrection prove,
 Rais'd to all the Life of Love.

5 What

5 What if here a while thou grieve,
GOD shall endless Comfort give:
Sorrow may a Night endure,
Joy returns as Day-Light sure:
Praise shall then thy Life employ:
Sow in Tears, and reap in Joy.

6 Doth thy LORD prolong his Stay?
Mercy wills the kind Delay:
Hides He still his lovely Face?
Lo! He waits to shew his Grace:
Seems He absent from thy Heart?
'Tis, that He may ne'er depart.

7 Gently will He lead the Weak,
Bruised Reeds He ne'er will break;
Touch'd with sympathizing Care,
Thee He in his Arms shall bear,
Bless with late but lasting Peace,
Fill with all His Righteousness.

8 Cou'dst thou the Redeemer see,
How his Bowels yearn on Thee!
How he marks with pitying Eye,
Hears his New-born Children cry,
Bears what every Member bears,
Groans their Groans, and weeps their Tears!

9 Cou'dst thou know, as thou art known,
JESUS would appear thy own:
Most abandon'd tho' it seem,
Darkly safe thy Soul with Him;
Farthest when from GOD remov'd,
Nearest then, and most belov'd.

10 Feebly then thy Hands lift up,
Hope, amidst Despairing hope:
Stand beneath thy Load of Grief,
Stagger not thro' Unbelief,

Make

Make thine own Election sure,
Faithful to the End endure,

11 GOD, to keep thee safe from Harms
Spreads his Everlasting Arms,
Feeds with secret Strength Divine,
Waits to whisper " Thou art Mine!"
His that thou may'st ever be,
Now He hides Himself from Thee.

12 Meekly then persist to mourn,
Soon He will, He must return:
Call on Him; He hears thy Cry,
Soon He will, He must draw nigh;
This the Hope, which nought can move,
GOD is Truth, and GOD is LOVE!

The Just shall live by FAITH.

1 COME hither all, who serve the LORD,
Who fear and tremble at his Word,
Hear me his Loving-Kindness tell;
Hear what He for my Soul hath done,
And look to prove it in your own;
Expect His promis'd Love to feel.

2 Come hither, all ye Slaves of Sin,
Ye Beasts without, and Fiends within,
Glad Tidings unto All I shew;
JESUS' Grace for All is free;
JESUS' Grace hath found out me,
And now He offers it to you.

3 Dead in the midst of Life I was;
Unconscious of my *Eden*'s Loss,
Long did I in the Grave remain,

A fallen

A Fallen Spirit, dark, and void,
Unknowing, and unknown of GOD,
 I felt not, for I hugg'd, my Chain.

4 He call'd: I answer'd to his Call,
Confess'd my State, and mourn'd my Fall,
 And strove, and groan'd to be renew'd:
With gradual Horror then I saw
The Nature of the fiery Law,
 But knew not then a SAVIOUR's Blood.

5 For ten long, legal Years I lay
An helpless, tho' reluctant Prey
 To Pride, and Lust, and Earth, and Hell:
Oft to Repentance vain renew'd,
Self-confident for Hours I stood,
 And fell, and griev'd, and rose, and fell.

6 I fasted, read, and work'd, and pray'd,
Call'd Holy Friendship to my Aid,
 And constant to the Altar drew;
'Tis there, I cried, He *must* be found!
By Vows, and new Engagements bound,
 All his Commands I Now shall do.

7 Soon as the Trying Hour return'd,
I sunk before the Foes I scorn'd;
 My firm Resolves did all expire:
Why hath the Law of Sin prevail'd?
Why have the Bonds of Duty fail'd?
 Alas, the Tow hath touch'd the Fire.

8 Hardly at last I all gave o'er,
I fought to free my self no more,
 Too weak to burst the Fowler's Snare;
Baffled by twice ten thousand Foils,
I ceas'd to struggle in the Toils,
 And yeilded to a just Despair.

9 'Twas

9 'Twas then my Soul beheld from far
The glimmering of an orient Star,
    That pierc'd, and chear'd my Nature's Night;
Sweetly it dawn'd, and promis'd Day,
Sorrow, and Sin it chas'd away,
    And open'd into glorious Light.

10 With other Eyes I now could see
The Father reconcil'd to me,
    JESUS the Juſt had ſatisfied:
JESUS had made my Sufferings His,
JESUS was now my Righteouſneſs;
    JESUS for *me* had liv'd and died.

11 From hence the Chriſtian Race I ran,
From hence the Fight of Faith began:
    O, 'tis a good, but painful Fight!
When Heavineſs o'erwhelms the Soul,
When Clouds and Darkneſs round me roll,
    And hide the SAVIOUR from my Sight.

12 Convinc'd my Work was but begun,
How did I ſtrive, and grieve, and groan,
    Half yielded, yet refus'd to yield!
Tempted to give my SAVIOUR up,
Deny my LORD, abjure my Hope,
    And baſely caſt away my Shield.

13 Mine Enemies and Friends were join'd,
GOD's Children with the World's combin'd
    To ſhake my Confidence in GOD:
Strongly they urg'd me to diſclaim
My weaker Title to the Lamb,
    My Intereſt in th' atoning Blood.

14 So frail, impure, and weak, could I
Purſume for *me* He deign'd to die,
    For *me* ſo cold, ſo void of Love!
                         JESU!

JESU! they bid me Thee refign,
They would not have me call Thee mine,
   Till the whole Power of Faith I prove.

15 What have I known fince Thee I knew!
What Trials haft Thou brought me thro'!
   Hardly I yet can Credit give:
Surely, my Soul, 'tis all a Dream;
Sav'd as by Fire (if fav'd) I feem,
   If ftill the Life of Grace I live!

16 What have I felt, while torn within,
Full of the Energy of Sin,
   Horror to think, and Death to tell!
The Prince of Darknefs rul'd his Hour,
Suffer'd to fhew forth all his Power,
   And fhake me o'er the Mouth of Hell.

17 But O! his Tyranny is o'er!
How fhall my refcued Soul adore
   Thy ftrange, thy unexampled Grace!
A Brand pluck'd from the Fire I am!
O SAVIOUR, help me to proclaim,
   Help me to fhew forth all thy Praife.

18 Fain would I fpread thro' Earth abroad
The Goodnefs of my loving GOD,
   And teach the World thy Grace to prove,
Unutterably Good Thou art!
Read, JESU, read my panting Heart,
   Thou feeft it pants to break with Love!

19 I only live to find Thee there:
The Manfion for Thyfelf prepare,
   In Love anew my Heart create:
The mighty Change I long to feel:
For this my vehement Soul ftands ftill,
   Reftlefs — refign'd – for This I wait.

20 I know

20 I know, my Struggling nought avails,
My Strength, and foolifh Wifdom fails,
    Vain is my Toil, and vain my Reft:
Only before thy Feet I lay,
The Potter Thou, and I the Clay,
    Thy Will be done, thy Will is beft.

21 I need not urge my eager Plea,
The Blood of Sprinkling fpeaks for me,
    JESUS for me vouchfafes t'appear,
For me before the Throne he ftands,
Points to his Side, and lifts his Hands,
    And fhews, that I am graven there!

22 Suffice it, LORD, I now Believe:
To Thee my ranfom'd Soul I give,
    Hide it, till all Life's Storms be o'er:
O keep it fafe againft that Day!
Thou ever liv'ft for me to pray:
    Thy Prayer be heard, I ask no more.

I SAIAH xlv. 22.

Look unto Me, and be ye faved, all ye
Ends of the Earth.

1   S INNERS, your SAVIOUR fee!
        O look ye unto Me!
Lift your Eyes, ye fallen Race!
    I, the Gracious GOD and True,
I am full of Truth and Grace,
    Full of Truth and Grace for you!

2   Look, and be fav'd from Sin!
        Believe, and be ye clean!

A a   Guilty

Guilty, lab'ring Souls draw nigh;
 See the Fountain open'd wide;
To the Wounds of JESUS fly,
 Bathe ye in my bleeding Side.

3 Ah dear, redeeming LORD,
 We take Thee at thy Word.
Lo! to Thee we ever look,
 Freely fav'd by Grace alone:
Thou our Sins and Curfe haft took;
 Thou for All didft once atone.

4 We now the Writing fee
 Nail'd to thy Crofs with Thee!
With thy mangled Body torn,
 Blotted out by Blood Divine;
Far away the Bond is borne;
 Thou art Ours, and we are Thine.

5 On Thee we fix our Eyes,
 And wait for frefh Supplies:
Juftified; we ask for more,
 Give th' abiding Spirit, give;
LORD, thine Image here reftore,
 Fully in thy Members live.

6 Author of Faith appear!
 Be Thou its Finifher,
Upward fti!l for this we gaze,
 Till we feel the Stamp Divine;
Thee behold with open Face,
 Bright in all thy Glory fhine.

7 Leave not thy Work undone,
 But ever love Thine own,
Let us all thy Goodnefs prove,
 Let us to the End believe;
Shew thine Everlafting Love;
 Save us, to the utmoft fave.

       8 O that

8   O that our Life might be
         One looking up to Thee!
Ever haft'ning to the Day
    When our Eyes fhall fee Thee near!
Come, Redeemer, come away!
    Glorious in thy Saints appear.

9   JESU, the Heavens bow,
         We long to meet Thee now!
Now in Majefty come down,
    Pity thine Elect, and come;
Hear in us thy Spirit groan,
    Take the weary Exiles Home.

10   Now let thy Face be feen,
        Without a Veil between:
Come and change our Faith to Sight,
    Swallow up Mortality;
Plunge us in a Sea of Light:
    CHRIST, be All in All to me!

Praife for REDEMPTION.

From the German.

1 HIGH Praife to Thee, All-gracious GOD!
       Unceafing Praife to Thee we pay:
Naked and wallowing in our Blood,
    Unpitied, loath'd of all we lay.
Thou faw'ft, and from th' Eternal Throne
Gav'ft us thy dear, thine only Son.

2 Thro' thy rich Grace, in JESU's Blood,
    Bleffing, Redemption, Life we find:
Our Souls wafh'd in this cleanfing Flood,
    No Stain of Guilt remains behind.
Who can thy Mercy's Store exprefs?
Unfathomable, numberlefs!

3 Now Christ in us doth live, and we,
    Father, thro' Him with Thee are one:
The Banner of his Love we see,
    And fearless grasp the Starry Crown:
Unutterable Peace we feel
In Him, and Joys unspeakable.

4 Now hast Thou giv'n us, thro' thy Son,
    The Power of living Faith to see,
Unconquerable Faith, alone
    That gains o'er all the Victory;
Faith which nor Earth nor Hell can move,
Unblameable in perfect Love.

5 Fully thy quick'ning Sp'rit impart,
    Thou who hast all our Sins forgiven;
O form the Saviour in my Heart;
    Seal of thy Love, and Pledge of Heaven:
For ever be his Name imprest
Both on my Hand, and on my Breast.

6 Thine is whate'er we are: Thy Grace
    In Christ created us anew,
To sing thy never-ceasing Praise,
    Thine unexausted Love to shew;
And arm'd with thy great Spirit's Aid,
Blameless in all thy Paths to tread.

7 Yea, Father, ours thro' Him Thou art,
    For so is thine Eternal Will!
O live, move, reign within my Heart,
    My Soul with all thy Fulness fill:
My Heart, my All I yield to Thee:
Jesus be All in All to me!

On the *Admiſſion of any Perſon into the* Society.

1 BROTHER in Christ, and Well-belov'd,
  To Jesus and his Servants dear,
Enter, and ſhew Thyſelf approv'd,
  Enter, and find that GOD is here!

2 'Scap'd from the World, redeem'd from Sin,
  By Fiends purſued, by Men abhor'd,
Come in, poor Fugitive, come in,
  And ſhare the Portion of thy Lord.

3 Welcome from Earth!—Lo! the Right-Hand
  Of Fellowſhip to Thee we give;
With open Arms, and Hearts we ſtand,
  And Thee in Jesu's Name receive!

4 Say, is Thy Heart reſolv'd as ours?
  Then let it burn with ſacred Love;
Then let it taſte the Heavenly Powers,
  Partaker of the Joys above.

5 Jesu, attend! Thyſelf reveal!
  Are we not met in Thy great Name?
Thee in the midſt we wait to feel,
  We wait to catch the ſpreading Flame.

6 Thou GOD, that anſwereſt by Fire,
  The Sp'irit of Burning Now impart,
And let the Flames of pure Deſire
  Riſe from the Altar of our Heart.

7 Truly our Fellowſhip below
  With Thee, and with thy Father is:
In Thee Eternal Life we know,
  And Heaven's unutterable Bliſs.

A a 3   8 In

8 In Part we only know Thee here,
　　But wait thy Coming from above,—
　And I fhall then behold Thee near,
　　And I fhall All be loft in Love!

Written after walking over Smith-field.

1 HAIL, Holy Martyrs, Glorious Names,
　　Who nobly *here* for Jesus ftood,
　Rejoic'd, and clap'd your Hands in Flames,
　　And dar'd to feal the Truth with Blood!

2 Strong in the Lord, Divinely ftrong,
　　Tortures and Death ye here defy'd;
　Demons and Men, a gazing Throng,
　　Ye brav'd, and more than Conqu'ring died!

3 Finifh'd your Courfe, and fought your Fight,
　　Hence did your mounting Souls afpire,
　Starting from Flefh, they took their Flight
　　Born upward on a Car of Fire.

4 Where Earth and Hell no more moleft,
　　Ye now have join'd the Heavenly Hoft,
　Entred into your Father's Reft,
　　And found the Life which here ye loft.

5 Father, if *now* thy Breath revives
　　In us the pure, Primeval Flame,
　Thy Power, which animates our Lives,
　　Can make us in our Deaths the fame;

6 Can out of Weaknefs make us ftrong,
　　Arming as in the antient Days,
　Loofing the ftammering Infant's Tongue,
　　And perfecting in Babes thy Praife.

7 Stedfaft

7 Stedfaft we then fhall ftand, and fure
   Thine Everlafting Truth to prove,
In Faith's Plerophory * fecure,
   In all th' Omnipotence of Love.

8 Come, Holy, Holy, Holy LORD,
   The Father, Son, and Spirit come!
Be mindful of thy changelefs Word,
   And make the faithful Soul thy Home.

9 Arm of the LORD, awake, awake!
   In *us* thy glorious Self reveal,
Let *us* thy Sev'enfold Gifts partake,
   Let *us* thy mighty Working feel.

10 Near us, affifting JESU, ftand,
   Give us the opening Heaven to fee,
Thee to behold at GOD's Right-hand,
   And yeild our parting Souls to Thee.

11 My Father, O my Father, hear,
   And fend the Fiery Chariot down,
Let *Ifrael*'s Flaming Steeds appear,
   And whirl us to the ftarry Crown!

12 We, we would die for JESUS too!
   Thro' Tortures, Fires, and Seas of Blood,
All, all triumphantly break thro',
   And plunge into the Depths of GOD!

The BELIEVER's TRIUMPH.

From *the* German.

1 JESU, thy Blood and Righteoufnefs
   My Beauty are, my glorious Drefs;
'Midft flaming Worlds in Thefe array'd
With Joy fhall I lift up my Head.   2 Bold

* i. e. *Full Affurance.*

2 Bold fhall I ftand in thy great Day ;
  For who ought to my Charge fhall lay?
  Fully thro' thefe abfolv'd I am
  From Sin and Fear, from Guilt and Shame.

3 The Deadly Writing now I fee
  Nail'd with thy Body to the Tree:
  Torn with the Nails that pierc'd thy Hands,
  Th'old Covenant no longer ftands.

4 Tho' fign'd and written with my Blood,
  As Hell's Foundations fure it ftood,
  Thine hath wafh'd out the Crimfon Stains,
  And white as Snow my Soul remains.

5 *Satan*, thy due Reward furvey,
  The LORD of Life why didft thou flay?
  To tear the Prey out of thy Teeth:
  To fpoil the Realms of Hell and Death.

6 The Holy, the unfpotted LAMB,
  Who from the Father's Bofom came,
  Who died, for *me*, ev'n *me* t'atone,
  Now for *my* LORD and GOD I own.

7 LORD, I believe thy precious Blood
  Which at the Mercy-Seat of GOD
  For ever doth for Sinners plead,
  For me, ev'n for *my* Soul was fhed.

8 LORD, I believe, were Sinners more
  Than Sands upon the Ocean Shore,
  For All Thou haft the Ranfom given,
  Purchas'd for All, Peace, Life, and Heaven.

9 LORD, I believe, the Price is paid
  For every Soul, th'Atonement made;
  And every Soul thy Grace may prove,
  Lov'd with an Everlafting Love.   10 Car

10 Carnal, and fold to Sin no more
   I am; Hell's Tyranny is o'er:
   Th'Immortal Seed remains within,
   And born of GOD I cannot fin.

11 Yet Nought whereof to boaft I have;
   All, all thy Mercy freely gave:
   No Works, no Righteoufnefs are mine;
   All is thy Work, and only Thine.

12 When from the Duft of Death I rife,
   To claim my Manfion in the Skies,
   Ev'n then, This fhall be all my Plea,
   "JESUS hath liv'd, hath died for me."

13 Thus *Abraham*, the Friend of GOD,
   Thus all Heaven's Armies, bought with Blood,
   SAVIOUR of Sinners Thee proclaim;
   Sinners, of whom the Chief I am.

14 Naked from Satan did I flee,
   To Thee, my LORD, and put on Thee:
   And thus adorn'd, I wait the Word
   "He comes: Arife and meet thy LORD."

15 This fpotlefs Robe the fame appears,
   When ruin'd Nature finks in Years:
   No Age can change its conftant Hue;
   Thy Blood preferves it ever New.

16 When Thou fhalt call in that Great Day
   For *my* Account, thus will I fay;
   "Thanks to my Gracious LORD, if ought
   "Of Good I did, glad I it wrought:

17 "And while I felt thy Blood within,
   "Cleanfing my Soul from every Sin,
   "Purging each fierce and foul Defire;
   "I joy'd in the refining Fire.

18 If

18 " If Pride, Defire, Wrath ftirr'd anew,
" Swift to my fure Refort I flew:
" See there my LORD upon the Tree!
" Hell heard: Inftant my Soul was free.

19 Then fhall Heaven's Hofts with loud Acclaim,
Give Praife and Glory to the LAMB,
Who bore our Sins, and by His Blood
Hath made us Kings and Priefts to GOD.

20 O ye, who joy to feed his Sheep,
Ever in your Remembrance keep;
Empty they are, and void of GOD,
'Till brought to the atoning Blood.

21 JESU, be endlefs Praife to Thee;
Whofe boundlefs Mercy hath for *me*,
For me, and All thine Hands have made,
An everlafting Ranfom paid.

22 Ah give me now, All-gracious LORD,
With Power to fpeak thy quick'ning Word;
That All, who to thy Wounds will flee
May find Eternal Life in Thee.

23 Thou GOD of Power, Thou GOD of Love,
Let the whole World thy Mercy prove:
Now let thy Word o'er all prevail:
Now take the Spoils of Death, and Hell.

24 O let the Dead now hear thy Voice,
Now bid thy banifh'd ones rejoice,
Their Beauty this, their glorious Drefs,
JESU, thy Blood and Righteoufnefs!

The.

The Love-Feast.

PART I.

1 COME, and let us sweetly join
   Christ to praise in Hymns Divine;
  Give we all with one Accord
  Glory to our Common Lord:

   Hands, and Hearts, and Voices raise,
   Sing as in the Antient Days,
   Antedate the Joys above,
   Celebrate the Feast of Love.

2 Strive we, in Affection strive:
   Let the purer Flame revive,
   Such as in the Martyrs glow'd,
   Dying Champions for their GOD.

   We, like them, may live and love,
   Call'd we are their Joys to prove;
   Sav'd with them from future Wrath,
   Partners of like pretious Faith.

3 Sing we then in Jesu's Name,
   Now, as yesterday the same,
   One in every Age and Place,
   Full for All of Truth and Grace.

   We for Christ our Master stand,
   Lights in a benighted Land;
   We our Dying Lord confess,
   We are Jesu's Witnesses.

4 Witnesses that Christ hath died;
   We with Him are crucified:
   Christ hath burst the Bands of Death;
   We his quick'ning Spirit breathe:

Christ

CHRIST is now gone up on high;
(Thither all our Wishes fly):
Sits at GOD's Right-hand above;
There with Him we reign in Love!

PART II.

1 COME, Thou High and Lofty LORD,
Lowly, meek, incarnate Word;
Humbly stoop to Earth again,
Come, and visit abject Man.

Jesu, dear, expected Guest,
Thou art bidden to the Feast;
For Thyself our Hearts prepare,
Come, and sit, and banquet there.

2 Jesu, we the Promise claim,
We are met in thy Great Name:
In the midst do Thou appear,
Manifest thy Presence here;

Sanctify us, LORD, and bless,
Breathe thy Spirit, give thy Peace,
Thou Thyself within us move;
Make our Feast a Feast of Love.

3 Let the Fruits of Grace abound,
Let in us thy Bowels sound;
Faith, and Love, and Joy increase,
Temperance, and Gentleness:

Plant in us thine Humble Mind;
Patient, pitiful, and kind,
Meek, and lowly let us be,
Full of Goodness, full of Thee.

4 Make

4 Make us all in Thee compleat,
Make us all for Glory meet,
Meet t' appear before thy Sight,
Partners with the Saints in Light.

Call, O call us each by Name
To the Marriage of the Lamb,
Let us lean upon thy Breaſt,
Love be there our endleſs Feaſt.

PART III.

1 LET us join (' tis **GOD** commands)
Let us join our Hearts and Hands;
Help to gain our Calling's Hope,
Build we each the Other up.

GOD His Bleſſing ſhall diſpenſe,
GOD ſhall crown his Ordinance,
Meet in His appointed Ways,
Nouriſh us with ſocial Grace.

2 Let us then as Brethren love,
Faithfully his Gifts improve,
Carry on the earneſt Strife,
Walk in Holineſs of Life;

Still forget the Things behind,
Follow CHRIST in Heart and Mind,
Toward the Mark unwearied preſs,
Seize the Crown of Righteouſneſs.

3 Plead we thus for Faith *alone*,
Faith which by our Works is ſhown;
GOD it is who juſtifies,
Only Faith the Grace *applies*,

B b

Active

Active Faith that lives within,
Conquers Hell, and Death, and Sin,
Sanctifies, and makes us whole,
Forms the SAVIOUR in the Soul.

4 Let us for This Faith contend,
Sure Salvation is its End;
Heaven already is begun,
Everlasting Life is won:

Only let us persevere
Till we see our LORD appear,
Never from the Rock remove,
Sav'd by Faith which works by LOVE.

PART IV.

1 PARTNERS of a glorious Hope,
Lift your Hearts and Voices up;
Jointly let us rise and sing
CHRIST our Prophet, Priest, and King.

Monuments of Jesu's Grace,
Speak we by our Lives his Praise,
Walk in Him we have receiv'd,
Shew we not in vain Believ'd.

2 While we walk with GOD in Light,
GOD our Hearts doth still unite,
Dearest Fellowship we prove,
Fellowship of JESU's Love;

Sweetly each with each combin'd,
In the Bonds of Duty join'd,
Feels the cleansing Blood *applied*,
Daily feels that CHRIST hath died.

3 Still, O LORD, our Faith increase,
Cleanse from all Unrighteousness,

Thee

Thee, th' Unholy cannot fee;
Make, O make us meet for Thee:

Every vile Affection kill,
Root out every Seed of Ill;
Utterly abolifh Sin,
Write thy Law of Love within.

4 Hence may all our Actions flow,
Love the Proof that CHRIST we know;
Mutual Love the Token be,
LORD, that we belong to Thee:

Love, thine Image Love impart,
Stamp it on our Face and Heart,
Only Love to us be given,
LORD, we ask no other Heaven.

PART V.

1 PETER i. 3. &c.

1 FATHER, hail, by All ador'd,
Father of our Bleeding LORD!
GOD of Mercy, Thee we praife,
Sav'd by thine abundant Grace:

To a lively Hope begot,
Into fecond Being brought,
Quicken'd by, and with, our Head,
Rais'd in JESUS from the Dead,

2 Rais'd t' inherit glorious Joys,
Happinefs that never cloys,
Happinefs without Allay,
Joys that never fade away;

Manna fuch as Angels eat,
Pure Delights for Spirits fit,

B b 2   All

All to us thro' JESUS given,
All for us referv'd in Heaven.

3 There we fhall in Glory fhine,
Kept on Earth by Power Divine;
Power Divine thro' Faith receiv'd:
We the Promife have believ'd;

Confident that CHRIST fhall come,
Make the Faithful Souls his Home,
Here in part Himfelf reveal,
Stamp us with the Spirit's Seal.

4 This we now rejoice to know,
Sorrowful howe'er we go,
Exercis'd, if Need require,
Purg'd in the Refining Fire:

Faith the Trial fhall abide,
Shine, as Gold, when fully tried,
Glory, Honour, Praife receive,
Which the Righteous Judge fhall give.

5 Him we love as yet unfeen:
(Flefh is interpos'd between:)
Only Faith's interior Eye,
Darkly can its LORD defcry:

Gladden'd by the partial Sight,
Swells our Soul with vaft Delight,
Glorious and unfpeakable:
Heaven begun on Earth we feel.

6 Here the Sinner that believes,
Everlafting Life receives,
Here Angelic Blifs we find,
Blifs, the fame with Theirs in *kind*,

Only differing in *Degree*:
Lengthen'd out it foon fhall be;

All

All our Heaven we then shall prove,
All th' Eternity of Love.

The Communion of Saints.

PART I.

1 FATHER, Son, and Spirit, hear
 Faith's effectual, fervent Prayer,
Hear, and our Petitions seal;
Let us now the Answer feel.

Mystically One with Thee,
Transcript of the Trinity,
Thee let all our Nature own
One in Three, and Three in One.

2 If we now begin to be
Partners with thy Saints and Thee,
If we have our Sins forgiven,
Fellow-Citizens of Heaven,

Still the Fellowship increase,
Knit us in the Bond of Peace,
Join, our new-born Spirits join
Each to each, and All to Thine.

3 Build us in One Body up,
Call'd in one high Calling's Hope;
One the Spirit whom we claim,
One the pure Baptismal Flame,

One the Faith, and Common LORD,
One the Father lives, ador'd
Over, thro', and in us all,
GOD Incomprehensible!

4 One with GOD, the Source of Bliss,
Ground of our Communion This;

Life

Life of All that live below,
Let thine Emanations flow,

Rife eternal in our Heart :
Thou our long-fought *Eden* art ;
Father, Son, and Holy Ghoft,
Be to us what *Adam* loft.

5 Bold we ask thro' CHRIST the Son,
Thou, O CHRIST, art All our own ;
Our exalted Flefh we fee
To the Godhead join'd in Thee :

Glorious now thy Heaven we fhare,
Thou art here, and we are there,
We participate of Thine,
Human Nature of Divine.

6 Live we now in CHRIST our Head,
Quick'ned by thy Life, and fed ;
CHRIST, from whom the Spirit flows,
Into Thee thy Body grows ;

While we feel the Vital Blood,
While the circulating Flood,
CHRIST, thro' every Member rolls,
Soul of all Believing Souls.

7 Daily Growth the Members find,
Fitly each with Other join'd ;
Clofely all compacted rife ;
Every Joint its Strength fupplies,

Life to every Part conveys,
Till the whole receive Increafe,
All compleat the Body prove,
Perfectly built up in Love.

PART

PART II.

1 CHRIST, the true, the Heavenly Vine,
  If thy Grace hath made us Thine,
Branches of a poison'd Root,
Fallen *Adam*'s evil Fruit;

If we now transplanted are,
If we of thy Nature share,
Hear us, LORD, and let us be
Fully grafted into Thee.

2 Still may we continue thus,
  We in Thee, and Thou in us;
Let us fresh Supplies receive,
From Thee, in Thee ever live;

Share the Fatness of the Root,
Blossom, bud, and bring forth Fruit,
With immortal Vigour rise,
Tow'ring till we reach the Skies.

3 CHRIST, to all Believers known,
  Living, precious Corner-Stone,
CHRIST, by Mortals disallow'd,
Chosen and esteem'd of GOD;

Lively Stones we come to Thee,
Built together let us be,
Sav'd by Grace thro' FAITH alone:
Faith it is that makes us One.

4 Other Ground can no Man lay,
  JESUS TAKES OUR SINS AWAY!
JESUS the Foundation is:
This shall stand, and only This:

Fitly fram'd in Him we are,
All the Building rises fair:

Let

Let it to a Temple rife,
Worthy Him who fills the Skies.

5 Hufband of thy Church below,
CHRIST, if Thee our LORD we know,
Unto Thee betroth'd in Love,
Always faithful let us prove,

Never rob Thee of our Heart,
Never give the Creature Part;
Only Thou poffefs the Whole,
Take our Body, Spirit, Soul.

6 Stedfaft let us cleave to Thee,
Love the Myftic Union be,
Union to the World unknown!
Join'd to GOD, in Spirit One,

Wait we till the Spoufe fhall come,
Till the LAMB fhall take us Home,
For his Heaven the Bride prepare,
Solemnize our Nuptials there.

PART III.

JOHN xvii. 20, &c.

1 CHRIST, our Head, gone up on high,
Be Thou in thy Spirit nigh,
Advocate with GOD, give Ear
To thine own effectual Prayer:

Hear the Sounds Thou once didft breathe
In thy Days of Flefh beneath,
Now, O JESU, let them be
Strongly eccho'd back to Thee.

2 We, O CHRIST, have Thee receiv'd,
We the Gofpel-Word believ'd,

Juftly

Juftly then we claim a Share
In Thine Everlafting Prayer.

One the Father is with Thee;
Knit us in like Unity;
Make us, O uniting Son,
One as Thou and He are One.

3 If thy Love to us hath given
All the Glory of His Heaven,
(From Eternity Thine own;
Glory here in Grace begun)

Let us now the Gift receive,
By the Vital Union live,
Join'd to GOD, and perfect be,
Myftically One in Thee.

4 Let it hence to All be known,
Thou art with thy Father One,
One with Him in Us be fhew'd,
Very GOD of Very GOD;

Sent, our Spirits to unite,
Sent to make us Sons of Light,
Sent, that we his Grace may prove,
All the Riches of his Love.

5 Thee He lov'd e'er Time begun,
Thee the Coeternal Son;
He hath to Thy Merit given
Us, th' Adopted Heirs of Heaven.

Thou haft will'd that we fhould rife,
See thy Glory in the Skies,
See Thee by all Heaven ador'd,
Be forever with our LORD.

6 Thou the Father fee'ft alone,
Thou to us haft made Him known:

Sent from Him we know Thou art,
We have found Thee in our Heart:

Thou the Father haſt declar'd:
He is here our great Reward,
Ours his Nature and his Name;
Thou art Ours with Him the ſame.

7 Still, O LORD, (for Thine we are)
Still to us his Name declare;
Thy Revealing Spirit give,
Whom the World cannot receive:

Fill us with the Father's Love,
Never from our Souls remove,
Dwell in us, and we ſhall be
Thine to all Eternity.

PVRT IV.

1 CHRIST, from whom all Bleſſings flow,
Perfecting the Saints below,
Hear us, who thy Nature ſhare,
Who thy Myſtic Body are:

Join us, in One Spirit join,
Let us ſtill receive of Thine,
Still for more on Thee we call,
Thee, who filleſt All in All..

2 Cloſer knit to Thee our Head,
Nouriſh us, O CHRIST, and feed,
Let us daily Growth receive,
More and more in JESUS live:

JESU! we thy Members are,
Cheriſh us with kindeſt Care,
Of thy Fleſh, and of thy Bone:
ove, for ever love Thine own.

3 Move, and actuate, and guide,
Diverse Gifts to each divide;
Plac'd according to thy Will,
Let us all our Work fulfil;

Never from our Office move,
Needful to the Others prove,
Ufe the Grace on each beftow'd,
Temper'd by the Art of GOD.

4 Sweetly now we all agree,
Touch'd with fofteft Sympathy,
Kindly for each other care:
Every Member feels its Share:

Wounded by the Grief of One,
All the fuffering Members groan;
Honour'd if one Member is,
All partake the common Blifs.

5 Many are we now, and One,
We who JESUS have have put on:
There is neither Bond nor Free,
Male nor Female, LORD, in Thee.

Love, like Death, hath all deftroy'd,
Render'd all Diftinctions void:
Names, and Sects, and Parties fall;
Thou, O CHRIST, art ALL in ALL!

PART V.

HEBREWS xii. 22, 23, 24.

1 KING of Saints, to whom are given
All in Earth, and All in Heaven,
Reconcil'd thro' Thee alone,
Join'd, and gather'd into One:

Heirs

Heirs of Glory, Sons of Grace,
Lo! to Thee our Hopes we raife,
Raife and fix our Hopes on Thee,
Full of Immortality!

2 Abfent in our Flefh from Home,
We are to Mount *Sion* come:
Heaven is our Soul's Abode,
City of the Living GOD;

Enter'd there our Seats we claim
In the *New Jerufalem*,
Join the countlefs Angel-Quire,
Greet the Firft-born Sons of Fire.

3 We our Elder-Brethren meet,
We are made with them to fit,
Sweeteft Fellowfhip we prove
With the General Church above;

Saints, who now their Names behold
In the Book of Life enroll'd,
Spirits of the Righteous, made
Perfect *here* in CHRIST their Head.

4 We with Them to GOD are come,
GOD who fpeaks the General Doom,
JESUS CHRIST, who ftands between
Angry Heaven, and guilty Men,

Undertakes to buy our Peace,
Gives the Covenant of Grace,
Ratifies, and makes it good,
Signs and Seals it with his Blood.

5 Life his healing Blood imparts,
Sprinkled on our peaceful Hearts:
Abel's Blood for Vengeance cried,
JESU's fpeaks us juftify'd:

Speaks

Speaks, and calls for better Things,
Make us Prophets, Priefts, and Kings,
Afks that we with Him may reign,
Earth and Heaven fay, Amen!

PART VI.

1 COME, ye Kindred Souls above,
    Man provokes you unto Love;
Saints and Angels hear the Call,
Praife the Common LORD of All:

Him let Earth and Heaven proclaim,
Earth and Heaven record His Name,
Let us Both in this agree,
Both his one great Family.

2 Hofts of Heaven begin the Song,
Praife Him with a tuneful Tongue,
(Sounds like yours we cannot raife,
We can only lifp his Praife)

Us repenting Sinners fee,
JESUS died to fet us free,
Sing ye over us forgiven;
Shout for Joy, ye Hofts of Heaven.

3 Be it unto Angels known,
By the Church, what GOD hath done:
Depths of Love and Wifdom fee
In a Dying Deity!

Gaze, ye firft-born Seraphs, gaze!
Never can ye found his Grace:
Loft in Wonder, look no more;
Fall, and filently adore.

4 Minifterial Spirits know,
Execute your Charge below:

C c   You

You our Father hath prepar'd,
Fenc'd us with a Flaming Guard:

Bid you all our Ways attend,
Safe convoy us to the End,
On your Wings our Souls remove,
Waft us to the Realms of Love.

5 Happy, Souls whose Course is run,
Who the Fight of Faith have won,
Parted by an earlier Death,
Think ye of your Friends beneath?

Have ye your own Flesh forgot,
By a common Ransom bought?
Can Death's interposing Tide
Spirits One in CHRIST divide?

6 No: for Us you ever wait,
Till we make your Bliss compleat,
Till your Fellow-Servants come,
Till your Brethren hasten home:

You in Paradise remain,
For your Testimony slain,
Nobly who for JESUS stood,
Bold to seal the Truth with Blood.

7 Ever now your speaking Cries
From beneath the Altar rise,
Loudly call for Vengeance due:
"Come, Thou Holy GOD, and True!

"LORD, how long dost Thou delay?
"Come to Judgment, come away!
"Hasten, LORD, the General Doom,
"Come away, to Judgment come!

8 Wait, ye Righteous Spirits, wait,
Soon arrives your Glorious State;

Rob'd

Rob'd in White a Seafon reft,
Bleft, if not compleatly bleft.

When the Number is fulfill'd,
When the Witneffes are kill'd,
When we All from Earth are driven,
Then with us ye mount to Heaven.

9 JESU hear, and bow the Skies,
Hark! we all unite our Cries;
Take us to our Heavenly Home,
Quickly let thy Kingdom come!

JESU come, the Spirit cries,
JESU come, the Bride replies;
One Triumphant Church above,
Join us All in Perfect Love.

ISAIAH lxiv.

1 O That Thou would'ft the Heavens rend!
O that Thou would'ft this Hour come down!
Defcend, Almighty GOD, defcend,
And ftrongly vindicate Thine own!

2 Now let the Heathens fear thy Name,
Now let the World thy Nature know,
Dart into All the melting Flame
Of Love, and make the Mountain flow.

3 O let thine Indignation burn,
The Lightning of thy Judgments glare,
Th' afpiring Confidence o'erturn
Of all that ftill thine Anger dare.

4 From

4 From Heaven reveal thy vengeful Ire,
    Thy Fury let the Nations prove,
  Confeſs Thee a confuming Fire,
    And tremble, till they feel thy Love.

5 Thy Power was to our Fathers known;
    A mighty GOD, and terrible;
  In Majeſty Thou cameſt down,
    The Mountains at thy Prefence fell.

6 The Wonders Thou for them haſt wrought
    Thy boundleſs Power and Love proclaim,
 Far above all they ask'd or thought:
    And now we wait to know thy Name.

7 We wait; for fince the World began
    To Men it ne'er by Men was fhew'd:
  Thou only canſt Thy felf explain,
    GOD only founds the Depths of GOD.

8 Eye hath not feen, Ear hath not heard,
    By Heart conceiv'd it cannot be,
  The Blifs Thou haſt for Him prepar'd,
    Who waits in humble Faith for Thee.

9 Thou meeteſt him that dares rejoice
    In Hope of thy Salvation near;
  Who wants, while he obeys thy Voice,
    The perfeƈt Love that caſts out Fear.

10 In Works of Rightoufnefs employ'd
    Who Thee remembers in Thy Ways,
  The ORDINANCES of his GOD,
    The facred Channels of thy Grace.

11 But lo! thine Anger kindled is,
    And juſtly might for ever burn;
  We have forfook the Path of Peace:
    How fhall our wand'ring Souls return?

12 In Thine appointed Ways we wait,
   The Ways thy Wisdom hath enjoin'd;
Thy saving Grace we here shall meet;
   For every one that seeks shall find.

13 Nor can we thus thy Wrath appeafe;
   We and our Works are all unclean,
As filthy Rags our Righteoufnefs,
   Our Good is Ill, our Virtue Sin.

14 Like wither'd Leaves we fade away,
   We all deferve thy Wrath to feel,
Swift as the Wind our Sins convey,
   And fweep our guilty Souls to Hell.

15 Not one will call upon thy Name,
   Stir himfelf up thy Grace to fee,
The LORD His Righteoufnefs to claim,
   And boldly to take hold on Thee.

16 For O! thy Face is turn'd afide,
   Since we refus'd t' obey thy Will;
Thou haft confum'd us for our Pride,
   Thy heavy Hand confumes us ftill.

17 But art thou not our Father Now?
   Our Father Now Thou furely art:
Humbly beneath thy Frown we bow,
   We feek Thee with a trembling Heart.

18 The Potter Thou, and We the Clay;
   Behold us at thy Footftool laid,
In Anger caft us not away,
   The Creatures whom thine Hands have made.

19 O let thine Anger rage no more,
   Remember not Iniquity;
See LORD, and all our Sins pafs o'er,
   Thine own Peculiar People fee.

20 *Jerusalem* in Ruins lies,
　　A Wildernefs thy Cities are ;
　A Den of Thieves thy Temple is,
　　No longer now the Houfe of Prayer.

21 Where humbly low our Fathers bow'd,
　　And Thee with joyful Lips ador'd,
　Idolaters profanely croud,
　　And take the Altar for its LORD.

22 The facred Means Thyfelf ordain'd,
　　Others rejeƈt with impious Hafte ;
　By Thefe blafphem'd, by Thofe profan'd
　　Our pleafant Things are all laid wafte.

23 And wilt Thou not this Havock fee,
　　For which we ever, ever mourn?
　Still fhall we cry in vain to Thee?
　　Return, our gracious LORD, return!

24 Hold not thy Peace at *Sion*'s Woe,
　　O caft not out thy People's Prayer,
　Regard thy fuffering Church below,
　　And fpare, the Weeping Remnant fpare.

25 Thy fallen Tabernacle raife,
　　Thy Chaftifement at laft remove,
　That all Mankind may fing thy Praife,
　　Thou GOD of Truth, Thou GOD of Love!

HEBREWS iv. 9.

There remaineth therefore a REST *to the People of* GOD.

1 LORD, I believe a Reft remains
　　To all thy People known,
　A Reft, where Pure Enjoyment reigns,
　　And Thou art lov'd Alone.

2 A

2 A Reſt, where all our Soul's Deſire
    Is fixt on Things above,
Where Doubt, and Pain, and Fear expire,
    Caſt out by Perfect Love.

3 A Reſt of Laſting Joy and Peace,
    Where all is calm within:
'Tis there from our own Works we ceaſe,
    From Pride, and Self, and Sin.

4 Our Life is hid with CHRIST in GOD;
    The Agony is o'er:
We wreſtle not with Fleſh and Blood,
    We *ſtrive* with Sin no more.

5 Our Sp'rit is right, our Heart is clean,
    Our Nature is renew'd,
We cannot, no, we Cannot Sin,
    For we are born of GOD.

6 From ev'ry evil Motion freed,
    (The SON hath made us free)
On all the Pow'rs of Hell we tread,
    In glorious Liberty.

7 Redeem'd, we walk on Holy Ground,
    In CHRIST we cannot err:
No Lion in that Way is found,
    No rav'nous Beaſt is there!

8 Safe in the Way of Life, above
    Death, Earth, and Hell we riſe;
We find, when perfected in Love,
    Our long-ſought Paradiſe.

9 Within that *Eden* we retire,
    We reſt in JESU's Name:
It guards us, as a Wall of Fire,
    And as a Sword of Flame.

10 O that I now The Reſt might know,
  Believe, and enter in!
Now, SAVIOUR, Now the Power beſtow,
  And let me ceaſe from Sin.

11 Remove this Hardneſs from my Heart,
  This Unbelief remove,
To me the Reſt of Faith impart,
  The Sabbath of thy Love.

12 I groan from Sin to be ſet free,
  From Self to be releas'd;
O take me, take me into Thee,
  Mine Everlaſting Reſt.

13 I would be Thine, Thou know'ſt I wou'd,
  And have Thee all mine own:
Thee, O mine All-ſufficient Good,
  I want, and Thee alone.

14 Thy Name to me, thy Nature grant;
  This, only this be given,
Nothing beſides my GOD I want,
  Nothing in Earth or Heaven.

15 Come, O my SAVIOUR, come away,
  Into my Soul deſcend,
No longer from thy Creature ſtay,
  My Author, and my End.

16 The Bliſs Thou haſt for me prepar'd
  No longer be delay'd:
Come my exceeding Great Reward,
  For whom I firſt was made.

17 Come, Father, Son, and Holy Ghoſt,
  And ſeal me thine Abode,
Let all I am in Thee be loſt,
  Let all I am be GOD!
                    F I N I S.

BOOKS

Publish'd by the REVEREND

Mr. JOHN and CHARLES WESLEY.

1 HYMNS and Sacred Poems, vol. 1.
2   Ditto, vol. 2, bound with Vol. 1. pr. together 3s
3 Ditto, vol. 3. pr. bound 3s.
4 A Collection of Psalms and Hymns, pr. bd. 1s.
5 Hymns on Gods everlasting Love, pr. 3d.
6 Ditto, price 4d
7 An Extract of the Rev. Mr. John Wesley's Journal, pr. bound 1s.
8 Ditto, vol. 2. pr. bound 1s
9 Ditto, vol. 3 pr. bound 1s
10 The Nature and Design of Christianity, pr. 2d 3d Edition.
11 A Collection of Forms of Prayers, pr. 3d 6th Edition.
12 The Doctrine of Salvation, Faith, and good Works, pr. 1d 6th Edition.
13 A Sermon on Salvation by Faith, pr. 1d 6th Edition.
14 Nicodemus: Or, a Treatise on the Fear of Man, pr. 3d 2d Edition.
15 Christian Prudence, pr. 3d 2d Edition.
16 Reflections upon the Conduct of Human Life, pr. 3d 2d Edition.
17 An Extract of the Life and Death of Mr. Tho. Haliburton, pr. 6d
18 An Extract of the Life of M. de Renty, pr. 4d
19 A short Account of the Death of Mrs Hannah Richardson, pr. 1d 4th Edition.
20 An Extract of Thomas à Kempis's Christian Pattern, pr. 8d.
21 The almost Christian, a Sermon, pr. 2d 2d Edit.

22 A

BOOKS publiſh'd.

22 A Sermon on Epheſians, verſe 14, pr. 2d *5th Edition.*
23 Chriſtian Perfection, a Sermon, pr. 6d
24 Free Grace, a Sermon, pr. 2d *3d Edition.*
25 Serious Conſiderations concerning Election and Reprobation, pr. 1d
26 Ditto, on Abſolute Predeſtination, pr. 1d
27 A Dialogue between a Predeſtinarian and his Friend, pr. 1d *2d Edition.*
28 The Scripture Doctrine concerning Predeſtination, &c. pr. 2d
29 The Character of a Methodiſt, pr. 2d *3d Edit.*
30 The Principles of a Methodiſt, pr. *3d.*
31 Thoughts on Marriage and Celibacy, pr. 1d
32 Rules of the United Societies, pr. 1d
33 A Word in Seaſon, pr. 1d
34 An Appeal to Men of Reaſon and Religion, pr. 6d
35 Publiſh'd by Subſcription, Three Volumes of Moral and Sacred Poems, pr. 7s 6d in Sheets.

Publiſh'd by

The Rev. Mr. HENRY PIERS,
VICAR of BEXLEY in KENT.

1 A Sermon preach'd *(in Part)* before the RIGHT WORSHIPFUL the Dean of the Arches, and the REVEREND the Clergy of the Deanery of *Shoreham*; aſſembled at *Sevenoaks* in KENT, on *Friday* the 21ſt of *May*, 1742. pr. 3d.
2 *Chriſt born, that we may be* born again. A Sermon, preach'd at BEXLEY in *KENT*, on *Chriſtmas-Day*, 1741, and on *Sunday* after *Chriſtmas-Day* 1742. pr. 8d.

E R R A T A.
Page 11. Line 22, *Give me to know.*—p. 25, l. 23, for *willy* read *wily.*—p. 213, l. 1, f. *But* r. *See.* —p. 250, l. 6, f. *yeid* r. *yield.*—p. 283, penult. f. *purſume* r. *preſume.*

The Wesleys have a pretty knack of versifying: Their Enthusiastick notions are best Cloathed in Poetick Diction; but stript of that Dress, they will often be found to be Nonsense, or Blasphemy, or Both. A thousand Instances might be given of this, in this Volume, but let us examine only the two last lines, by turning them into sober prose; & then, stript of that Enthusiasm of Poetry, w.ᶜʰ made them supportable, this will be found to be his Modest Prayer, viz

Let my Humanity be absorbed in thy Divinity
Let All yᵉ remains of me be GOD.

Let all I (John Wesley) am, in This be lost
Let all I John Wesley am, be GOD.
Let John Wesley be GOD! Monstrum H........

THE
CONTENTS.

PART I.

D d   After

The CONTENTS.

PART II.

The

The CONTENTS.

D d 2

Acts

The CONTENTS.

PART III.

The CONTENTS.

PART IV.

D d 3   Hymns

The CONTENTS.

THE

INDEX.

The INDEX.

The INDEX.

The INDEX.

The INDEX.

The INDEX.

Lightning Source UK Ltd.
Milton Keynes UK
UKOW07f0015140516

274222UK00011B/251/P